BECOMING CRIMINAL

Becoming Criminal

Transversal Performance and
Cultural Dissidence in
Early Modern England

Bryan Reynolds

THE JOHNS HOPKINS UNIVERSITY PRESS
BALTIMORE AND LONDON

The Johns Hopkins University Press
2715 North Charles Street
Baltimore, Maryland 21218-4363
www.press.jhu.edu

Library of Congress Cataloging-in-Publication Data

Reynolds, Bryan (Bryan Randolph)
Becoming criminal : transversal performance and cultural
dissidence in early modern England / Bryan Reynolds.
    p.   cm.
Includes bibliographical references and index.
    ISBN 0-8018-6808-4
    1. English literature—Early modern, 1500–1700—History
and criticism.   2. Criminals in literature.   3. Literature and
society—England—History—16th century.   4. Literature and
society—England—History—17th century.   5. England—Social
conditions—16th century.   6. England—Social conditions—
17th century.   7. Crime—England—History—16th century.
8. Crime—England—History—17th century.   9. Romanies in
literature.   10. Crime in literature.   I. Title.
PR428.C74 R49 2002
820.9′35206927—dc21   2001001332

A catalog record for this book is available from the British
Library.

Frontispiece: Image of "The Roaring Girle or Moll Cut-Purse,"
from T. Middleton and T. Dekker, *The Roaring Girl,* 1611.
Courtesy of the Harvard College Library.

In loving memory of
Dede
and
for Kim
without whom not

CONTENTS

MY FASCINATION with criminals began long ago. I was unusually mobile for a kid living in the New York City suburb of Scarsdale, riding my Honda SR75 (minimotorcycle) pretty much anywhere I pleased on quiet roads, bicycle paths, and horse trails—and, of course, ditching the cops whenever necessary. Mobility meant freedom, and for a curious adolescent with a penchant for everything transgressive, such freedom meant exposure to exciting new people: small-time criminals of all sorts. I found these people not in the village of Scarsdale, where the criminals were mostly white-collar and less accessible to an adolescent, but in the school yards, parks, and shopping malls of the neighboring city of New Rochelle.

It was in New Rochelle that I met my motorcycle-riding buddies Benny and John, the two guys responsible for my participation in the evening that was a powerful precursor to my interest in early modern England's criminal culture. It was a freezing March night, three days after my fifteenth birthday. John, then sixteen, and Benny, eighteen, picked me up in John's new jet-black Pontiac Trans Am. They were taking me to the infamous Enzo's apartment in downtown New Rochelle, but for what purpose was going to be a surprise.

We parked a few blocks away so that no one could connect us to our car. When we arrived at a metal door at the end of an alley located behind a commercial building, Benny knocked. A minute later a voice hollered from behind a screened window above. Benny blurted out the magic words and we were buzzed in. At the top of the stairs we were greeted by a large man who Benny introduced to us as Tony. Tony silently padded us down, then ushered us along. We entered a spacious combination kitchen and living room with leopard-, zebra-, and tiger-patterned furnishings, from shag carpets and kitchen chairs to sofas and love seats. The walls were covered with pictures of naked women from pornographic magazines, often posing next to or astride souped-up cars and motorcycles. On one wall a stuffed buffalo head was mounted beside a collection of rifles.

There were also four real women, scantily clad in diaphanous blouses, lingerie, or topless, with "big hair," much makeup, and high heels, either leaning against something, dancing go-go-like to the disco music, or just strutting around. They observed our entrance, smiled, but said nothing. There were also six men, not including Tony, all snugly couched in the safari decor. Only Enzo, a short, olive-skinned Italian immigrant in his mid-twenties, and another guy, a taller, plumper Italian-American about the same age, acted happy to see us. The rest, also Italian-Americans wearing white tanks, gold chains, unbuttoned disco shirts, and polyester suits, were preoccupied with their torches, glass pipes, and baking soda while freebasing cocaine. They were pleasantly indifferent to our arrival, throwing us no more than a glance, nod, and smirk.

At this point I wanted to sit down somewhere unnoticed or merge with the wallpaper and disappear. I was nervous about what might happen next yet could do nothing but continue to perform the macho coolness expected of me, which meant saying little and looking unaffected. Enzo demanded that space be cleared for us on one of the couches. He also told the women to pay attention to us, and to bring us piña coladas. The other friendly guy, named Lilo, offered us a joint and cut us several massive cocaine lines. The climactic moment, however, occurred when one of the other guys attempted to drive some cocaine and freebasing equipment over to us in a remote-control toy truck; to his embarrassment and my relief, he accidentally tipped it over.

My discomfort with what was happening, combined with my fear of what might happen, was exacerbated by the fact that half of the conversation between our hosts and Benny was incomprehensible to me. I knew the discussion was about real estate, since it was prompted by the announcement that I was from Scarsdale, but I couldn't understand the details because I didn't know most of their slang words and phrases. After a while, when it became clear to Enzo that I had no idea what was going on, he let me in on the surprise, the reason why I was brought there: Enzo wanted to "honor" me with employment as his drug dealer in my high school. I thanked him but declined the offer. I'm sure my life would have been very different had I accepted. A year later Benny was convicted of manslaughter for killing a man with a chair in a bar fight. Ten years later, after establishing himself as a drug dealer, John was shot six times at close range in his car during a deal. He survived, but without the use of his right arm.

Later, as a student, I became intrigued by the many structural similarities between the organized criminality I had experienced and its transhistorical representation in various literary genres. I became especially fascinated by the criminal culture portrayed in the literature of early modern England, where the comparison was strongest and the representation was abundant, consistent, and multifaceted. I wanted to learn more about the relationship between actual criminals and the popular media. Why was criminal culture such marketable subject matter? How did criminal culture function dynamically in the workings of early modern English society? These were the same kinds of questions I had about criminal culture today. As my research about early modern English criminal culture progressed, my need to develop a theoretical lens through which to analyze and make sense of its unusual influence became more pressing and important. This book represents my attempt to explain the existence, both real and imaginary, of this criminal culture using my own critical approach that I call "transversal theory."

ACKNOWLEDGMENTS

I AM GRATEFUL to Harvard University, the Andrew W. Mellon Foundation, and the University of California, Irvine, for their support. I also want to thank many people for helping me in various ways to write this book. Among family members are my grandparents, Louis and Helen Goldberg; my parents, Don and Donna Reynolds; and my brother, Greg. Other individuals to whom I owe thanks include: Dede and Bob Savelson, Scott Gordon, Evan Livingstone, Tony Kubiak, Leo Damrosch, David Perkins, Tom Augst, Candace Carey, Douglas Stewart, Dan Donoghue, Scott Albertson, Amy Engel, Kate Rubin, Rich Busgang, Rodney Byrd, Alan Sinfield, Michael Eliel, Jay Ward, John Bishop, Paul Alpers, Emily Rubin, Don Hedrick, Homer Lusk, and Maura Burnett, my editor. I am especially grateful to Marge Garber, Stephen Greenblatt, Marc Shell, James Intriligator, Ian Munro, Jeff Masten, Matt Grant, Barry Crittenden, Nina Venus, and Kris Lang. Most of all, I am indebted to Kim Savelson for her love that sustained me, for her brilliance that inspired me, and for her friendship that continues to guide me.

Portions of this book have appeared in *Theatre Journal* 49.2 (1997): 142–67, and *Literature, Interpretation, Theory* 9.4 (1999): 369–95, and are here reprinted by kind permission.

BECOMING CRIMINAL

CHAPTER ONE

State Power,
Cultural Dissidence,
Transversal Power

BEGINNING IN sixteenth-century England, a distinct criminal culture of rogues, vagabonds, gypsies, beggars, cony-catchers, cutpurses, and prostitutes emerged and flourished. This community was self-defined by the criminal conduct and dissident thought promoted by its members, and officially defined by and against the dominant preconceptions of English cultural normality. In this book I argue that this amalgamated criminal culture, consisting of a diverse population with much racial, ethnic, and etiological ambiguity, was united by its own aesthetic, ideology, language, and lifestyle. In effect, this criminal culture constituted a subnation that illegitimately occupied material and conceptual space within the English nation. With its own laws and customs, it was both independent of and dependent on England's official (mainstream) culture. It was self-governing but needed the law-abiding populace for food and shelter and as a social entity against which to define itself. I also argue that the enduring presence of this criminal culture markedly affected the official culture's aesthetic sensibilities, systems of belief, and socioeconomic organization. It was both conducted by and a conductor for what I call "transversal power."[1]

Before describing my "transversal theory" that explains "transversal power" and accounts for the terms, methods, and arguments that drive this study, I want to consider, as a point of entrance, the remarkable resemblance between discussions of the sociohistorical actuality, representation, and influence of early modern England's organized crime and that of today's Italian-American mafia. Both topics are controversial and important to studies of criminality and sociocultural differentiation within their respective periods and geographies, and many of the historiographical issues with which my analysis must contend would also pertain to analysis of the Italian-American mafia.

Mafia Presence

What do most Americans today really know about the Italian-American mafia? According to the *Oxford English Dictionary* (*OED*), the term "mafia" originated in nineteenth-century Sicily, where it was used to describe "the spirit of hostility to the law and its ministers prevailing among a large portion of the population and manifesting itself frequently in vindictive crimes"; today it also refers to "the body of those who share in this anti-legal spirit (often erroneously supposed to constitute an organized secret society existing for criminal purposes)." Ethnicities with distinguishable groups allegedly among this mafia "body" today in the United States include Jews, Russians, Mexicans, Irish, and Italians. However, of these, the Italian mafia receives the most attention in the media. Americans are most familiar with the consistent representation of the criminal operations and culture of the mafia in popular films.[2] But do the films constitute adequate evidence for the real-life existence of this mafia? In other words, why do people believe that the mafia exists? Of course, we know more about the mafia than what the films tell us. From printed, broadcasted, televised, and internet news and information sources we know about the crimes allegedly committed by such mafiosi as Carlo Gambino, Joseph Colombo, Paul Castellano, and John Gotti. Moreover, supporting references and commentary on the information provided by these sources often surface in popular literature and music.[3] If we were to add to our list of possible sources some FBI, police, and court records, as well as testimonies from convicted mafiosi, most people would probably agree that we could make a plausible argument for the existence of an Italian-American mafia, especially if the sources corroborated each other and presented a largely cohesive picture. But if there were a scholar writing, say, in the twenty-fourth century, would he or she have ample material for a sociohistorical study of the twentieth-century's Italian-American mafia's criminality and culture?

Even though historical evidence becomes more debatable as time passes, and firsthand (eyewitness) accounts based on personal experience become unavailable, this question, I think, calls for a resolute yes. Such an affirmative response makes sense when considered in light of the implications of this question in regard to the general enterprise of sociohistorical inquiry. Indeed, this response recalls the long-standing debate over the "fictionality" or relativity of history. According to the *OED,* history is a narrative, a story, or a chronological record of events. Hence, for a history to exist, there must be at least one storyteller or chronicler—the historian—who records, synthesizes, and creates a particular story out of the artifacts (art pieces, architectural remnants, literature, personal belongings, etc.), all of which can be considered the textual evidence and materiality for that history.[4] Put differently, as Frederic Jameson says in a statement representative of today's literary-cultural critics, "History—Althusser's 'absent cause,' Lacan's 'Real'—is *not* a text, for it is fundamentally non-narrative and nonrepresentational; what can be added, however, is the proviso that history is inaccessible to us except in textual form, or in other words, that it can be approached only by way of prior (re)textualization [reinsertion into its historical context]."[5] Like an actual historical event (what Jameson refers to as "history"), for which we have no unmediated access, a given history, such as that of early modern England's criminal culture or the Italian-American mafia, can never be a monolithic, hermetic, or absolute text that will read the same to everyone. A history's textuality, like its occurrence, can never be exclusive or isolated; rather, it is necessarily informed by and connected to various sociohistorical determinations endemic to the historical moment and social experience of both the subject matter and the historian. Therefore, a history's historical, social, and material embedding and mediations, both past and present, must be excavated, analyzed, and contextualized in order to understand the processes by which this history is made relevant.

The job of historians is to assemble the historiographical evidence, determine which texts are significant and credible, and construct an overarching text, that is, their own (narrative) account of the history in question. It is to their advantage that this account be convincing and accepted by most people. Even more important is that it be recognized and at least professionally and provisionally accepted by the "right" people: other "authorities" with equal or more sociopolitical status and, by extension, "social power." Social power is achieved by individuals and groups when they occupy, through discourse and action, social spaces that are important to the functioning of a society. In sum, social power is demonstrated through authoritative presence and legitimation of perspective in a society's institutional and noninstitutional social spaces that work to affect the society's members.

Insofar as history is intertwined with diverse and competing conductors of social power, which to some degree must always be the case, there can never be just one history or a pure, correct history. History is an ultimately uncontainable, cumulating process of occurrence and the recording of events; it is a process that is always already contingent on the interpretations of historians, which might be as different and as idiosyncratic as the historians themselves. There are and can only ever be multiple histories, some more coherent and cogent than others, whose status must always be dependent on the individual wills and ideologies of the historians, the legitimating powers of the interpretive communities with whom the historians are affiliated, and the sociopolitical mechanisms that influence these interpretive communities. Thus, the complex circumstances ineluctably surrounding and directly involved in the making of a history call for a critical approach that remains aware and sensitive to the situation and contingency of that history's production.

To meet this historiographical demand, I developed, with the help of cognitive neuroscientist James Intriligator, the "investigative-expansive mode" of analysis, which is an important methodological component of my transversal theory.[6] Intriligator and I wanted to offer an alternative to the methodology characteristic of most dialectical argumentation, scientific investigation, and Western historiography. Our name for this traditional methodology is the "dissective-cohesive mode" of analysis. This analytical approach first breaks its subject matter into constituent parts and then categorizes and examines those parts with the goal of reassembling them into a unified and accountable whole. We determined that the historian should not be constrained by preconceived parameters, the pursuit of totality, or the fantasy of singular truth. Instead, the historian should be a traveler, a self-consciously marginal figure who transgresses the boundaries of tradition as well as of time and place, not in search of wholeness but of new leads, (dis)connections, and tangents, even if this requires trespassing on the memories, methodologies, and histories of others. But this traveler must also be a cartographer, mapping out his or her journey, revealing the nexuses, both material and thematic, so that others can follow along and intersect according to the parameters of their own quests.

Unlike the dissective-cohesive mode, then, the investigative-expansive mode insists that the subject matter under investigation be partitioned into variables according to essentially *ad hoc* parameters. The internal connectedness (among themselves) and external connectedness (to other forces, such as the subject matter's social history) of the partitioned variables are then examined with a readiness to reparameterizing as the analysis progresses. The historian must be prepared to adjust his or her focus and direction as unexpected problems, information, and ideas surface. Whereas the objective of the dissective-cohesive mode is to (re)construct conclusively, the investigative-expansive mode seeks comprehension of the subject matter's fluid, plural, and evolving relationships to its own parts and to the greater environments of which it is a part. Whereas our hypothesized twenty-fourth-century scholar researching the Italian-American mafia may not employ the investigative-expansive mode, it is the approach I have chosen for the present study of early modern England's criminal culture. By using the investigative-expansive mode, I hope to make my analysis more responsible and valuable for scholars in a number of fields, and wish it to serve as a critical model, especially for other historiographical and literary-cultural work on performance, social identity, and subcultures.

Given the preponderance of evidence, it is almost certain, however, that our hypothesized twenty-fourth-century scholar would have little difficulty establishing that there was an Italian-American mafia, that is, a criminal organization comprised predominantly of Italian-Americans and some recent Italian immigrants that operates on local and regional levels, such as in neighborhoods of Brooklyn and Queens and in the hubs and vicinities of Atlantic City, Las Vegas, New York City, Chicago, and Boston. But there are also some widely "known" twentieth-century claims made about the mafia that might be somewhat difficult to substantiate. These include: (1) the mafia is a monolithic, hierarchically structured organization; (2) the mafia is a worldwide organization; (3) the mafia is in cahoots with the Roman Catholic church; (4) the mafia runs the Teamsters and other national unions; (5) the mafia has a direct influence on the U.S. government, particularly the White House and the FBI; and (6) the U.S. government collaborated with the mafia in the World War II war effort. While there will be historians who support these claims, there will be those who adamantly oppose them. It is rare, if not impossible, for a history to be determined beyond a reasonable doubt. (I am imagining Jacques Derrida as the judge.)

Nevertheless, the pervasiveness of these claims in the popular mind makes them essential analytical material for any sociohistorical study of twentieth-century America's mafia. Ideas are the stuff of subjectivity; they influence people. The ubiquitous dissemination of these and other claims about the mafia, ones that have been commodified and romanticized in the popular media, have undoubtedly influenced many Americans. Not only does the plurality of popularly marketed media about the mafia testify to this influence, but this influence is often at the thematic core of the mafia's representations in this media. Consider the protagonists of Martin Scorsese's *Goodfellas* (1990) and Robert De Niro's *A Bronx Tale* (1993), both of whom, as youngsters, want to become gangsters. As indicated by the popularity of films like these, and the award-winning HBO series *The Sopranos,* many young Americans today are fascinated with the prospect of becoming a gangster. The point is that regardless of whether the mafia exists as it is most often depicted, the popular image of the mafia plays a significant role in various aspects of American culture. For example, The Smithereens, a rock 'n' roll band, compare what I call the mafia's "affective presence" to that of cultural icon Santa Claus in their 1994 song "Gotti" about the notorious mafioso John Gotti: "Tell me there's no mafia, / I'll tell you there's a Santa Claus."[7] By "affective presence" I mean the combined material, symbolic, and imaginary existence of the mafia that influences the circulation of social power and thus the identity formation and worldview of many people, especially the mainstream moviegoing population and other consumers of mafia-related media and products.

I have been discussing the Italian-American mafia to illustrate a similarity between my present investigation of early modern England's criminal culture and that of our hypothesized twenty-fourth-century scholar, which will become apparent as my analysis progresses. Basically, this similarity relates to the fact that some popular "truths" have a profound impact on people without also having much credibility in terms of an academically approved history or a readily substantiated historical reality. If a society believes in a "truth," such as the Christian concept of God, and its members live in accordance with that "truth," then in many respects one could say that that "truth" might as well be fact. A commonly believed "truth" is often *this* society's "reality" since, as an everyday operative "truth," it informs the lived experience of the society's members. The "truth" becomes another buttress in the society's ideological infrastructure. When the "truth" in question relates to mysterious subject matter, such as the supernatural force of a god, the metaphysics of being, romantic love, or a (less abstract) secret society like the Italian-American mafia or early modern England's criminal culture, the possibility of its material substantiation is diminished and its potential for conceptual influence is increased. In other words, the more amorphous and intangible the subject matter, the easier it is for people in power, which is to say the "authorities," to exploit their subordinates based on what they do not and cannot know about it.

In the case of early modern England's criminal culture, there are two facts that serve as considerably stronger evidence than those supporting the existence of today's Italian-American mafia. The first is that although it was typical for the competing commercial writers during the period to critique each other for presenting fallacious or dubious information, the early modern English chroniclers of the criminal culture never do this. Instead, they claim to be supplementing each other's accounts, sharing additional information derived from their more extensive experience and knowledge. Their accounts corroborate each other in greater detail than those of the Italian-American mafia and are almost entirely consistent. The second point is that this consistency of representation occurred in many varieties of media—including etchings, songs, theater, and commercial, popular, and state literature—for over one hundred years, which is almost double the length of time the Italian-American mafia has been a presence in popular culture. In fact, the original accounts of early modern England's criminal culture went virtually unchallenged until the second half of the nineteenth century, when (as I discuss in the next chapter) scholars began to the make claims for racial and etiological differences among criminal groups.

The interests of my project, however, extend well beyond establishing that there was a distinct criminal culture in early modern England. I am most concerned with the connections between the conceptual influence, social power, and literary-cultural implications of the criminal culture's presence in the popular imagination. The "history" I pursue is that of the relationships between the criminal culture's representation, the processes of identity formation and subjectification with which the populace had to cope, and the general circulation of sociopolitical power that made this period in English history so exceptionally innovative and transformational. This brings me to the specific theoretical parameters that inform and are supported by my analysis of early modern England's criminal culture.

Transversal Theory

According to my transversal theory,[8] there are processes of identity formation that work within and in response to configurations of social power that lead to the construction and destruction of societies. Transversal theory observes that all societies are governed by an assembly of sociopolitical "conductors": mental and physical movers, orchestrators, and transmitters. These include the educational, juridical, and religious structures, as well as the institutions of marriage and family, which powerfully affect the circulation of social power. In agreement with its investment in cultural, social, political, and economic fluctuations and determinations, this organizing machinery functions over time and space, sometimes consciously and sometimes unintentionally, to channel and transform social power into "state power," which, both ideologically and materially fueled, works discursively to produce cohesive government. Put differently, the ultimate purpose of the organizing machinery that runs on the state power it must generate is to configure society and manufacture "the state": the totalized "state machinery."

I coined the term "state machinery" to refer to a society's governmental assembly of conductors as a corrective to the political philosophy of Louis Althusser that has informed much recent Marxist scholarship, particularly that of cultural materialists and new historicists in the field of early modern studies. By "state machinery," a term that simultaneously connotes singularity and plurality, I am adapting Althusser's conception of what he calls the "(Repressive) State apparatus," which includes the governmental mechanisms, such as the military and the police, that work to control our bodies, and fusing it with his subsidiary "Ideological State Apparatuses," the inculcating mechanisms that work to control our thoughts and emotions.[9] My purpose is to emphasize that the overall desire for governmental coherence is driven by diverse conductors of state-oriented organizational power that are, at different times and to varying degrees, always both repressive and ideological. This is a socio-power dynamic in which various conductors work, sometimes individually and sometimes in conjunction with other conductors, to substantiate their own positions of power within the sociopolitical field. This field is where social and political discourse and actions negotiate and coalesce. In the process, the conductors work, sometimes intentionally and sometimes inadvertently, to advance the image of and development toward the totalized state.

Hence, my use of the term "state machinery" should make explicit the multifarious and discursive nature of state power and thus prevent the misperception of the socio-power dynamic as resulting from a conspiracy led by a monolithic state. This is not to say, however, that conspiracies do not occur and take the form of state factions. On the contrary, this must be the case for the more complex machinery to run. The upper echelon of early modern England's state machinery, for instance, consisted of such state factions as the monarch (with members of court), the church, the Privy Council, and Parliament. Parliament, the Privy Council, and the monarch enforced, with their respective legislation and punitory capacity, the ideology of the church. In turn, the church justified, with its sacred dogma, the power of these state apparatuses. Church and state attempted, together and separately, to reinforce and promote the existing sociopolitical hierarchy upon which their superior status relied.[10] They did this notwithstanding internal contradictions and conflicts, such as those between and within the courts of Elizabeth and James, the church, Parliament, and other loci of state power (London's mercantile elite, local constabularies and judiciaries, educational institutions). Nevertheless, the monolithic, Leviathan, or absolute state can only ever be a fantasy goal whose realization would preclude this socio-power dynamic. This is because "the state" (like the concept of historical totality discussed in the previous section) is an impossibility or, at the very least, inaccessible and unobservable by even its most powerful conductors. This is the case insofar as social structures and systems evolve in relation to ongoing natural processes, such as environmental changes, genetic mutations, and anarchist tendencies, that remain unaffected by human intervention.

Although research in many disciplines, both sociological and scientific, seems to have made huge strides since the early modern period in its quest to understand and influence natural processes, the organizing machinery of all modern states is still unable to account for all inconsistencies and ruptures in the "conduction"—the dissemination and management—of social order. Precisely for this reason, the machinery focuses on what it knows it must, and often can, control: the range of thought, which I call the "conceptual territory," of the populace. More specifically, the machinery continually needs to reestablish the scope of personal experience and perception of the populace's members. This scope, which I refer to as their "subjective territory," must be navigated so that notions of identity cease to be arbitrary and transitory and acquire temporal constancy and spatial range for the subsistence of what is perceived to be a healthy individual and, by extension, a cohesive social body. Regardless of how originally or actually heterogeneous the subject population, either genetically, ethnically, or philosophically, the state machinery needs to imbue this population with a common state-serving subjectivity, indeed, a shared ideology, that would at the same time give this social body the assurance of homogeneity and universality.

My term "subjective territory" schematizes personal conceptualization in spatial terms. It is related to Immanuel Kant's notion that it is our in-tuited acknowledgment of ourselves (as mental beings) as objects to our-selves within space and time that allows for both internal and external ex-perience. Our experiences are predicated on the understanding of ourselves as objects existing in space and time.[11] In regard to conceptual-ization, like Kant (but to a greater extent) I am privileging the spatial over the temporal aspect of experience. Hence my use of the word "territory." I am merging Kant's notion of space with that of Henri Lefebvre, who sees space as a mental, physical, and social determinant that is primary to personal experience.[12] For the subject, then, the relationship between space and time is biunivocal (two into one) with the subject becoming cog-nizant of his or her existence first in space, next in time, and then together in almost instantaneous succession. (I am writing in my home office, at 11:24 P.M., yet I'm not sure of the exact date.) In this view, moreover, con-ceptualization encompasses space, and thus allows for expansion of the subject's conceptual territory and, by extension, emotional territory, which often leads to overlap with, trespass against, and flight from the conceptual and emotional territories of others. This happens because the relationship between the conceptual and the emotional is also biunivocal, with the emotional trailing immediately behind the conceptual, inasmuch as there are shared regions of conceptual and emotional territory that could become social and interactive. Thus, it is territory that permits oc-cupation by subjects and objects. I posit subjective territory as a correc-tive to the idea of subjectivity as wholly individual, hermetic, or station-ary. Subjective territory acknowledges the processual, interactive nature of social identity.

Notwithstanding what may, in fact, be liberating in potential within this viewpoint, subjective territory usually refers to the scope of the concep-tual and emotional experience of an individual within any hegemonic soci-ety or subsociety (the university or criminal organizations, for example),[13] as well as to subjectification by state machinery. It refers to those whose subjectivity has developed under the influence of both traditional educa-tional and governmental institutions and what Pierre Bourdieu calls the "symbolic power" of particular organizational social structures, whether mainstream, subcultural, or countercultural. According to Bourdieu:

Symbolic power—as a power of constituting the given through ut-
terances, of making people see and believe, of confirming or transforming the vision of the world and, thereby, action on the world
and thus the world itself, an almost magical power which enables one
to obtain the equivalent of what is obtained through force (whether
physical or economic), by virtue of the specific effect of mobiliza-
tion—is a power that can be exercised only if it is *recognized*, that
is, misrecognized as arbitrary. This means that symbolic power does
not reside in "symbolic systems" in the form of an "illocutionary
force" but that it is defined in and through a given relation between
those who exercise power and those who submit to it, i.e., in the very
structure of the field in which *belief* is produced and reproduced.[14]

The efficacy of symbolic power corresponds directly to the maintenance
of the belief system of the society in which it operates. Regardless of how
they benefit or suffer from the exercise of symbolic power, that society's
members must contribute to it in one form or another, and thus to their
own subjectification.

For instance, regardless of whether a female stripper is aware of how
her occupation contributes to the further sexual commodification of
women in a male-dominated society—and consequently to the privileging of women as sex objects and the subsequent oppression of women as
intelligent, emotional beings—by its very practice alone her occupation
exercises symbolic power that contributes to both the sexual objectification and the corresponding oppression. The stripper's participation in the
sex industry symbolizes in a positive manner all women who seek to profit
from their own sexual exploitation; it affirms the value of reducing women
to the status of sex object and therefore contributes to the discrimination
against women who resist such objectification or cannot measure up
anatomically to the standards set by the industry. The symbolic power of
the stripper reinforces the subjective territory of those socialized to promote the ideology that appreciates her and her socioeconomic position-
ing within the society's hierarchy. It is an individual's prescribed subjective territory, typically based on the class status into which he or she is
born, that enforces the acceptance of the society's hierarchy; it is also what

prevents the individual from recognizing that the hierarchy is, in fact, an arbitrary social construction, reinforced by actions that exercise symbolic power and serve the interests of some people more than others.

Subjective territory incorporates conceptual and emotional boundaries that are defined by the prevailing science, morality, and ideology. These boundaries bestow a spatiotemporal dimension, or common ground, to an aggregate of individuals or subjects, and work to ensure and monitor the cohesiveness of this social body or, to borrow a phrase from Benedict Anderson, this "imagined community."[15] It is "imagined" because there are usually no actual social relationships or communal experiences connecting *most* of its members, thereby substantiating the boundaries. Yet the conceptual and emotional boundaries, thematically linked and experienced as real by members of the populace through frustration, guilt, shame, and anxiety, demarcate the specific coordinates for the interaction of sociocultural and ideological centers and conductors. These conductors are most often the same evaluative assemblages that define the state machinery, such as the educational, juridical, and religious structures, that were implemented or appropriated by the state machinery to institute the conceptual and emotional boundaries in the first place. In short, subjective territory is the existential and experiential realm in and from which a given subject of a given hierarchical society perceives and relates to the universe and his or her place in it, constraining the subject's ability to imagine himself or herself as anything other than what he or she may already be.

To maintain their privileged status and not allow the populace's imagination to wander, the state's machinic constituents need to exercise their sociopolitical power carefully and strategically. Their movements, whether symbolic or explicit, must dominate the circulation of social power within the often clustering but ultimately acentered, unpredictable network of interaction within the sociopolitical field. Every sociopolitical field is necessarily dominated by a particular ideology, such that its discursive ideological system controls significant conceptual territory. To this end, the state machinery supports and is supported by the dominant culture, so that this particular culture becomes "official" culture. However, since official culture is not always dominant in all circumstances, such as in a subcultural ghetto, official culture is primarily defined by its agreement with state power and not by the pervasiveness and constancy of its superiority. For me culture consists of the aesthetics, ideology, and sociopolitical conductors common to and cultivated by a certain group of people at a specific historical moment; and official culture is the culture of a distinguishable or imagined group of people characteristically aligned with the aesthetics, ideology, and sociopolitical conductors that mutually support state power. Official culture's sociopolitical conductors work to formulate and inculcate subjective territory with the appropriate culture-specific and identity-specific zones and localities. This sets common boundaries for personal and group expression along certain socioeconomic lines, such that a connecting, overarching subjectivity that substantiates the state machinery is simultaneously shared, habitually experienced, and believed by each member of the populace to be natural and its very own. In a clever twist on Descartes's famous formulation, André Glucksmann epitomizes the axiomatic goal for state philosophy: "I think, therefore the State is."[16]

For the subjectified populace of early modern England, socialization and indoctrination were conclusively grounded in Christian philosophy and its concept of God. The most pragmatic enterprise of the state machinery in the sociopolitical field, where competing agencies vied for the monopoly of the power to legitimate, was to (re)produce, harness, and consecrate the doxological illusion that the Christian God is the supreme transcendental signified: the source of all meaning across space-time. As a result, all explanation could be conveniently deferred to the readily accepted idea that God must have intended things to be this way or they would not be like this, since the way things are must reflect the allpowerful God's intentions. This idea is epitomized in a homily entitled "Exhortacion concernyng Good Ordre and Obedience to Rulers and Magistrates" (first printed in 1547 and reprinted frequently throughout Elizabeth's reign), which is characteristic of the legion of homilies that the state fashioned for preaching in church services, where weekly attendance by all members of the populace was mandatory (although apparently not strictly enforced). The homily reads as follows:

> Almightie God hath created and appointed all thinges in heaven, yearth and waters in a moste excellent and perfect ordre. . . . Every

degre of people, in their vocacion, callyng and office, hath ap-
poynted to them their duetie and ordre. Some are in high degre,
some in lowe, some kynges and princes, some inferiors and subjects,
priestes and laimen, masters and servauntes, fathers and chyldren,
husbandes and wifes, riche and poore, and every one hath nede of
other. . . . Where there is no right ordre, there reigneth all abuse,
carnall libertie, enormitie, syn and babilonicall confusion.[17]

Nevertheless, as with most efforts to (re)configure conceptual territory
and solidify subjective territory and, in effect, to consolidate a narrowly
defined social body and nation-state, there was resistance. There is almost
always resistance of some kind when people are forced to think, value, and
desire the "proper" things. The construction of subjective territory can be
painstaking, especially when the subject already exists in a competing subjective territory that must be radically transversed and reconfigured rather
than just redefined in order for the imposing subjective territory to take
form. And because there has yet to be implemented a mode of hegemony
that can fully control or sufficiently accommodate the relative unpredictability and diversity that seems fundamental to the experience of all
things, resistance and change seem to relate symbiotically.

In human society resistance to control and change occurs diversely in
modes of response and expression deemed abnormal, unconventional, or
illegal according to the dominant ideology. In early modern England resistance often took the form of occultism (witchcraft and paganism), random and organized crime (mugging, prostitution, racketeering), and sexual immorality (fornication, adultery, sodomy). Simply put, resistance
occurs because the boundaries of subjective territory are challenged, al-
tered, or expanded by the individual, a social collective, or an external
force. Like the disparate and often diffuse sociopolitical conductors that
support official culture and state power, those that resist the state machinery need not work together as part of an instituted or monolithic
movement against the state, even though collaborative resistances and
even traditions are common. Like the state machinery, conductors of resistance are typically discursive and not necessarily deliberate; but unlike
the state machinery, whose conductors point toward an idealized total-

ity, these conductors collectively often point toward a plurality or a decentralized power. Although they are structurally related in that they defy convention, they are barely related in regard to overall purpose.

To be a conductor of resistance or of state power, one, or, more appropriately, one's practice or expression, neither has to be wholly against or wholly supportive of the official ideology, nor against or supportive of this ideology at all times. To be identifiably influential, however, sociopolitical conductors must be predominantly and recognizably on one side or the other at a given moment. Furthermore, regardless of whether an individual in early modern England who practices a dissident act, such as adultery or witchcraft, does so intentionally as an act of resistance to state power, such behavior, because of its symbolic power within the sociopolitical field, nonetheless constitutes resistance. As with the example of the female stripper, the effect of coalition occurs even without an established coalition. To take another example (discussed in greater detail in chapter 5), the fears of the early modern English antitheatricalists were grounded not so much in the idea that the transgressive acts and characters portrayed on stage would be imitated offstage but rather in imagined coalition whose effects would be achieved by different means. These effects, moreover, might be intentional or not, for it is frequently the case that people (like the female stripper) inadvertently oppose or support a power structure and thus unwittingly contribute to their own emancipation, on the one hand, or oppression, on the other.

Many new historicist and cultural materialist critics—who have dominated early modern studies for the last two decades—argue that, inadvertently or otherwise, early modern England's hegemonic forces fostered dissidence, only to suppress it eventually and thereby further reinforce the dominant power structure. Although such entrapment is a common scheme of all state machinery, this subversion/containment paradigm[18] does not account for or acknowledge the full complexity of the sociopolitical situation at hand, no more than it is fully transferrable, as some argue, to any historical period. It is especially significant that this paradigm, as it is often applied, tends to preclude or ignore microsubversions or small revolutionary changes of the sort that a transversal model allows. In some cases the state machinery may have manufactured or inspired these changes but either chose not to contain them or was unable to contain them. Furthermore, while uncontained microsubversions did occur on various sociopolitical levels, they occurred most significantly, with the most immediate ramifications, at the level of conceptuality. If a particular microsubversion (such as the early modern English female-to-male transvestism fashion analyzed in chapter 5) was thought-provoking and generated polemics and legal action, it was more consequential than a different microsubversion, such as a seditious but esoteric play, that generated little or no response. (I am thinking of the "positive value," as Terry Eagleton puts it, of the witches' subversiveness in *Macbeth*.)[19] Both the contained and uncontained dissidence of early modern England's public theater received tremendous attention and generated vehement conceptual and physical responses from both popular and official sources. The public theater was so influential that, as I hope to demonstrate, it developed into and was inspired by what I call "transversal territory."

Initially introduced by Félix Guattari, the terms "transversal" and "transversality" were used rather narrowly. In his collection of essays (1971–77) entitled *Molecular Revolution: Psychiatry and Politics,* Guattari uses these terms to discuss the phenomenon of group desire, in particular the way in which the degree of awareness of others in space and time serves to govern movement and change.[20] Guattari's metaphor for this is a field of horses that wear blinkers, whose awareness of what is outside themselves depends upon the degree to which the blinkers are open or shut, which in turn determines their collisions, avoidance, maneuvering, and movement in general. Related to collective fantasy, Guattari thus writes of transversality as "the whole aspect of *social creativity.*"[21] Helpful, too, is a brief borrowing of the term by Gilles Deleuze after being criticized for capitalizing on his theoretical positions by means of the figures of drug users, alcoholics, lunatics, and others without having shared their experiences himself. He responds that transversality ensures that "any effects produced in some particular way (through homosexuality, drugs, and so on) *can always be produced by other means.*"[22] While Guattari's initial use of the term is incorporated in my own, I extend his definition of transversality from accounting for the phenomenon of group desire to include conceptuality and its territories, and apply it to the existential processes of individuals as well as of groups getting outside themselves through various means.

As with my use of the word "territory," I am expanding the *OED*'s spatial definitions of "transversal" as "something lying athwart" and a "deviation" to include conceptual spaces. Transversal territory is thus the nonsubjectified region of one's conceptual and emotional territory. It is entered through the transgression of the conceptual boundaries, which are not necessarily tangible ones, and, by extension, the emotional boundaries of subjective territory. Most conceptual and emotional boundaries, like those of subjective territory, are historically and socially determined *modi operandi* that decide, normalize, and monitor individual and collective conceptualization and experience of the world; as a result, these same *modi operandi* are often successfully perpetuated throughout space-time.

Transversal territory is entirely different. Although also firmly linked to its sociohistorical moment, transversal territory neither requires determination or regulation nor does it serve any specific structures, conductors, dispositions, methods, or objective outcomes. In a sense, transversal territory is an antisubjective territory: the power of transversal thought produces or informs the transgressive *modi vivendi* of sociopaths, schizoids, criminals, philosophers, artists, and various other social, cultural, and political nonconformists. Transversal territory is entered through departures from and subversive intersections with subjective territory. It is where someone goes conceptually and emotionally when they venture, through what I call "transversal movements," beyond the boundaries of their own subjective territory and experience alternative sensations, thoughts, and feelings. Typical ways by which transversal movements occur are through the process of empathizing (or attempting to emphasize) with another or by performing the unfamiliar social identity of another. In these cases, one passes into, and usually through, transversal territory, the amorphous and ephemeral space in between subjective territories, while journeying into and out of the subjective territories of others. Transversal movements can also be launched by extraordinary actions, astonishing occurrences, and traumatic events that challenge subjective territory, permeate its borders, make the familiar strange, and turn the world topsy-turvy.

Transversal territory, therefore, is the spontaneous product of the "transversal power" that causes transversal movements. Transversal power, as a mechanism for experiential alterity, energizes and is energized by the enunciation and amplification of transition states, as when one empathizes, performs, transgresses, or, to cite more far-reaching examples, when one copes with transformations spurred by tragic happenings, sociopolitical uprisings, or natural disasters. Consequently, transversal territory transcends, fractures, or displaces the constantly affirmed world of subjective territory. By extension, since subjective territory is a mechanism of subjectification for the state machinery, transversal territory threatens an ideologically ordered "official territory": the ruling properties of a society's interiority that work to meld the overlap between the respective subjective territories of individuals. The "rational State," as Glucksmann opines, is a Machiavellian "machine consciously organized on the basis of permanent awareness that the fatherland, that is, the State itself, is in danger."[23] Transversal territory is not a mechanism of this machine; it is not a hobgoblin that the state needs and constructs strategically or paranoiacally; it is not simply a factor in a subversion/containment operation. Instead, transversal territory is diametrically opposed to the state machinery and a *real* enemy of state power, whatever the progressive or nonprogressive status of that power might be. As we will see, it is reflected in the great metamorphic themes and topoi of historical narratives: woman into man, criminal into actor, actor into anything, citizen into gypsy, gypsy into revolutionary philosopher—in the innumerable instances of spectacular, experimental alterity.

To reiterate, people occupy transversal territory when they defy or surpass the conceptual boundaries of their prescribed subjective addresses, opening themselves, as it were, to subjective awareness outside the self that is currently principal. Transversal territory invites people to deviate from the hierarchizing assemblages—whether vertical or horizontal—of any organizational social structure. Its transversal power inspires multiplicities of conjunctions and disjunctions within official territory and may even stimulate the production of a counterculture, which is to say a subculture that actively and intentionally challenges official culture. Of course, transversal power need not stop at a single social formation: a counterculture itself would, by the logic of the transversal, be subject to further movements leading members outside the subjective territories of a hegemonic subculture. In other words, transversality is the indispensable traveler's aid, inducing travel conceptually and emotionally across the organized space of subjectivity. It expands subjective territory through entrance into a disorganized, possibly unlimited, space by means of processual movement through performances of iconoclasm, impropriety, immorality, criminality, and insanity.

In effect, transversality often accounts for the historical fact of heterogeneous social configurations and asymmetrical or erratic social development. Although I agree with the Lacanian post-Marxists Ernesto Laclau and Slavoj Žižek, who respectively identify this fact as a "radical indeterminacy" that is historically conditional and necessarily challenges all attempts to effectuate hegemonic order,[24] I disagree with their claim that this fact originates in and is symptomatic of humankind's traumatic acknowledgment that "there is no return to the natural balance" and the consequent "radical antagonism through which man cuts his umbilical cord with nature, with animal homeostasis."[25] For them it is this "pure antagonism" (Laclau's phrase), caused by humankind's estrangement from nature, that inspires all social change.[26] In contrast, I see the sociohistorical process as a phenomenon fueled by humankind's desire to control its own experience *in relation to* the natural world. Moreover, I see transversal power, however present and potent in different historical moments and situations, as a major player behind heterogeneous social evolution. Although transversal territory may surface as a result of antagonism between humans or between humans and natural events (atrophic, seismic, or meteorological transformations), it cannot be defined against or in response to nature because transversality reflects nature's apparent capriciousness and multifariousness while at the same operating adjacent to it.

Under the regime of subjective territory, desire, whether for pleasure, consumption, or change, is constructed and manipulated by and for state power in order to perpetuate official culture. By contrast, transversality produces and expresses desire in the dynamic form of what Deleuze and Guattari term "becoming."[27] Becoming is a desiring process by which all things (energies, ideas, people, societies) change into something different from what they are. If the things had been identified and normalized by some dominant force, such as state law, religious credo, or official language, then any change in them is, in fact, becomings-other. The metamorphosis of becoming-other-social-identities confounds such concepts as the essential, the normal, the unified, and the universal, which are fundamental to subjective territory. It thereby undermines the supposedly fixed terms, binary distributions, and dialectics that are culturally and historically widespread, as in the constructs male and female, good and evil, normal and abnormal, natural and unnatural, real and unreal.[28] The occurrence of identity becomings corresponds to a negotiation and transformation in the modes of power and knowledge from which official models for subjectivity are drawn. Considering the social and political potential of becomings, it is important to remember that neither revolutionary change, containment, nor return, whether on individual or collective levels, ever happens instantaneously or totally. Rather, they happen as a result of various microsubversions and microcontainments. Just as there can be no autonomous future, there can be no complete return to past systems; for now, this is the nature of the spatiotemporal, endlessly reverberating continuum in which we live. In contradistinction to subjective territory, transversality necessitates the conceptual space-time for identity becomings, and advances heterogeneity, mutability, performance, expansion, nomadism, and indeterminacy.[29] Finally, one can even imagine a kind of transversal universality: the ideal state in which transversal power is pure and pervasive and in which everyone values difference, transformation, and indeterminacy. Hence what I imagine to be the transversal chorus: "We think, therefore we can be anything."

Yet it is precisely this chorus that we hear through the subtexts of representations of early modern England's criminal culture. The next chapter opens with a conductor according to which this chorus melodiously sings. The conductor is the assemblage of literature and analysis that is the product of my research on the relationship between early modern England's rogues and vagabonds and its allegedly recent immigrant gypsy population. Historians, cultural anthropologists, sociolinguists, and literary-cultural critics who have written on this relationship mainly focus on the differences between them rather than on their similarities. In fact, these scholars usually insist on a rigid distinction, if not total separation, between these alternative sociocultural categories.[30] In contrast to this approach, I hope to establish that there was a substantially unified criminal culture of rogues, vagabonds, beggars, cony-catchers, cutpurses, prostitutes, *and* gypsies that emerged in the 1520s and continued to develop until and possibly beyond the Puritans' rise to power in the early 1640s. (Historiographical evidence is scant during the interregnum.) By doing so, I want to make the corresponding argument that this criminal culture was commodified and fetishized by official culture such that its influence on official culture's members is not only recognizable but measurable. I want to argue that early modern England's criminal culture was both informed by and a medium for transversal power: the social and conceptual forces that stimulate movement outside the parameters imposed on people socially or physically by any organizational social structure. Criminal culture's transversality was exemplified by its members' individual and collective realizations of the antistate concepts of heterogeneity, mutability, performance, expansion, nomadism, and indeterminacy that characterize all transversal movement. To varying degrees and in diverse ways, these realizations inspired becomings-criminal.

CHAPTER TWO

Becoming Gypsy, Criminal Culture, Becoming Transversal

BY THE 1620S the floating signifier "gypsy," which was short for "Egyptian," had become a totalizing catchphrase or euphemism for members of early modern England's criminal culture. This does not mean that every rogue, vagabond, beggar, cony-catcher, cutpurse, and prostitute was immediately or regularly lumped under the umbrella category "gypsy," nor that the word "gypsy" indiscriminately referred to all of these criminal types. In such a social milieu, in which resistance to totalization and specificity in linguistic expression were commonplace, this could not have been the case. But it does mean that anyone referred to as a "gypsy" also could have been considered a criminal. Nevertheless, in spite of its implicit reference to all members of criminal culture, the signifier "gypsy" usually denoted people who traveled nomadically in groups, had dark skin, read fortunes, were performers, and acquired a reputation for immorality. The connotation or signified to the signifier "gypsy" was the paganism, sorcery, nomadism, profane sexuality, theatricality, deception, thievery, indeed, the multifarious criminality, the "gypsyism" with which "gypsy" is typically associated in literary texts, statutes, legal records, and personal letters of the period.

In conjunction with my argument for the existence of a criminal culture for which "gypsy" was an important signifier, I hope to demonstrate that the gypsy sign—the biunivocal expression of the signifiers (the media of representation) and the signifieds (the concepts represented) that together constituted this sign—became a compelling sociopolitical conduc-

tor that was transversally empowered and fetishized (imbued with magical power, sexual or otherwise) such that its circulation created and expanded space for criminal culture and transversality in official territory.[1] I
mean to show that the gypsy sign was exceptionally endowed with the socially and historically contingent phenomenon of transversal power *and*
with the hallucinatory and symbolic power of a fetishized object. It is my
hypothesis that it was precisely the gypsy sign's exceptional endowment
and subsequent "objective agency" that made it so transversally influential.

Objective Agency and the Gypsy Hypothesis

I have coined the term "objective agency" to refer to the power of a
sign to frustrate or transcend the effectual parameters and expectations
generally ascribed to that sign by a system of codification within which it
functions. Objective agency often occurs on minor levels when there is ig-
norance, presignification, and miscommunication. For instance, consider
the psychological and social effects (delusion, fanaticism, disillusionment)
of the social category "Christian," often believed to be someone who has
a personal relationship with the historical or supernatural Jesus Christ. A
sign is especially likely to achieve considerable objective agency when it
is simultaneously both fetishized, as Jesus Christ often is, and caught up
in transversal movement (which is seldom the case for the Christian sign-
object in a predominantly Christian culture). Through the fetishization of
the sign-object—the idolization of, obsession with, and submission to the
sign-object—the fetishist conceptually and emotionally opens himself up
to and even welcomes the sign-object's objective agency. In the case of the
gypsy sign, the profound cathexis (the libidinal and/or mental concentra-
tion) on the gypsy sign that fetishism requires made members of early
modern England's official culture (the fetishists) more vulnerable to the
actual transversal power for which the gypsy sign was already a conductor. The signifying modes by which the concept of gypsyism presented itself, or was represented, ceased to combine with this concept (the signified) to constitute a sign that referred solely to the conventionally expected
referent: dark-skinned immigrants whose existence was primarily distinct
from yet nonetheless dangerous to English society and official culture.

Instead, the signifying modes combined with the concept of gypsy-ism to produce a different sign, one that was more ideological and abstract and consequently obscured or displaced the expected referent. To be sure, the case of the gypsy sign concretely supports Jean Baudrillard's and J.-M. Lefebvre's similar theories on the general nature of all referents. Follow-ing Lefebvre, Baudrillard maintains that since it is formed and conducted through a sign, our relationship to the referent is necessarily mediated, ideologically informed, and abstracted: "The referent has no other value than that of the signified, of which it wants to be the substantial reference *in vivo,* and which it only succeeds in extending *in abstracto.*"[2] As Lefebvre puts it, as a result of the sign's primacy in our conceptual relationship to our environment, "the referent is not reality (i.e., an object whose exist-ence I can test, or control): we relate to it as real, but this intentionality is precisely an act of mind that belies its reality, which makes a fiction, an artificial construction out of it."[3] Having been exceptionally endowed, and not having an easily recognizable or tangible referent, the gypsy sign it-self, as "an act of mind," became the fetishized object as well as a trans-versal message for which it was the vehicle. It was the conceptual medium for "gypsyism" and, as Marshall McLuhan would argue, was therefore not just primarily the message but the *massage:* its objective agency acted upon its environment.[4]

Consequently, the gypsy sign became a sociopolitical conductor whose transversal power and objective agency made it an unusually trenchant mechanism for the expansion of transversal territory. It stimulated the tres-pass from subjective territory into transversal territory and initiated the dynamic sociocultural process of becoming gypsy. In other words, the gypsy sign's exceptional endowment caused members of official culture to fetishize the sign itself rather than the supposed referent. The added sus-ceptibility produced by such fetishization (by the worship of and resig-nation to the fetish-sign-object) made these members especially sensitive to the transversal power conducted by and through the gypsy sign. In this interpretive situation, as I shall attempt to show with diverse textual evi-dence, the gypsy referent lurks elusively and ambiguously beyond the gypsy sign. It lurks predominantly or perhaps only as a *potential* reality that constantly haunts the sign's hermeneutic existence. If it was the case that the gypsy referent was merely a fantasy or a specter, we would need to reevaluate the now pervasive claims to the actual existence in early modern England of a dark-skinned immigrant population whose members called themselves gypsies. Indeed, I want to argue that there were few, if any, gypsy immigrants in early modern England, and that both those people referred to as gypsies and those people that called themselves gypsies were not only actually disguised English rogues and vagabonds, but were also a major component of a greater criminal culture.

My larger purpose is to show that the members of official culture who fetishized the gypsy sign really fetishized the transversal, antistate concepts of heterogeneity, mutability, expansion, nomadism, performance, and indeterminacy that the gypsy sign embodied and articulated as gypsyism. And, that it was their intense exposure to transversal power through this act of fetishism that precipitated their own infection with transversal thought. This causality is evident in the literary expression and social realization of their desires to become gypsy members of criminal culture. Members of official culture wanted to actualize the gypsy sign for and by themselves and thereby personally experience gypsyism. They sought the incarnation of the sign and indirectly caused the further estrangement, enlargement, or replacement of the expected referent. Official culture greeted the gypsy sign's influence with a variety of perpetually faltering defense mechanisms, both material (laws and punishments) and conceptual (moralistic, Christian, and English nationalistic discourse). These defense mechanisms are revealed in, just as they themselves reveal, the transversal movement, fetishism of the gypsy sign, and the process of becoming gypsy that I mean to disinter and chart in the period's personal, popular, commercial, and state literature. To facilitate this undertaking, I have chosen Ben Jonson's court masque *The Gypsies Metamorphos'd* (1621) as a point of entrance into my discussion.[5] This text powerfully illustrates both the amalgamation that was criminal culture and the influential fetishization of the gypsy sign.

Gypsy Vogue and the Language Connection

During the 1620s, with nearly one hundred years of legislation against them still on the books, gypsies were, for the first time in English history, acceptable subject matter for a court masque.[6] Without question, in 1621 *The Gypsies Metamorphos'd* accomplished an extraordinary feat in the field of royal entertainment: King James liked the masque so much that he ordered it performed for him on three separate occasions (at Burley, Belvoir, and Windsor). Citing both a letter from John Chamberlain to Sir Dudley Carleton and the repeat performances as his primary evidence, Stephen Orgel claims that *The Gypsies Metamorphos'd* "was the king's favorite masque, and the court's. It is difficult to believe that it was not Jonson's favorite as well."[7] However, rather than attribute the masque's immense popularity to its gypsy subject matter, Orgel concludes: "The great interest provoked by the masque must have been generated partly by the aptness of the fortunes, but mainly by the rowdy good humor that was so much to the king's taste."[8] Richard Dutton adds: "Some of its popularity with the King undoubtedly lay in its providing a perfect vehicle for the histrionic talents of his last and most powerful favorite, the Duke of Buckingham."[9] Although King James probably liked *The Gypsies Metamorphos'd* for these reasons, as well as for the fact that it is a splendidly crafted masque, it is my postulate that the strange topicality of gypsyism, caused by the gypsy sign's objective agency, contributed significantly to its appeal and success.

In her essay "Critically Queer" Judith Butler purposefully extends Jacques Derrida's understanding of the performative to encompass issues of social identity. She claims that any performative utterance is not the function of the originating will of an individual but is always a derivative utterance following, and thus reliant upon, some previously codified act. Derrida writes: "Could a performative utterance succeed if its formulation did not repeat a 'coded' or iterable utterance, or in other words, if the formula I pronounce in order to open a meeting, launch a ship or a marriage were not identifiable as conforming with an iterable model, if it were not then identifiable in some way as a 'citation'?"[10] Butler explains the "citationality" or historical contingency of performativity that Derrida suggests: "If a performative provisionally succeeds (and I will suggest that 'success' is always and only provisional), then it is not because an intention successfully governs the action of speech, but only because that action echoes prior actions, and *accumulates the force of authority through the repetition or citation of a prior, authoritative set of practices.*"[11] This means that the probability of conveying an intended meaning with a performative act, even with a theatrical performance on the stage, or with basically any speech act or gesture, is dependent on one's ability to conform to or echo, indeed, cite preconceptions about the intended meaning. These preconceptions are, of course, themselves historically and socially conditional. They are the products of a citational history that is itself an infinite network of citationality or, as Nietzsche put it, like all things or customs they are the historical culmination of "a continuous sign-chain of ever new interpretations and adaptations whose causes do not even have to be related to one another but, on the contrary, in some cases succeed and alternate with one another in a purely chance fashion."[12] Concerning the present status in the sign-chain of the term "queer," Butler asks: "When and how does a term like 'queer' become subject to an affirmative resignification?" Her question assumes that "much of the straight world has always needed the queers it has sought to repudiate through the performative force of the term."[13] The present analysis pursues a similar question with regard to the resignification or increasing celebration of the signifier "gypsy" in early modern English literature and culture. What, by the 1620s, made the term so popularly affirmative, interesting, and voguish? Why gypsies at this historical moment?

To answer these questions, I must first turn to Jonson's text.[14] *The Gypsies Metamorphos'd* begins with the following stage directions: "*Enter a Gypsie leading a horse laden with five little children bound in a trace of scarfes upon him, a second leading another horse laden with stolne poultrie & c.,*" and "*The first leading Gypsie speakes, being the Iackman*" (121). The Jackman declares that the children are "the fiue Princes of Ægipt mounted all vpon one horse," and requests that the audience "Gaze vppon them as on the ofspringe of Ptolomçe begotten vppon seuerall Cleopatra's in theire seuerall counties" (121). In doing so, he pokes fun at what he implicitly suggests is the contrived or mistaken Egyptian history that was commonly assigned by contemporaries to England's allegedly immigrant gypsy population ("seuerall counties" refers to English counties). This initial implication is reflected throughout the text. *The Gypsies Metamorphos'd* contends, both tacitly and overtly, that there is really nothing Egyptian about the history of gypsies in England, and that English gypsy culture, with its mythologized Egyptian lineage, is a novel invention that is the composite outcome of criminal self-production and the popular construction of an alternative, criminal culture. To be sure, according to *this masque,* gypsy culture is almost identical to the culture of English rogues, vagabonds, beggars, cutpurses, cony-catchers, and prostitutes.

Yet this view is very different from that of some early chroniclers of criminal culture, the most prominent of whom were the Kentish justice of the peace Thomas Harman and English annalist William Harrison. In his groundbreaking account of criminal culture *A Caveat or Warening, For Commen Cursetors vulgarely called Vagabones* (1567), Harman distinguishes between rogues and vagabonds and "the wretched, wily, wandering vagabonds calling and naming themselves Egyptians."[15] In *The Description of England* (1587) Harrison says that English rogues and vagabonds copy "the Egyptian rogues" in devising their own language, called "canting."[16] Unlike Harman and Harrison, Jonson's gypsies possess the traits and speak the language characteristic of most personal, popular, commercial, and state representations of the rapidly flourishing criminal culture. Jonson's representation of gypsies, together with other contemporary representations, completely disavows all possible convenient or superficial differentiations between early modern England's gypsies and rogues and vagabonds and epitomizes the popular fetishism of the gypsy sign. It illuminates the seductive transversal gateway connecting gypsy identity to everyone else.

In its literary representation, the prevalent factor unifying criminal culture is the language, commonly called "cant," which was created and spoken by its members. Although this language is the subject of the next chapter (where I analyze its multiple uses for criminal culture), it here relates to the gypsy-rogue-vagabond alliance in the early modern "popular mind" as well as the gypsy-rogue-vagabond disconnection asserted by twentieth-century historians, cultural anthropologists, sociolinguists, and literary-cultural critics. Cant is the indicative solder for the gypsy-rogue-vagabond fusion in Jonson's masque which led Frank Aydelotte to exclaim in his seminal study *Elizabethan Rogues and Vagabonds,* "It is true that Ben Jonson in the *Masque of the Metamorphosed Gypsies,* working entirely at second hand, completely confuses two classes."[17] If Jonson was "working entirely at second hand," which is unlikely yet impossible to determine, it seems that he was working from reliable sources. His depiction of criminal culture is not confused but in fact consistent with practically every source utilized by Aydelotte, whose own work, like mine, is worlds away from first-hand experience.[18]

Jonson uses cant terms throughout *The Gypsies Metamorphos'd,* beginning with the introduction of the character called "Iackman."[19] "Iackman" is one of several functional names used by Jonson's gypsies, like the real-life speakers of cant, to denote their specific criminal occupation and social status within their own community. The functional names employed by Jonson's gypsies are included among the numerous functional names allegedly vernacular to early modern England's criminal culture. These are cataloged in such widely circulated texts as John Awdeley's *The Fraternitye of Vacabondes* (1561), which describes "*The Fraternitye of Vacabondes, both rufling and beggarly, Men and Women, Boyes and Girles, with their proper names and qualities*"; Thomas Harman's *A Caveat or Warening, For Commen Cursetors vulgarely called Vagabones* (1567), which describes all aspects of the criminal culture; William Harrison's *The Description of England* (1587), which describes "the several disorders and degrees amongst our idle vagabonds"; Thomas Dekker's *The Belman of London* (1608), which describes many of the same criminal types, "with their severall *qualities and manners of life*"; and Samuel Rid's *Martin Markall, Beadle of Bridewell: His Defense and Answers to the Bellman of London* (1610), which describes "the long-concealed Original and Regimen of Rogues."[20] Some examples given by Awdeley and Dekker that appear in *The Gypsies Metamorphos'd,* as well as in Harman and Harrison, are an "upright man" (gang leader), a "jackman" (counterfeiter), a "kintchin mort" (young whore), a "doxy" (older whore), and a "rogue" (gang member/criminal).[21]

Jonson's employment of the canting language, however, is not limited to functional naming. His gypsies use cant in discussion as well. At the conclusion of his introductory speech, Jonson's Jackman displays his proficiency in cant when he speaks of a young gypsy—the offspring of a sheriff's daughter and a gypsy captain—who must "marche in the infantes equipage . . . till with his painefull progenitours he be able to beate it on the hard hoofe to the bene bowse or the stauling ken, to nip a ian or cly the iarke."[22] Translation: The Jackman says that the young criminal must associate and operate with the other inexperienced criminals ("marche in the infantes equipage") until he learns enough to participate with his elders ("painefull progenitours") in the hard life of crime ("hard hoofe"), to cut a purse or be whipped (to nip a ian or cly the iarke"), and go with them to the alehouse ("bene bowse") or place in which stolen goods are received and disposed of ("stalling ken").[23] More important than this display of proficiency is the fact that the Jackman also informs the audience about the role of cant in gypsy-criminal culture: "If here we [the gypsies] be a little obscure, it is our pleasure, for rather then wee will offer to be our owne interpreters, we are resolued not to be vnderstood: yet if any man doubt of the significancie of the language, wee refer him to the third volume of reports sett forthe by the learned in the lawes of cantinge, and published in Gypsie tounge" (123, 125). And later in the narrative, rustic Pvp inquires about the gypsies's usage of cant: "Can they cant and mill? are they masters in theire artes?" ("mill" means "rob" or "steal" in the canting dictionaries of Harman, Dekker, and Head and Kirkman).[24] Since there is no evidence to suggest that he conflates the two languages for satiric or analogical purposes, for Jonson the "cantinge" or "cant" language and "Gypsie tounge" are the same. Middleton seems to have shared this view. In his play *More Dissemblers Besides Women* (1619) the gypsy band, complete with their "Captain," "doxies," and "dells," speaks "cant."[25] Therefore, according to Jonson as well as Middleton, for gypsies to be "masters in theire artes" they must be able to "cant and mill" like other members of criminal culture.

Nevertheless Frank Aydelotte asserts that language difference is key to differentiating between gypsy and English rogue-vagabond cultures. He concludes his analysis of the relationship between them with the following statement: "But the gipsies and the English rogues were two different classes. . . . The history of gipsy life in England and the measures employed against them is quite distinct from the history of English vagabond life, and far less important" (20). Why must Aydelotte introduce his conclusion with the conjunction "But"? The answer is that the evidence supplied by Aydelotte to support his conclusion falls drastically short of what appears to have been his intention: to uphold the longstanding historical, cultural, and biological distinction between what he considers the gypsy and English rogue-vagabond "races" (18). Such a motivation is wholly congruous with his assertion that "gipsy life" is "far less important" than "English vagabond life." The traditional formulation of Aydelotte's argument backfires because the evidence for a gypsy-rogue-vagabond alliance that he provides initially is far more compelling, though less developed, than his later evidence for their disconnection.

"Modern gipsies," claims Aydelotte, "use a few words belonging to the cant language of the sixteenth-century rogues, and, no matter from which they were borrowed, there must have been some intercourse between the two races"; he also accepts the "fact" that this enduring linguistic affiliation "indicate[s] that there was some connexion between the gipsies and the English rogues." But he nonetheless insists that "there is ample evidence that the two races were not identical." Aydelotte presents as his strongest argument against "the two races" being "identical" the fact that "the rogues' cant given by Harman is entirely distinct from Romany, the gypsy language."[26] For Aydelotte language equals "race." In her excellent book *The Traveller-Gypsies* cultural anthropologist Judith Okely observes that this sort of logic, which she treats with much skepticism, is fairly common among scholars of gypsy history and culture: "Language has been equated by the Gypsiologists with 'race.' . . . The underlying assumption is that language is transmitted or learnt only through biological descent."[27] Like Okely, I do not equate language with "race," but if I did I would argue that early modern England's gypsies, rogues, and vagabonds must have been "racially" identical since they spoke the same canting language. As I demonstrate in the next chapter, this point is further supported by the consistent claims in texts about gypsies, rogues, and vagabonds that cant was an exclusive language, and that it was only taught to and used by bonafide members of criminal culture.[28]

Aydelotte's line of argument for a gypsy-rogue-vagabond distinction is similarly proffered by A. L. Beier in his book *Masterless Men: The Vagrancy Problem in England, 1560–1640*. Beier claims: "Gypsies were different from English vagrants in having a language of their own, Romany."[29] To support this claim, he quotes two passages from Samuel Rid's *Martin Markall, Beadle of Bridewell* (1610), which occur within the following sentence: "Romany was 'spun out of three other tongues, viz. Latin, English and Dutch,' and was invented 'to the end their cozenings, knaveries, and villainies might not so easily be perceived,' according to one Jacobean writer" (60). Beier not only decontextualizes these passages but does so without providing a citation for them apart from indicating that they were written by a "Jacobean writer" discussing "Romany." To facilitate the "establishing of their new-found government" comprised of the two criminal factions, and to assist them when committing crimes, Rid says that the criminals invented their own language. He provides two examples of this language, the functional names "clapperdudgeon" and "counterfeit crank," both of which are attributed to the canting language by Awdeley, Harman, Dekker, and Head and Kirkman, as well as by Rid himself.[30] The following quotation from *Martin Markall: Beadle of Bridewell* includes the passages decontextualized by Beier:

> In the northern parts another sort of vagabonds (at the Devil's Arse A-Peak in Derbyshire) began a new regiment, calling themselves by the name of Egyptians. These were a sort of rogues that lived and do live by cozening and deceit, practising the art called legerdemain. . . . After a certain time that these upstart losels had got unto a head the two chief commanders [Giles Hather and "Cock Lorel, the most notorious knave that ever lived"] of both these regiments [the "Egyptians" and "Quartern of Knaves, called the five-and-twenty orders of knaves"] met at the Devil's Arse A-peak, there to parley and entreat of matters that might tend to the establishing of their new-found government. And first of all they think it fit to devise a certain kind of language, to the end their cozenings, knaveries, and villainies might not so easily be perceived and known in places where they come. And this their language they spun out of three other

tongues, viz., Latin, English and Dutch—these three especially, notwithstanding some few words they borrowed of Spanish and French. They also gave names to such persons of their company according to the kind of life that he undertook, as for example: a common beggar or rogue, they termed a clapperdudgeon; one that counterfeited the falling sickness, they termed him the counterfeit crank, for *crank* in their language is the falling sickness, and so counterfeit crank is the false falling sickness; and so of the rest.

This Cock Lorel continued among them longer than any of his predecessors before him or after him; for he ruled almost two-and-twenty years, until the year A.D. 1533.[31]

Beier's omission of relevant citation information can be explained by the fact that *Martin Markall, Beadle of Bridewell* never mentions Romany or any language exclusive to a gypsy population.[32] I underscore Beier's dubious use of important evidence not so much to censure him as to illustrate how such an application of historiographical evidence can lead to an authoritative communication of a fabricated historical reality that readily serves the interests of those inclined to believe and espouse the falsehood that there were only negligible miscegenational, exogamous, and interpersonal relations between the dark-skinned members of the gypsy population and the allegedly truly English population.

For instance, consider the fact that Beier cites T. W. Thompson's extremely well researched article in the *Journal of the Gypsy Lore Society* only to point out that the average size of a traveling gypsy band was "15.7 members." Beier uses this text only as a source of statistics and makes no reference to Thompson's main point, which pertains directly to the English gypsy-rogue-vagabond relationship that is the topic of Beier's own discussion. From his cross-examination of numerous constables's accounts and other sources, Thompson reveals that such prototypical English surnames as Brown, Smith, Bannester, Reynolds, Lawrence, Rowland, Thomas, and Jackson were also already or initially common gypsy surnames in early modern England. This suggests that early modern England's gypsies either assumed English names or, like its rogues and vagabonds, were of English heritage and thus were not recent immigrants.

Thompson concludes that this sameness in surnames—which he sees as the result of miscegenation—supports the fact that "Gypsy blood" flows through the veins of a great number of today's English populace: "From my own knowledge," remarks Thompson, "I can say that there have been Jacksons with at least a dash of Gypsy blood in them on the English roads in recent years."[33] Like most scholars who specialize in gypsy history and culture (often called "Gypsiologists"), Thompson spent years associating with and interviewing Britain's gypsies.[34] Hence, according to Thompson's credible, firsthand "knowledge," there is much "English" and "gypsy" blood flowing together in harmony today, even if those who identify themselves as English or gypsy deny it.

Contrary to Beier, while recounting the history of what I have termed early modern England's criminal culture, Rid mentions the crucial merging of two different groups of rogues and vagabonds, those led by Giles Hather and Kit Callot and those led by Cock Lorel. In his book *The Elizabethan Underworld* Gamini Salgado reminds us that Giles Hather and Kit Callot "had long been traditional English names before gypsies arrived in England," so Hather and Callot may very well have been of domestic and not immigrant parentage. "Cock Lorell, the hero," Aydelotte notes skeptically, "has been regarded by many early and modern writers as a real person—a famous leader of rogues and vagabonds."[35] Although Aydelotte's skepticism about the validity of Cock Lorel's "real" status is reasonable since stories told in early modern popular literature sometimes seem outlandish or farfetched—such as the accounts of incubi recounted by Reginald Scott in *The Discoverie of Witchcraft* (1584)—it is curious that he supplies no explanation for his skepticism. Instead he asserts without substantiation that Cock Lorel "occurs" in *Martin Markall, Beadle of Bridewell* "in the midst of a jumble of evident myth and hopelessly inaccurate history."[36] Since the information presented by most literary-cultural artifacts is of questionable validity, we have no way of knowing whether the legendary Cock Lorel was ever a real person. But we do know from the many contemporary references to him—such as in *Cocke Lorelles Bote* (n.d.), *A Strange Banquet, or the Devil's Entertainment by Cock Laurel at the Peak in Derbyshire* (n.d.), *The Treatyse Answerynge the Boke of Beardes* (n.d.), Robert Copland's *The Highway to the Spital-House* (1535–36), Awdeley's *The*

Fraternitye of Vacabondes (1561), and Jonson's *The Gypsies Metamorphos'd* (1621)—that he played a significant role in the popular conception of the genealogy of criminal culture. For this reason alone Rid's account should be taken seriously, but not necessarily as fact. Like the apparently fictional Robin Hood, whose legend is analogous, Cock Lorel occupied special space within official territory: he was notorious yet celebrated and highly romanticized. This is not because of his benevolence and allegiance to the king, which is the case of Robin Hood, but because of his infamous status as a revolutionary leader of criminal culture. Unlike Robin Hood, Cock Lorel is usually unambiguously represented as a real person (as in the passage from Rid quoted earlier).[37]

Beier notes: "Modern scholars have demonstrated that Romany is the product of many languages: the gypsy hegira from India through Europe can be charted linguistically from the vocabulary picked up along the way. But Romany was also the result of isolation from the culture of the society in which they had come to rest. This segregation, together with gypsy links with vagrants and crime, is seen in correlates between Romany and canting vocabulary."[38] To which Salgado adds, "It is worth noting that the confusion between the gypsy language and the canting tongue continued into the eighteenth century [a longtime association that renders the term "confusion" inappropriate]. *The English Rogue,* first published in 1665, gives as Romany speech a vocabulary which is almost wholly that of English vagrants, as does the life of Bamfylde Moore Carew published in the next century."[39] Like Beier, Salgado wrongly claims that a text, in this case Head and Kirkman's *The English Rogue,* calls the vocabulary it attributes to the language spoken by gypsies "Romany speech." Head and Kirkman never mention Romany, but the vocabulary they do attribute to gypsies is, as Salgado states, "almost wholly" consistent with other recordings of the canting language of "English vagrants." In his book *The Canting Crew: London's Criminal Underworld, 1550–1700,* John McMullan provides a brief etymological history of cant, which he deduces from the fact that popular and state literature began to represent or address issues relating to the canting language and gypsies at the same time: "The origins of cant coincided with the arrival of gypsies in the fourteenth and fifteenth centuries, and some cant terms derived from gypsy lore and language."[40] (Incidentally, this is all McMullan has to say about the gypsy-rogue-vagabond connection in his study.) I do not want to belabor the point that Aydelotte, Salgado, and Beier are resistant to the fact that the criminal population was either ethnically or "racially" integrated or comprised almost entirely of English rogues and vagabonds.[41] Rather, I highlight the fact that their work (inadvertently) demonstrates that the criminal population was English. Together with McMullan's deduction that the emergence of cant and gypsies "coincided," Aydelotte, Salgado, Beier, and McMullan make a convincing argument for a "racially" (or ethnically) integrated or native criminal population.

The Disguise Factor

The evidence discussed thus far, establishing that cant was used by all members of criminal culture, including gypsies (especially when read in light of Rid's historical account of the origin of this amalgamated criminal culture), indicates that there was substantial integration between dark- and white-skinned rogues, vagabonds, and gypsies. But what, then, do we make of Rid's statements that the vagabonds comprising the "new regiment" were "calling themselves by the name of Egyptians" and "causing their faces to be made black, as if they were Egyptians." What, exactly, does Rid mean by "as if"? It is suggested here that there were no immigrant gypsies with naturally dark skin in early modern England, and that the people "calling themselves by the name of Egyptians" were really white-skinned rogues and vagabonds who, "causing their faces to be made black," pretended to be Egyptians or gypsies. Posing a rhetorical question, I want to recall briefly the elusiveness and spectrality of the gypsy sign's referent outlined in the introduction to this chapter. If people were merely pretending to be dark-skinned gypsy immigrants, and if such an undertaking was truly simply a theatrical component of gypsy signification, then to what extent are we to accept the veracity of any claim, whether by Harman or Aydelotte, for a referent to the gypsy sign?

With this question in mind, I want to investigate the possibility that there were either just enough dark-skinned immigrant gypsies living in Britain, or suficient knowledge of continental gypsies circulating, to have served as inspiration and models for the emergent criminal culture.[42] I intend to prove that it was common for white-skinned rogues and vagabonds to blacken their faces, fancifully attire themselves, practice fortune-telling, and label themselves Egyptians. Moreover, they did this not to mock gypsies, as was the case with the use of blackface by white people to travesty black people in the nineteenth and twentieth centuries, but to pass as or become gypsies.[43] As Aydelotte states, "There are several statutes against English vagabonds disguising themselves as gipsies or wandering in company with them, which indicates that there were some relations between the two races."[44] Over time, as I shall show, the statutes concerned with gypsies, rogues, and vagabonds differentiated less and less between them. Authorities became progressively more aware of the masquerade confusing these social categories, of the similarities actually existing between them, and of the fact that gypsies were actually rogues and vagabonds who distinguished themselves from the rest of the English populace with an alternative society and culture that they invented for themselves.

Early modern England's gypsies, as Beier is quick to assert, formed "a genuine alternative society," albeit not in the same terms "as many do today."[45] Today's recognizable or unambiguous English gypsy population, as Brian Vesey-Fitzgerald and Okely respectively document, is behaviorally identified and allegedly consanguineously related. To be a member of a gypsy community today, one must not only look and act like a gypsy—which was the case for gypsies in early modern England—but also meet the standard for kinship through a sanguineous connection to an accepted, authentic member.[46] England is now much more ethnically diverse, and it is less economically advantageous and desirable to be a member of a gypsy community than it was in early modern England. Therefore, according to Vesey-Fitzgerald and Okely, today's gypsy population is more exclusive, relatively smaller, and prefers to pass unnoticed, which it can now do more easily than ever before. By contrast, early modern England's gypsy population, or the population that called themselves gypsies or Egyptians, was more inclusive and popularly desirable, spectacularly blatant, both unavoidably and necessarily criminal(ized), and (predominantly) white-skinned or already integrated to the extent that skin color was ambiguous.

Of course, as I have argued, gypsy culture was all of these things because gypsyism was transversally empowered and fetishized.

The precedential gypsy statute of 1530, entitled "An Act concerning Egyptians," was passed sixteen years after the first known literary reference to gypsies in England. This literary reference occurs as a short discussion on an "egypcyan" fortune-teller in Thomas More's *A Dyalog of Syr Thomas More Knyghte* (1514).[47] The act orders the expulsion from England of the "dyverse and many outlandysshe People callynge themselfes Egyptians [who] so many tymes by crafte and subtyltie had deceyved the People of theyr Money and also had comytted many and haynous Felonyes and Robberies."[48] In addition to the lack of evidence by which to ascertain the size of the gypsy population at the time, there is insufficient evidence to assess the degree to which their banishment was enforced.[49] On 5 December 1537, in a letter addressed to "my lorde of Chestre, president of the Counsaile of the Marches of Wales," Henry VIII's chief minister, Thomas Cromwell, chastises local officials for not dealing with the gypsies and commands them: "Laye diligent espiall throughowte all the partes there aboutes youe and the shires next adjoynyng whether a of the sayd personnes calling themselfes Egipsysans shall fortune to enter or travayle in the same. And in cace youe shall here or knowe of any suche, be they men or women, that ye shall compell them to repair to the nexte porte of the see to the place where a shellbe taken . . . without sparing uppon a commyssion licence or placarde that they may shewe or aledge for themselfes."[50]

Not only does this letter indicate some laxity of state power with regard to the gypsy problem; as Salgādo points out, it also indicates "the existence of the trade in forged licenses . . . (we may remember that the speaker in Jonson's masque is the Jackman, a counterfeiter of seals) [and] also perhaps that some local officials at least were not averse to granting gypsies a license, if only to see them safely off the parish."[51] For instance, a letter dated 19 January 1549 from the Justices of Durham to the Earl of Shrewsbury, indicates that "John Roland oon of that sorte of people callinge themselffes Egiptians" accused "*Baptist Fawe, Amy Fawe,* and *George Fawe,* Egiptians," of having "counterfeate the Kyngs Maties Greate Seale," and that when apprehended the accused persons were found with "one wryting with a greate Seall moche like to the Kings Maties greate Seall, which we bothe by the wrytinge and also by the Seall do suppose to be counterfeate and feanyd."[52] That gypsies had access to counterfeit licenses means that they could have traveled freely throughout the realm. Such exceptional travel privileges would have given gypsies, as promulgators of transversal thought and criminal culture, the opportunity to commingle with a wide variety of people, use their anonymity to their advantage, solicit new gypsy members, and set up criminal operations in numerous towns.

The Philip and Mary Act of 1555, entitled "An Act against certain Persons calling themselves Egyptians," and the Elizabethan Act of 1562, entitled "An Act for the further punyshement of Vagabondes callyng them selues Egiptians," reconsider and revise the 1530 statute.[53] And a directive in 1569 from the Privy Council to the London Aldermen, which establishes the rhetoric for most future gypsy-rogue-vagabond statutes (even as late as the Derbyshire order of 1629), further undermines the exclusive or immigrant status of gypsies by lumping them together or homogenizing them with English rogues and vagabonds.[54] The 1562 statute abolishes the practice of banishment of native-born gypsy offspring since they are technically, by birthright, English citizens. It also stipulates that these offspring or any people will be condemned if found "counterfaityng, transformyng, or disguising them selues by theyr apparell, speeche, or other behauiour, lyke vnto suche vagaboundes cõmonly called or callyng them selues Egiptians."[55] Here it seems that immigrant gypsies and "vagaboundes cõmonly called or callyng them selues Egiptians" might have been different. The 1569 directive demands the apprehension of "all vacabonds, sturdy beggers comonlie called Roges, or Egiptians, and all other idle vagrant personnes hauinge no masters nor any certainie howe or wherby to lyve, and theime cause to be imprisoned in stockes and suche like, and according to the qualities of there faultes to procede againste theyme."[56] As Aydelotte, Salgado, Beier, and Randall emphasize, the state was under the impression that gypsies, whoever they were, posed a grave threat to the social order.[57] But how many people really disguised themselves as or became gypsies?

By the end of the sixteenth century, the phrasing of the Elizabethan Act of 1562, which, as Salgado puts it, "seems to take note of the genuine gypsy and the fake," was typical of all legal documents pertaining to gypsies and their alleged counterfeits.[58] For instance, the 1597 Elizabethan "Acte for Punyshment of Rogues, Vagabondes, and Sturdy Beggars" demands: "All such persons . . . wandering and pretending themselves to be Egipcyans, or wandering in the Habbite, Forme or Attyre of counterfayte Egipcyans; shalbe taken adjudged and deemed Rogues, Vagabondes and Sturdy Beggars."[59] This statute says nothing of immigrant gypsies since it equates "counterfayte Egipcyans" with "Rogues, Vagabondes and Sturdy Beggars." Consider the following examples from the state papers with references to gypsies:

1539, Feb 2. John Vernon (Sheriff of Staffordshire) to Cromwell. "This Candlemas they, George Fas and Michael Meche, 'two Egyptians as they say,' came to his house . . .

[20 May] 1540. Nicholas Robertson to Cromwell. "Master Paynell, bailiff of Boston, as come hither to convey up certain persons 'namynge themsellffes Egiptians' in prison here. On Monday in Rogation Week four Egyptians came hither from Lenn and were carried up to London by the Undermarshal of the Marshalsea.

Westminster, Feb. 21, 1542–3. "Letters wer written to George Paullett and Jhon Norton to avoyde the countrey off a certayne nombre off vagabondes going upp and downe in the name off Egiptians."

1576, March 10. "A letter to the Lord Keper that where they are given tunderstand that there are . . . apprehendid certen lewde vagabundes, men and women, namyng themselfes Egiptians, wandring under colour of a counterfett licence . . .

1577. "A letter to the Sherif of Bucks . . . certifieng the apprehencion in that countie of certein rogues namyng themselfes Egiptians . . .

1589, June 17. "A letter to the Justices of Assize for the county of Hereford; whereas theire Lordships were given to understand of certaine lewd and badd persons terminge them selves Egiptians, that lived by deceitfull shiftes, pilfering and abusing of the people, going from place to place . . . about the countie with a counterfaicte passeport.[60]

Every one of these representative documents intimates uncertainty about the authenticity of the "vagabondes" and "rogues" who called themselves "Egiptians" and wandered "under colour of a counterfett licence." In fact, except for the one dated 1540, which speaks of "four Egyptians" incarcerated "On Monday in Rogation Week," which was when officials conducted a manhunt for rogues and vagabonds, none of the documents refer to Egyptians without skepticism about the authenticity of their identity. Although it is occasionally ambiguous as to whether this skepticism pertains to their status as Egyptians from Egypt, it is usually clear that it pertains to their status as something other than English rogues and vagabonds. The issue is typically whether or not they are dark-skinned immigrants.

This skepticism is understandable, given the fact that many of the Egyptians apprehended did eventually confess to being fakes, that is, they confessed to being English rogues and vagabonds disguised as gypsies. For example, Thompson found that Robert Hylton, who appears in Harman's 1567 list of rogues and vagabonds, "was convicted of felony 'for callinge himself by the name of an Egiptian' in 1591."[61] Was Hylton a rogue or a gypsy or both? Salgado notes that "on 27 November 1618 a witness deposed before two Justices at Manchester that on his way to Heppenstall fair in Yorkshire he met a company of counterfeit Egyptians one of whom he believed was called William Waller. Waller, a shoemaker of Newcastle-upon-Tyne, was examined and duly confessed that he was born in Newcastle and that he 'traveled under the pretence of counterfeit Egyptians.'"[62] What was so compelling about being a gypsy that a shoemaker would risk his life to travel as one? As specified by the state, Egyptian impersonation did not go unpunished. For instance, "Manchester Constables' Accounts also record a payment of two shillings and eight pence 'for whipping of eight counterfeit gypsies that were taken with a private search.'"[63]

Unclear in the state records regarding gypsies are the criteria by which officials differentiated between "real" and "counterfeit" gypsies. By almost always discussing Egyptians with skepticism, the records imply that there may have been no immigrant gypsies. The popularized skepticism about gypsy identity that the records reflect was eventually attenuated or obviated by a new definition of gypsy identity that took for granted its performative nature. For instance, in *The Guide to Tongues* (1617) John Minsheu tells of "a counterfet Egyptian" or "cousening Fortune-teller" who clarifies: "Egyptians are in our Statutes and Lawes of England, a counterfet kinde of roagues, that being English or Welsh people, accompanie themselves together, disguising themselves in strange roabes, blacking their faces and bodies, and framing to themselves an unknowen language, wander up and downe, and under pretense of telling of fortunes, curing diseases, and such like, abuse the ignorant common people, by stealing all that is not too hot, or too heavie for their carriage."[64]

The constant expression of skepticism about gypsy identity over so many years leaves little room for the belief in the existence of immigrant gypsies in early modern England. Certainly gypsies could not have existed in the huge numbers posited by Beier, which are exaggerated only if it is assumed, as Beier does, that all gypsies had naturally dark skin and were immigrants or of immigrant parentage. "But whatever the explanation," asserts Beier, "the conclusion is inescapable that gypsies travelled in much larger groups than other vagrants."[65] In line with this point is the fact that early modern English descriptions of gypsy culture are in many respects consistent with descriptions of gypsy culture from the Renaissance to the present, which also claimed that gypsies traveled nomadically in groups, were performers and palmisters, and practiced immorality and thievery. Therefore there may have been some immigrant gypsies living in early modern England, or certainly enough people talking about the lifestyle of continental gypsies to have made a significant impression on, as Minsheu maintains, many "English or Welsh people." Either way, however disseminated and manifested, the gypsy concept was attractive and potent.

Early modern England's popular and commercial literature about gypsies, as we have seen in Jonson, takes the skepticism of the state papers even further. This literature exposes the gypsy-forgery trend by not only highlighting the ways in which rogues and vagabonds disguised themselves as gypsies but also by furnishing an explanation for why they would want to assume gypsy identities. By making gypsies the subject of so much literature, these writers reveal gypsyism's immense popularity and transversal attraction. In *Lanthorne and Candle-Light* (1608), for example, Thomas Dekker vividly and cogently describes the gypsies, *all* of whom he claims are counterfeits. Generally speaking, Dekker says: "They are a people more scattred then Jewes, and more hated: beggerly in apparell, barbarous in condition, beastly in behavoir: and bloudy if they meete advantage. A man that sees them would sweare they had all the yellow Jawndis, or that they were Tawny Moores bastardes, for no Red-oaker man caries a face of a more filthy complexion."[66] He explains that the gypsies's dark skin—their "filthy complexion"—is artificial: "[Y]et are they not borne so, neither as the Sonne burnt them so, but they are painted so: yet they are not good painters neither, for they do not make faces, but marre faces" (236). He is just as sure that "they never discended from the tribes of any of those people that came out of the land of *Egypt: Ptolomy* (King of the Egiptians) I warrant never called them his Subjects: no nor *Pharaoh* before him" (236). Dekker denies gypsy authenticity, that is, as a people who have migrated from Egypt, and maintains that English gypsy culture is despicable and entirely contrived.

Dekker says gypsies are "in mockery" called "*Moon-men*" because "*a Moonman* signifies in English, a mad-man," yet they are not "absolutely mad, not yet perfectly in their wits"; like the moon, he explains, they are "never in one shape two nights together" and they "never tary one day in a place" (235–36). According to Dekker, gypsies granted themselves the luxury of forever changing their appearance and geographical location. This nomadic aspect of their transversality set them apart from others who abided by the law, which disallowed travel outside of one's parish without a permit. In a statement wrongly employed by Aydelotte and Salgado to illuminate the "racial" difference between gypsies and English rogues and vagabonds,[67] Dekker maintains that there is as much difference between "a civell cittizen of Dublin and a wilde Irish Kerne" as there is "betwéene one of these counterfeit Egiptians and a true English Begger."[68] His analogy indicates not "racial" but moral or class difference. For Dekker both the "civell cittizen" and "wilde Irish Kerne" (a foot soldier or loutish person) are Irish, just as both the "counterfeit" Egyptian and "true" (honest) English beggar are English.

Dekker describes in some detail the garb of the gypsies, which is distinct from that of the average English beggar, as well as the purposefulness of this alternative garb: "Their apparell is odd, and phantasticke, tho it be never so full of rents: the men weare scarfes of Callico, or any other base stuffe, *hanging* their bodies like Morris-dancers, with bels, and other toyes, to intice the countrey people to flocke about them, and to wounder at their fooleries or rather rancke knaveryes" (237–38). Although Dekker says this with an ironic and annoyed tone, he subtly exposes his own envy for the popularity of the gypsy men (for their seductive, ornate "bodies"). He expresses similar sentiments for the gypsy women. Like the gypsy men, who don "apparell" that "is odd, and phantasticke," the women, too, "intice the countrey people to flocke about them," with their deceptive practices and embellished appearance; the latter is also theatrically inspired: "The women as ridiculously attire themselves, and (like one that plaies the Roague on a stage) weare rages, and patched filthy mantles upermost, when the under garments are hansome and in fashion" (238). In other words, Dekker maintains that gypsy women, like gypsy men and stage actors, dress and play the part of their choice. That they could afford "handsome" and "fashion[able]" undergarments implies that they were financially successful. Dekker aligns himself with other early modern writers who wrote about criminal culture by exposing, often in the midst of an otherwise harsh description, his attraction for the gypsy persona and the gypsies's criminal way of life. This brings us back to the attractiveness of Jonson's gypsies, which is so strikingly apparent and alluring for his rustics. Jonson's rustics' response to the gypsies is wholly consistent with Dekker's account.

Upon first seeing the gypsies, rustic Towneshead declares: "These are a couie of Gipsies, and the brauest newe couie that euer constable flewe at; goodlie game, Gipsies! they are Gipsies o' this year, o' this moone, in my conscience."[69] For Townshead, most of all, the gypsies are an abstraction; they exist positively in his "conscience." Rustic Clod responds, "O, they are calld the Moone men, I remember now" (155). The rustics are very excited by the arrival of the "Male Gipsies all," and so eager to carouse with them that they immediately call for "some musique" and "take out the wenches" (157). Although they are not naïve—they are aware that they must protect themselves against the thievery of the gypsies, as Pvp insists: "But looke to our pockettes and purses for our own sake"—the rustics nonetheless celebrate the gypsies wholeheartedly: "Come girls," yells rustic Cock, "here be Gipsies come to towne: letts dance 'em town!" (159). The rustics praise the gypsies with such adulatory words as "wise," "learned" and "diuine" (161–63), and the "fine fingered Gypsies" tell them their fortunes while they slyly and surreptitiously steal their purses and other belongings" (165–69). In this scene Jonson captures the essence of the gypsies' fetishized status. For the opportunity to associate even for a short time with the all-male gypsy band, the rustics are willing to share their women, whom they treat possessively and who are presumably their usual objects of desire, and sacrifice their belongings to the gypsies' thievery. But this is really not a matter of willingness or sacrifice. The rustics perceive the gypsies as possessing a mysterious yet irresistible charm, of which they are envious. The rustics see the gypsies as wondrous products of humanity or God—they are "wise," "learned" and "diuine"—and consequently relate to them with astonishment and servility. Pierre Bourdieu uses the term "political fetishism" to describe this situation: "Political fetishism lies precisely in the fact that the value of the hypostatized individual, that product of the human brain, appears as charisma, a mysterious objective property of the person, an elusive charm, an unnameable mystery."[70] The fetishism of the gypsies or, rather, this fetishism of everything intangibly associated with gypsyism (the gypsy sign) dominates the rustics' field of desire to such an extent that they no longer merely desire the gypsies' company. The gypsies' affective presence is so powerful and seductive that the rustics want to subjugate themselves to them.

After the Patrico returns their stolen goods, the rustics enthusiastically express their desire to become gypsies themselves. In a characteristically transversal move, the rustics want to dissolve their conventional identity and reconstitute themselves as gypsies. This way they would immerse themselves in the aura of the fetishized gypsy sign. They would no longer desire, as rustics, the company of gypsies, which is an association that must always be slippery, amorphous, and ephemeral. The desire to abandon their rustic existence and become gypsy, and thus adopt a gypsy lifestyle, is transversal because it would require deterritorialization from official territory rather than the accepted socioeconomic position into which the rustics were born. It would have been significantly less threatening to official culture and state power for a rustic to pursue a career as an artisan, a merchant, or a clergyman than to become a gypsy.

In response to the rustics's plea, the Patrico gladly supplies a litany of procedures they must perform and traits they must acquire in order to become gypsies. Among these is the special formula for blackening their faces to which Dekker alludes when he talks of their artificial skin color:

> Of our Ptolomęes knott,
> It is, and 'tis not;
> To change your complexion
> With the noble confection
> Of wall nuttes and hoggs greace.[71]

Once again gypsy identity is depicted as a performative identity, available to anyone willing and capable of playing the part. Patrico's understanding of the performativity of gypsy identity as a citational enterprise (as Butler would put it)—including his special complexion-blackening formula for proper gypsy codification—is similarly expressed by the anonymously authored ballad *The Brave English Gipsy,* which was probably written sometime between 1600 and 1625, when it was in circulation. The supposed gypsy singer of the ballad indicates the solution for the gypsies' white skin: "The walnut tree supplies our lacke; / What was made faire, we can make black.... We can paint when we command, / And looke like Indians that are tand."[72] The singer also gives voice to the gypsy credo: "To drinke, be drunke, and tipsie, / Delights the English Gipsie: / We live to love all those / Who are no Gipsies foes" (186). As in Jonson's masque, the gypsy community is here represented as a relatively open community, accepting all people as long as they are tolerant of the gypsy aesthetic and lifestyle. This positive view of gypsyism, expressed with playful irony but no obvious critique, is also given in the play *The Spanish Gypsy,* which was performed for Prince Charles at Whitehall in 1623 and 1624.[73] That *The Spanish Gypsy,* like *The Gypsies Metamorphos'd,* was repeatedly performed for the aristocracy further attests to the widespread, trans-class popularity and fetishized status of the gypsies.

In this play the Spanish gypsies distinguish themselves from the English gypsies by claiming that they do not practice thievery; earning their money only as entertainers and fortune-tellers. When Alvarez, the benevolent leader of the Spanish gypsies, summons his cohorts, he adjures: "Be not English gipsies, in whose company a man's not sure of the ears of his head, they so pilfer!" To which his buddy Carlo replies in agreement, "Gipsies, and yet pick no pockets?" (2.1.38–44). However ironic this line may seem, when read in light of the constant positive depiction of honest gypsies in this play, it is clear that it should be taken literally. The Spanish gypsies also distinguish themselves from their English counterparts by not changing the hue of their skin; while they do wear flamboyant clothing characteristic of gypsies and travel nomadically, they do not blacken their faces. When Diego tells Louis of the gypsy woman with whom he is infatuated, he proclaims that she is a gypsy "in her condition, not in her complexion" (1.5.106). Alvarez concretizes this distinction when he boasts to his gypsy band, "The tailor's shears has cut us into shapes fitting our trades. . . . Gipsies, but no tanned ones; no red-ochre rascals umbered with soot and bacon as the English gipsies are" (2.1.1–7). In *The Spanish Gypsy,* what is most appealing about the gypsies, including English gypsies, is their entertainment value and their nomadic and communal lifestyle. Least appealing, according to this author, is their criminality and artificially darkened skin.[74]

Although Jonson champions the gypsies throughout *The Gypsies Metamorphos'd,* the play's epilogue discloses an apparent ambivalence regarding the gypsies's artificially darkened skin:

> But least it proue like wonder to the sight
> To see a Gipsie, as an ÆEthiop, white,
> Knowe that what dide our faces was an oyntment
> Made and laid on by Master Woolfs appointment,
> The Courtes *Lycanthropos,* yet without spelles,
> By a meere barbor, and no magicke elles:
> It was fetcht of with water and a ball;
> And to our transformation this was all,
> Saue what the master fashioner calls his,
> For to a Gypsies metamorphosis
> (Who doth disguise his habit and his face,

And takes on a false person by his place)
The power of poesie can neuer faile her
Assisted by a barbor and a taylor.[75]

According to this epilogue (probably delivered by the actor who played the Jackman), gypsy metamorphosis, whether experienced by a gypsy at large or an actor playing gypsy on the stage, requires one to "disguise his habit and his face, / And takes on a false person by his place." But if the offstage gypsy, the one who indulges in gypsyism in everyday life, is always pretending to be a gypsy, then this gypsy is indeed a "false person." The performative identities of all gypsies, whether onstage or off, make them "false" gypsies. In other words, regarding early modern England's gypsies, the "false person" and the "real person" are one and the same since there were only performative gypsies. Thus, the "place" occupied by and demarcating the "false person" must be a radical locality somewhere within transversal territory. The gypsy transcended both conceptually and materially his or "her" subjective territory, as well as the spatiotemporal and sociopolitical mandates of official territory; the gypsy moved into or crossed over into transversal territory.

Magnetic Criminal Culture

When one considers the austere conditions of subjectification generated by the period's state machinery, official culture, and state power, it is not surprising that *The Spanish Gypsy*'s author and others who wrote about criminal culture celebrated the alternative, liberated, transversal existence of gypsies. They fetishized the gypsy sign both because it was the spirit of gypsyism that they sought and because the gypsy referent was always absent, always obscured by the disguise, the deception, and the theatricality that was so essential to being a gypsy. The absence of the referent left imaginary room for both the gypsy sign's expansion and fulfillment.[76]

In *The Spanish Gypsy* Carlo points out that the gypsy "trade" is as "free as a mason's."[77] And Alvarez proclaims, "If one city cannot maintain us, away to another!" (2.1.51). Gypsies were free and would not be contained. Transversally inspired, gentleman Sancho entreats gentleman Soto: "We'll live as merrily as beggars; let's both turn gipsies" (2.2.171–72). And Soto eagerly accepts the proposal: "Come, then, we'll be gipsified" (2.2.176). Later on Sancho confesses to Roderigo that he has abandoned his prescribed subjective address as "gentleman": "But now-a-days 'tis all the fashion [to become gypsy]. . . . I have thus transformed myself out of a gentleman into a gipsy" (3.1.77, 90–91). Like Sancho and Soto, Middleton's Dondolo in *Dissemblers* is eager to gypsify and appeals to the sensibilities of the gypsy captain: "I pray take me into some grace amongst you too. . . . I had two uncles that were both hanged for robberies . . . and a brave cut-purse to my cousin-german. If kindred will be taken, I am as near a kin to a thief as any of you that had fathers and mothers."[78] As in Harman's *A Caveat or Warening, For Commen Cursetors vulgarely called Vagabones* and Jonson's play *Bartholomew Fair* (1614), "kindred" here is determined through a family history of thievery;[79] the fact that kindred is not determined through sanguinity alone, as with continental and modern gypsies, is further evidence that early modern England's gypsies were different. Dondolo emphasizes, "The naked truth is, sir, I would be made a Gypsy as fast as you could devise" (4.2.120–21). To which the Captain responds, "With rusty bacon thus I gypsify thee," as he dabs Dondolo with the bacon used to "black our faces" (4.2.186, 199).

Hence, like Jonson's rustics, Middleton's Dondolo and *The Spanish Gypsy*'s Madrid gentlemen want to and, indeed, become gypsies, for as gypsies they are "free" to live "merrily" wherever they please, and "if one city cannot maintain" them, they simply depart "away to another." As the singer of *The Brave English Gipsy* poetically rejoices, "English Gipsies live all free, / And love and live most jovially."[80] This sentiment is echoed by Middleton's gypsy captain:

> We have neither house nor land,
> Yet never want good year. . . .
> Come live with us, come live with us,
> All you that love your eases.
> He that's a Gypsy
> May be drunk or tipsy
> At what hour he pleases.[81]

But perhaps most compelling, as Sancho announces, is that "now-a-days" (the 1620s) it was "all the fashion" to abandon one's conventional identity and become a gypsy. Becoming gypsy was so popular that, as we have seen, the catchphrase "gypsify" was invented to describe the process. In one way or another, many people were influenced by gypsyism—were becoming gypsified. If people were not adventurous enough to gypsify themselves in everyday life, to become a gypsy for all the world to see, they gypsified themselves ephemerally as an actor on the public stage, vicariously as a spectator of a play about gypsies, as a devoted fan or fetishist of gypsyism, or perhaps as a literary-cultural critic writing about gypsies.

The opportunity to demonstrate some radical independence by violating the law and roaming freely and merrily throughout the realm with one's gypsified pals must have been enticing for both common people dissatisfied with the era's troubled socioeconomic system and upper-class people who were bored or adventurous (as in *The Spanish Gypsy*). But what, in addition to the delightful feeling of empowerment that such a rebellious communal enterprise facilitates, fueled the popular longing for knowledge of and association with the gypsy community and criminal culture in general? To some extent, the answer to this question, as just implied, must lie with socioeconomic concerns, for unprecedented overpopulation, extensive poverty, and unemployment characterized this remarkable historical moment. Certainly criminality had its economic advantages, and it was especially economically advantageous to be a gypsy. The generally exotic disposition of gypsies or those pretending to be gypsies in England—exemplified by their dark skin, ostentatious clothing, nomadic and communal lifestyle, and foreign canting language—made it easier for them to deploy some cons (such as in fortune-telling, astrological readings, and herbal remedies) and to intimidate people, inadvertently or otherwise, into giving them alms. In fact, as evinced by constables' records, it was common for town officials and landowners to pay gypsies to leave or stay away from their town or property. As a result, gypsies made money by doing nothing other than simply venturing where they were not wanted. They inspired a transversal economy in which people were paid to effect their own disappearance and estrangement from official culture: their own nomadism.

The following sample of gypsy-related entries in the constables' records from the parishes of Market Harborough, Melton Mowbray, Wymeswold, Stathern, and Ecclesfield testifies to the enduring popularity of the pay-the-gypsy-to-go-away practice:

1606.   Itm payed to the Echipsions the xxvij day of July in there passage to Cumberlande . . . ij[s]

1610.   layd out to the Gipsyes . . . iij[s] iii[d]

1612.   payd the 17 of February 1612 for Jipses that had a passe . . . viii[d]

1613.   Gyven to the gippsis to ride the towne of them . . . xij[d]

1618.   Itm given to the Gipseyes the 8th of Junne . . . ij[s] vj[d]

1623.   Given to the Egyptians . . . 6[d]

1632.   Given to a great Companie of gipes 16 August . . . 1[s] 4[d]

1640.   Given to twellve gippsies to pass them away . . . 1[s][82]

Although obviously the by-products of gypsy discrimination and fetishization, people became gypsies to take advantage of the privileges exclusive to the gypsy-criminal population. After all, if the many texts that depict them are reliable, and I think their consistency shows that they are, the gypsies were fortunate in comparison to the bulk of early modern England's population, which consisted of hardworking poor folk and beggars. As the gypsy ballad singer crows:

Our fare is of the best;
Three times a weeke we feast,
Nay, sometimes every day,
And yet for nothing pay,
For beefe or bacon, geese or hens;
What we eate is other mens. [83]

This view of criminal culture's decadence is supported by Somersetshire Justice Edward Hext's letter to a member of the Privy Council in 1596:

And I maye Iustlye saye that the Infynyte numbers of the Idle wandrynge people and robbers of the land are the chefest cause of the dearthe [of food], for thowghe they labor not, and yet they spend dobly as myche as the laborer dothe, for they lye Idlely in the ale howses daye and nyght eatinge and drynkynge excessively. And within these iij monethes I tooke a thief that was executed this last assises that confessed vnto me that he and too more laye in an Ale-house three weeks in which tyme they eate xx^{ti} fatt sheepe wherof they stole every night on, besydes they breake many a poore mans plowghe by stealing an Oxe or too from him and not beinge able to buy more leaseth a great parte of his tyllage that yere, others leese ther shepe owt of ther folds by which ther grounds are not so frute-full as otherwyse they wold be.[84]

The criminals' luxurious lifestyle is celebrated in many popular texts, often without the accompanying contradictory disparagement and admi-ration that characterizes much gypsy-rogue-vagabond literature.[85] This is especially true of texts written during and after the 1620s, such as Jonson's *The Gypsies Metamorphos'd* (1621), John Fletcher and Philip Massinger's play *Beggars Bush* (first performed at court in 1622), the poetry of John Taylor (the Water Poet) (1630), Richard Brome's play *A Jovial Crew: or, The Merry Beggars* (1641), and James Shirley's play *The Sisters* (1642). It was during this period that criminal culture's transversal power culminated contemporaneously with the English populace's dissatisfaction with the monarchical state machinery and shortly before criminal culture's trans-versal power was diluted, neutralized, or simply eclipsed by the English civil war. For the most part, all of the texts cited straightforwardly express their fascination with criminal culture.

The rogues and vagabonds in Fletcher and Massinger's *Beggars Bush* sing a song that epitomizes criminal culture's worldview or, more accu-rately, the popular view of criminal culture:

In the world look out and see: where so happy a Prince as he
    [their leader, Higgen]
Where the Nation live so free, and so merry as do we?
Be it peace, or be it war, here at liberty we are,
And enjoy our ease and rest; To the fields we are not prest;
Nor are call'd into the Towne, to be troubled with the Gowne.
Hang all Officers we cry, and the Magistrate too, by;

When the Subsidie's encreast, we are not a penny sest.
Nor will any goe to law, with the Beggar for a straw.
All which happinesse, he brags, he doth owe unto his rags.[86]

Throughout the early modern period "beggar" was often used synonymously with "rogue" and "vagabond" to indicate a member of the criminal community.[87] About beggars John Taylor similarly writes in his poem
"The Beggar":

He liues in such a safe and happy state. . . .
He nothing feares, nor nothing hath to lose.
Let Towns and Towres with batt'ry be o're-turn'd,
Let women be deflowr'd and houses burn'd:
Let men fight pell-mell, and lose life and lim,
If earth and skies escape, all's one to him. . . .
Thus is a Begger a strange kinde of creature,
And begg'ry is an Art that liues by Nature:
For he neglect all Trades, all Occupations. . . .
Hee's his owne Law, and doth euen what he list.[88]

Richard Brome's *A Jovial Crew: or, The Merry Beggars* (1641), which depicts
a community of rogues and vagabonds (complete with its gypsy Patrico),
also wonderfully captures both the immorality and transversality of criminal culture. Gentleman Hilliard exclaims, "Beggars! They are the only
people can boast the benefit of a free state, in the full enjoyment of liberty,
mirth and ease, having all things in common and nothing wanting of nature's whole provision within the reach of their desires."[89] And Springlove,
steward to the aristocrat Master Oldrents, declares to the beggars, "You are
a jovial crew, the only people whose happiness I admire" (34). Like *The
Spanish Gypsy*'s gentlemen Sancho and Roderigo and *Dissemblers*' Dondolo,
Oldrents's daughters Rachel and Meriel become happy members of criminal culture. Rachel vaunts, "Such as we saw so merry, and you concluded
were th'only happy people in a nation" (44). To which Meriel cheerfully
adds, "The only free men of a commonwealth; free above scot-free; that observe no law, obey no governor, use no religion, but what they draw from
their own ancient custom, or constitute themselves, yet are no rebels" (44).

Brome's rogues and vagabonds negate every aspect of the state machinery and official culture (they "observe no law, obey no governor, use no religion"), but they are not interested in rebellion (they "are no rebels"). It is not in their interest to overthrow the state but rather to live parasitically off it, like fleas on the back of a dog. Frapolo, the chief bandit in James Shirley's play *The Sisters,* reminds his men, "You shall live grandees, till the State fangs catch you."[90]

The Sexual Initiative

Economic motivations, however, cannot adequately or primarily explain the becomings-gypsy-rogue-vagabond phenomenon. There was clearly much more behind the dynamic process of becoming criminal than economic impetus in the strict, monetary sense. There was also an economy of sexual desire that informed this process. Fortunately, when taking the next investigative step into sexual issues, we do not need to uncover or piece together the sexual infrastructure lurking subtextually within representations of the gypsy fetish. This is because the public's sexual interests in criminal culture permeates the surface meaning of almost all popular literature about gypsies and rogues and vagabonds. Transgressive sexuality is the window through which criminal culture's chroniclers scrutinize their fetishized gypsy-sign-object. The relationship of the chroniclers to criminal culture was much like that of an envious, rejected, hostile lover. They claim to be disclosing, often at great personal risk, clandestine aspects of criminal culture so that their readers will be equipped with information with which to better defend themselves against criminals. And while they often speak contemptuously about gypsies and rogues and vagabonds, they also seductively sensationalize their sexual and criminal practices. Yet the paradoxically critical and celebratory discussion of criminal culture's sexuality—the discrepant popular representation of the sexual desires, gender roles, and sexual behavior supposedly endorsed and encouraged by criminal culture—exposes much mainstream cultural anxiety over what may have been a foreseeable transition. Because sexuality is a tremendous preoccupation for human civilization, its construction, manipulation, and evaluation informs most subjectifying strategies, especially those related to the moral impositions of the state's ideological conductors. This information makes sexuality important to most identity-related leaps into the uncharted territory of transversality. In this section I will argue that the contradictory discourse on the sexuality of criminal culture signifies a conceptual transcendence of official culture's moral boundaries. It also indicates that the writers themselves were infected with transversal thought and therefore constitutes their own approximation or crossing of the threshold to transversal territory.

Stimulated by various reasons or forces, the popular desire to become gypsy—the becoming criminal of English citizens—was at least partially a desirous and concerted endeavor to have sex in new, forbidden, and exciting ways. Criminal culture is typically described as patriarchal, but in terms very different from England's official culture. According to its chroniclers, monogamous heterosexuality, marriage, and marital sex were neither compulsory nor the status quo. Some heterosexual criminal couples did marry, but only under the jurisdiction of the criminal community and not the church, and without any obvious faithfulness to Christian ideology. In a controversial passage in *The Fraternitye of Vacabondes,* Awdeley tells of one type of rogue called a "Patriarch co"—ordinarily spelled "Patrico" in canting dictionaries (as in Jonson)—who "doth make marriages, & that is vntil death depart the married folke, to which is after this sort: When they come to a dead Horse or any dead Catell, then they shake hands and so depart, euery one of them a seuerall way"; the "married folk" could divorce at any time over the body of a dead animal.[91] This divorce ceremony, as Aydelotte notes, is well documented as a gypsy custom by historians writing about gypsies living in England after the Restoration. Yet Aydelotte opines that Awdeley confuses the gypsy and rogue-vagabond cultures by attributing this custom to rogues and vagabonds. To support this claim, he wrongly refers to *A Caveat or Warening, For Commen Cursetors vulgarely called Vagabones* (1567): "Harman denies that any such custom existed among the rogues and that there was any such name as Patrico."[92]

Although Harman displays some resistance to ascribing this or any marriage-related ritual to criminal culture, Harman corrects Awdeley's misspelling of "Patriarch co" with "Patrico" and states, "For I put you out of doubt that not one amongst a hundred of them [the vagabonds] are married; for they take lechery for no sin, but natural fellowship and good liking, love: so that I will not blot my book with these two that be not."[93] Harman stresses that since so few vagabonds marry, there is no need for him to provide details ("blot my book") about the Patrico as he does for other criminal types. But he does deem the type important enough to be included in his canting dictionary: under the entry for "patrico" we find "a priest" (114). In support of Harman's rationale, Beier found that "unmarried or dubiously joined couples were common among vagabonds."[94] Beier concludes that "at least half were probably unmarried by the strict rules of the church" (65). However, considering the illegality of fornication and thus the advantage in lying about it, it is likely that the actual number of criminal couples traveling out of wedlock was much higher. All things considered, I must accept Awdeley's account of the vagabond divorce as fact: the divorce ceremony is attributed elsewhere to rogues and vagabonds, as in *The Belman of London*,[95] and the hedge priest is called a "Patrico," as we have seen, and is mentioned in almost every text portraying early modern England's criminal culture. For instance, Dekker writes: "a *Patrico*, who amongst *Beggers* is their priest; every hedge beeing his parish, every wandring harlot and *Rogue* his parishioners" (101). Hence, the marriage and divorce ceremonies are additional cultural connections between rogues and vagabonds and gypsies.

However common marriages were, and despite the official connotation of marriage in regard to sexual fidelity, popular and state literature dealing with gypsies and rogues and vagabonds indicates that there was much sexual freedom among criminals, with "casual sex" being the norm. Because female criminals were expected to have sex on demand with their superiors, according to the criminal social hierarchy, their freedom must have been limited. And since the most powerful criminals were usually men, they were at the mercy of men. This was especially true of the "*Upright men*," for they were the "*Chiefest*." Dekker reports: "Whersoever an *Upright-man* is in presence, the *Doxye* [female criminal] is onely at his command" (84, 104). In Middleton's *More Dissemblers Besides Women*, the gypsy Captain informs Dondolo that once he becomes a gypsy,

Thou shalt have all thy heart requires.
First, here's a girl for thy desires.
This doxy fresh, this new-come dell,
Shall lie by thy sweet side and swell.[96]

Unfortunately, there are few representations of how the female criminals felt about their situation in the criminal community. We are led to believe that their sexual subservience was consensual. For instance, Aurelia tells Dondolo, "I'll be thy doxy and thy dell. With thee I'll live, for thee I'll steal" (4.2.208–9). Evidence suggests that sexual promiscuity, that is, the luxury of being able to freely wander "without shame" (as Dekker puts it) from sex partner to sex partner, was a decisive nomadic characteristic of criminal culture.[97]

Criminal culture was transversal in many ways. It was a culture that undermined and challenged the state's efforts to ground and monitor the populace, both ideologically and spatiotemporally; it subverted the conventional obligation to "settle down" with a particular person (a spouse) in a particular locality. In Head and Kirkman's *The English Rogue,* the narrator says of gypsies: "Jealousy was a thing they never would admit of in their society, and to make appear how little they were tainted therewith, the males and females lay promiscuously together, it being free for any of the Fraternity to make choice of what doxy he like best, changing when he pleased."[98] Higgen, the criminal leader in *Beggars Bush,* makes the following promise to his male followers:

Each man shall eate his own stolne eggs, and butter,
In his owne shade, or sun-shine, and enjoy
His owne deare Dell, Doxy, or Mort, at night
In his own straw, with his owne shirt, or sheet,
That he hath filch'd that day."[99]

Higgen merely promises his followers what they already desire and expect on a daily basis (each "night" and "day") as individual members of a criminal community.

In *O per se O* Dekker informs us that "the cause why so many of this wicked generation wander up and down this kingdom is the free command, and abundant use they have of women; for if you note them well in their marching, not a tatterdemalion walks his round, be he young, be he old, but he hath his mort, or his doxy, at his heels (his woman, or his whore)."[100] Moreover, Dekker maintains that the sexual activity of the criminals is complemented and vastly augmented by the plenitude of haunts established by criminals in various towns to better facilitate their criminal operations: "And this liberty of wenching is increased by the almost infinite number of tippling-houses, called bousing kens, or of stalling kens; that is to say, houses where they have ready money for any stolen goods" (367). The "liberty of wenching" hardly describes the degree of sexual freedom assigned criminal culture by Dekker and others. In a discussion of "those Innes" in which the criminals "lodge every night," Dekker sums up the dominant perception of the criminals' sexual experience: "In all Shires have they such Innes as these [he lists eight]; and in all of them and these recited, shall you find sometimes 40 *Upright-men* together ingendering beggars with their *Morts.* No sinne but is here committed without shame. Adultery is common amongst them, Incest but laughed at, *Sodomy* made a jest."[101] Specifically about gypsies Dekker similarly declares: "These Barnes" where the gypsies dwell at night "are the beds of Incests, Whoredomes, Adulteries, and of all other blacke and deadly-damned *Impieties.*"[102] Although Dekker renders unspeakable the "other blacke and deadly-damned *Impieties,*" and therefore relegates them to the wild recesses of his reader's imagination, the fact that he contemplated such forbidden "blacke and deadly-damned *Impieties*" at all shows that his own thoughts had been influenced by the wayward subject matter that so enthralled him.

Sexuality was not only a variable in the popular construction of criminal culture but was also a determining factor in the individuation of identity by and for members within that culture. This is evident in criminal culture's use of sexually informed nicknames. Just as each criminal was assigned a functional name appropriate to his or her criminal occupation and hierarchical status (upright man, rogue, doxy, etc.), so each was assigned a nickname supplementary to his or her state-recorded, official name—if he or she had an official name. "Every one of them," Dekker says, "hath a peculiar nickname proper to himself, by the which he is more known, more enquired after by his brothers, and in common familiarity more saluted, than by his own true [official] name."[103] Many criminals were born, as opposed to initiated, into the criminal community and therefore did not have official, baptismal names. Sometimes an alias, which was commonly assumed by criminals, became their official name through widespread circulation and/or false testimony. As Dekker puts it, "Yea, the false is used so much that the true is forgotten" (378). In any case, the nicknames given to the criminals normally referred, as they do today, to a particular aspect of their personality, behavior, or physique—for example, Mary Frith aka Moll Cutpurse, or Jonson's gypsy "Captaine, Charles the tall man"—and that aspect often related to their sexual disposition.[104] After listing numerous examples of criminal nicknames, such as Dimber Damper, Hurly Burly, General Nurse, and High Shrieve, Dekker continues: "And some nicknames are either upon mockery, or upon pleasure given onto them: as the Great Bull, the Little Bull, and many other suchlike. The Great Bull is some one notable lusty rogue, who gets away all their wenches; for this Great Bull by report had in one year three and twenty doxies, his jockey was so lusty. Such liberty they have in sinning, and such damnable and detestable manner of life do they lead."[105] When considering Dekker's emphasis on "Great Bull" (the only nicknamed person whom he describes in detail) and mention of "many other suchlike" in light of the other sexually titillating passages he quoted earlier, it is clear that sexuality and lust were a major component of his interest in criminal culture.

The exceptional sexual license of gypsies, rogues, and vagabonds was, in fact, a preoccupation for Dekker and the others who wrote about criminal culture, all of whom were men (as far as we can tell from their first names). From their writings it seems they thought conventional sexuality boring and deficient in comparison to that of criminals, and that their own sexual conventionality reflected poorly on them. As men in a society preoccupied with sexual-gender issues, especially with the ability of men to adequately demonstrate their masculine prowess, they might have felt somewhat emasculated and threatened by the more sexually adventurous and voracious criminal men and women. Therefore, any transversal wandering by them through their expression of desires antithetical to those officially sanctioned and permitted within their subjective territory, such as in the production of the provocative poetics with which they describe the criminals's sexual experience, may have been spurred by the wanting and consequent void they felt vis-à-vis that experience. Their subjectification was endangered by the transversality that criminal culture symbolized and promoted, for the sexuality of the criminals pointed toward a drastic departure from or overstatement of their masculine subject position. This transversal influence may have led them to novel and officially unacceptable subject positions, such as that of a gypsy-criminal. (Recall the transversal slogan "Become what you aren't.") From official culture's point of view, criminal sexuality was pathological masculinity and femininity; it threatened subjective territory and, by extension, the sociopolitical conductors that typically worked to support state power, like church teachings and the institutions of marriage and family.[106]

Dekker's contradictory commentary on the "liberty they have in sinning," the sexual verve of the criminals, both his admiration and condemnation of it, is characteristic of popular portrayals of criminal culture. Even Harman, the harshest of the chroniclers of criminal culture, writes about their conduct with a mixture of contempt and enthusiasm. In an account that reminds me of Hunter S. Thompson's sensational descriptions of the pagan rituals of the Hells Angels, Harman recalls that an acquaintance of his observed a ritual profoundly aberrant and frightening to official culture. In the barn of a recently deceased man, he witnessed a company of "wayfaring bold beggars" engaged in an orgiastic shindig: "Seven score persons of men, every of them having his woman, except it were two women that lay alone together for some especial cause. Thus having their makes to make merry withal, the burial was turned to bousing and bellycheer, mourning to mirth, fasting to feasting, prayer to pastime and pressing of paps, and lamenting to lechery."[107] Similarly, when describing the traits of a "wild rogue" ("A wild rogue is he that is born a rogue"), Harman maintains: "He is a more subtle and more given by nature to all kind of knavery, as beastly begotten in barn or bushes, and from his infancy traded up in lewd lechery . . . but that is counted amongst them no sin" (78). Harman portrays a Dionysian criminal culture that willy-nilly converts—indeed, desecrates—a Christian funeral by turning it into a wild party in which "seven score persons of men" each have their own female sex partner, unless "two women" choose to have sex with each other instead (they "lay alone together for some especial cause") (64). The funeral transformation, as Harman insists, was not unusual in criminal culture, for it "is their custom, that when they meet in barn at night, every one getteth a make to lie withal, and there chance to be twenty in a company. . . . For to one man that goeth abroad there are at the least two women, which never make it strange when they be called, although she never knew him before" (78). Harman depicts a sexually indulgent, indiscriminate, and satiated criminal culture in which all its members, the women as well as the men, have multiple sex partners. This is a culture whose norms were vastly different from that of official culture, which punished people for fornication and adultery.[108]

Harman's racy description of criminal culture could easily be generically categorized as early modern erotica or fantasy rather than, say, investigative journalism or moralistic pomp. This is not simply because of its sexually explicit content but rather its seductive diction and gripping rhythmic style. Consider the alliteration, assonance, and end rhyme in "bousing and belly-cheer, mourning to mirth, fasting to feasting, prayer to pastime and pressing of paps, and lamenting to lechery" and in "all kind of knavery, as beastly begotten in barn or bushes, and from his infancy traded up in lewd lechery" (78). Consciously or not, Harman was smitten with criminal culture and wanted his readers to be pulled into his passion. Like Dekker, he writes poetically when recounting the sexual activities of the criminals; he romanticizes criminal culture's transcendence of official cultural normalcy and state law. Under the auspices of his prescribed duty as a Kentish justice of the peace and as a supposedly fully subjectified and authorized member of official culture, Harman exalted and advanced, however inadvertently, the aesthetic and lifestyle of criminals. Harman's *A Caveat or Warening, For Commen Cursetors vulgarely called Vagabones* was tremendously successful commercially and critically. The numerous allusions to it in subsequent popular literature about gypsies, rogues, and vagabonds testify to its influence. It was a catalyst for the invigoration and radiation of the transversal power that was only beginning to develop *as* and *through* criminal culture at the time of its initial publication.

After the publication of Harman's work, as documented by Ian Archer, "the Elizabethan reading public was saturated in the image of a deviant counterculture," which indicates that "contemporaries firmly believed there to be a counterculture of deviants," just as the many statutes against this criminal counterculture indicate that "legislators were also convinced of the existence of an organized underworld."[109] To illustrate the latter, Archer quotes a 1567 act against pickpocketing. The act asserts the existence of "a certain Kind of evil-disposed Persons, commonly called Cutpurses or Pick-purses who do confeder together, making among themselves as it were a Brotherhood or Fraternity of an Art or Mystery, to live idly by the secret Spoil of the good and true Subjects of the Realm" (205). It is precisely this "Art or Mystery," a theme common to most representations of criminal culture, that must be further investigated in order to comprehend how the criminals managed "to live idly by the secret Spoil of the good and true Subjects of the Realm." Crucial to understanding criminal culture, then, is the mysterious cant language that facilitated the manifestation of the art. An art form in itself, cant worked to enable criminal culture's members to secretly and mysteriously "confeder together" and thus regularly to perpetrate crimes while simultaneously living and operating in the same public spaces as the members of official culture who were their victims.

CHAPTER THREE

Communal Departure, Criminal Language, Dissident Consolidation

IN A REMARKABLE and ingenious transversal movement, early modern England's criminal culture of gypsies, rogues, vagabonds, beggars, cony-catchers, cutpurses, and prostitutes transgressed the sociolinguistic hegemony of official culture by inventing its own language, called "cant." Among other sociocultural variables, criminal culture was unified by this unique spoken language. In effect, cant was analyzed, commodified, and fetishized in the period's popular, commercial, and state literature. It was imbued with a mysterious and alluring nature and history that heightened both criminal culture's infamy and the conduction of the transversal power for which this culture was a manifestation and vehicle.[1] Through a social semiotic analysis of cant's literary representation, I hope to show that cant worked in a complex fashion to connect criminal culture not just on the level of communication but also on aesthetic, ideological, and practical levels; and that by facilitating crimes and inspiring dissidence, cant significantly affected English society.

My approach reflects Robert Hodge and Gunther Kress's understanding of Michael Halliday's concept of "antilanguages." In purely linguistic terms, antilanguages are highly developed jargons: languages spoken by subcultures that have the syntactical and morphological structure of the dominant language but use essentially different lexical words (those carrying meaning), often with no recognizable etymology. Like Halliday, Hodge and Kress maintain: "These are languages generated not by agents of the state but the opposite: criminals, prisoners, groups that have been marginalized by the state, who express their opposition by creating a language which excludes outsiders."[2] But, unlike Halliday, who insists that the "interpersonal function" of antilanguages "predominates over the ideational," Hodge and Kress maintain that antilanguages "simultaneously exclude outsiders, and express the ideology of the antigroup" because this "antigroup" developed the antilanguage to articulate and promote its ideational, and thus its ideological, differences in the first place (87).

My own comprehension of "antilanguages" differs from Hodge and Kress's as well as Halliday's understanding. In general, I see the use of "antilanguages" by alternative groups as expressions of difference and resistance and not of antithesis to the dominant or official group. I also want to argue that although cant meets Hodge and Kress's criteria for an antilanguage insofar as it served criminal culture's need to create internal solidarity and exclude others, in a very real way cant eludes the binary opposition that drives their view. Cant is not about negation. It is about assertion and promotion. Whereas for Hodge and Kress "antilanguages characteristically are built up by a series of transformations whose meaning is negation, opposition, inversion," cant promoted a culture that both thrived on difference from and dependence on official culture even as it rebelled against it.[3]

The Language Imperative

The early modern English state perceived vernacular multilingualism as a threat to state power and national integrity, instead promoting monolingualism as the ideal.[4] Like most governments, especially in Europe, where language differences have historically been associated with the distinguishable territories of individual nation-states, that of England pursued a standardized language as a symbol and instrument for the sociopolitical unification and maintenance of its nation-state and official culture. With the idea of "one nation, one language" as its goal, the state sought, by means of its sociopolitical conductors (juridical, religious, and educational structures) to increase literacy and thereby further standardize the East Midlands dialect of Middle English that had already surfaced as England's official language.[5] Commonly referred to today as the "London standard," this dialect acquired superior status over the many other dialects spoken in England at the time because the Midlands region was most important in terms of wealth and population. It contained the commercial center of London, with its flourishing middle class and mercantile elite; the court, with its royalty and aristocracy; and Oxford and Cambridge Universities, the leading ideological assemblages for higher learning and technological advancement. Like most standardized languages, the London standard arose, together with the upper layers, in a stratified, hierarchical arrangement of sociopolitical determinations. It was the speech variety advanced by the state and official culture (the dominant speech community), for it was the linguistic medium through which this culture articulated and disseminated its ideology.

The English state first addressed the issue of linguistic variety in 1535 when Henry VIII prohibited the use of Welsh because a "great Discord Variance Debate Division Murmur and Sedition" had arisen since the Welsh people "have and do daily use a Speech nothing like, nor consonant to the natural Mother Tongue within this Realm."[6] Cultural debate over the linguistic variety to which Henry VIII alludes was just beginning in the 1530s, and it continued heatedly throughout the early modern period, reaching its climax around 1600. During the early modern period, England experienced extraordinary growth in population, domestic and foreign migration and travel, industry, international commerce, poverty, and crime.[7] This growth caused the English language to expand and diversify as foreign words became increasingly popular and new words were invented to accommodate the changing social atmosphere. The compulsion to standardize simultaneously increased because, as Steven Mullaney puts it, the changes in language usage precipitated the breakdown of the medieval period's "dual language hierarchy," which consisted of "on the one hand, a stable monolithic Latin for learned and official society, and on the other, the metamorphic, plural, and largely oral vernacular, a plethora of local dialects, idioms, and jargons that was the province of popular culture."[8] It was the imminence of this breakdown, most evident in the fact that scholars and clergymen began writing in English instead of Latin, that initially spurred the language debate among scholars. But as the breakdown became more pronounced, the stakes rose, and more people with prestige, power, and an investment in the language hierarchy got involved. While many intellectuals and popular writers participated in the debate,[9] the state dealt with the problem primarily at the grassroots level through the institutionalization of an official public school system designed to educate the populace—though the education of females was limited to elementary ("petty") school—and thereby consolidate the entire social order.[10] In *The Description of England* (1587), chronicler William Harrison provides an account of this situation: "There are a great number of Grammar schooles through out the realme, and those verie liberallie indued, for the better reliefe of poore scholers, so that there are not manie corporat townes now under the queenes dominion, that hath not one Gramar schoole at the least, with a sufficient living for a maister and usher appointed to the same" (87). As noted by Carl Bridenbaugh, David Cressy, and Joan Simon, grammar schools were free or relatively inexpensive, and grammar-school curriculum included the teachings of the church, classical literature and language, and basic skills for reading and writing the London standard. Thus, rather than allowing the language debate to hinder its consolidation procedures, the state took strategic official action to ensure the preservation of the standard by diminishing the related problem of illiteracy. The more proficient the populace became in reading, writing, and speaking the London standard, the more pervasive that language became.

This pedagogical approach worked to increase cultural cohesion among the populace since it marginalized the languages and cultures of minority and immigrant peoples living in England, such as the Welsh and Irish. At the same time, it empowered the literate quantitative minority since English literacy became increasingly more valuable, especially as a vehicle to higher socioeconomic echelons. Surprisingly, the higher value that official culture placed on literacy and adherence to the standardized language in both speech and writing did not guarantee that everyone learned it. There were those who were not interested in learning the London standard—possibly, as Cressy says, because they did not think such an endeavor worth their time and energy (23)—or were unable to take time off from work to learn it, and there were also those who challenged it. I am here arguing that the emergent criminal culture challenged official culture's language-standardization movement through its use of cant.

Commodification, Fetishization, Intervention

Official culture sought to safeguard its power by recording, co-opting, and commodifying cant in legal documents and commercial literature.[11] As I shall demonstrate, this treatment of cant paradoxically effectuated a romanticization and fetishization of cant that contributed to the overall romanticization and fetishization of criminal culture. It precipitated a positive desire among members of official culture to learn and speak cant. This desire led to extended dissidence and transversal movement, particularly in the adoption of criminal modes of thought, expression, and action, which seems to have been symptomatically related and roughly proportional to the degree of knowledge of cant acquired.

Criminal culture was marketable subject matter for popular plays, pamphlets, and ballads, and cant was central to its marketability. Cant was one of criminal culture's most intriguing and attractive features. It was the most tangible aspect of this sneaky and enigmatic culture that depended so greatly on its own performance, intangibility, and elusiveness. It was the public mask worn by a private subculture, and this mask proved to be endlessly fascinating to the populace at large. The popular fascination with criminal culture and cant was motivated by curiosity of the illicit and subterranean. For both defensive and offensive purposes, people wanted to learn about the mind and nature of the criminal underworld. Cant was a window through which people hoped to see—and possibly saw the mirrored reflection of—many of English society's most hidden, profound, or unconscious desires.

The popular fascination with cant is clear from the numerous commercial texts about criminal culture that include dictionaries of cant vocabulary as well as representations of its use. This fascination is even evident within the texts; cant appears to have intrigued members of both criminal and official cultures. Among the most successfully marketed were those by John Awdeley, Thomas Harman, Robert Greene, William Harrison, Thomas Dekker, Thomas Middleton, Samuel Rid, Richard Head, and Francis Kirkman, the anonymously authored *Street Robberies consider'd* (n.d.), and the anonymously authored work entitled *The Catterpillers of this Nation anatomized* (1659).[12] In *Martin Markall, Beadle of Bridewell* (1610), for instance, Samuel Rid maintains that Thomas Dekker's texts are hugely popular, and that their popularity can be measured by the fact that people everywhere are learning to speak cant: "These volumes and papers now spread everywhere, so that every jack-boy now can say as well as the proudest of that fraternity: 'Will you wap for a win, or trine for a make?'" (386). Although Rid exaggerates the popular knowledge of cant, cant may have been well enough known for the average person to test a passing beggar of his moral status and authenticity. According to Dekker in his *Lanthorne and Candle-Light* (1608), when "a poore common Rogue come to a mans doore, but he shall be examined if he can *cant*" (194). In Rid's "Canters' Dictionary," he provides many examples of "rogues in their native language"; he says that he has "enlarged his dictionary (or Master Harman's) with such words I think he never heard of," because they are new words—invented after Kentish Justice of the Peace Thomas Harman published his groundbreaking account of rogue-vagabond culture, *A Caveat or Warening, For Commen Cursetors vulgarely called Vagabones* (1567)—and he promises the "true Englishing" (the correct translation) for all words (406–10). But cant was so evasive, bountiful, and fast-evolving that, as Dekker claims, it was "impossible to imprint a *Dictionarie* of all Canting phrases" (*Lanthorne* 181). Harman agrees: "And as they [the rogues and vagabonds] have begun of late to devise some new terms for certain things, so will they in time alter this, and devise as evil or worse" (117). Therefore, popular knowledge of cant, however common, was not a serious threat to its legitimate speakers, but it was fuel for cant's increasing popularity as a fetishized commodity.

A concrete example of cant's popularity is found in Dekker and Middleton's play *The Roaring Girl* (1611), which is one of several popular texts about the notorious London personality Mary Frith (who was a female-to-male transvestite, a prostitute, and the leader of a criminal gang).[13] In this play cant is depicted as a defining attribute of criminal culture's members. In the scene that follows, Moll Cutpurse (the character based on

Mary Frith) is walking through the streets of London with some members of official culture's gentry, including Jack Dapper, Lord Noland, Sir Thomas Long, and Sir Beauteous Ganymede. During their walk, they encounter two rogues: Trapdoor, disguised "like a poor soldier with a patch o'er one eye," and Tearcat, "all tatters" (looking homeless). Because of the abundance of cant in this scene, critics have found it baffling and impenetrable. Through a discussion of the sociolinguistics involved, I hope to make some sense of it.

Pretty sure that they are criminals pretending to be legitimate beggars (this was a common con), Moll seeks to expose their status within the criminal community. She suspects that Trapdoor is an "upright man,"[14] a term denoting a criminal of high rank who governs the actions of other criminals (a gang leader):

> *Moll:* I hope, then, you can cant, for by your cudgels, you, sirrah, are an upright man.
> *Trapdoor:* As any walks the highway, I assure you.
> *Moll:* And, Tearcat, what are you? A wild rogue, an angler, or a ruffler?
> *Tear:* Brother to this upright man, flesh and blood; ruffling Tearcat is my name, and a ruffler is my style, my title, my profession.
> (5.1.155–62)

It is not enough for Moll that Trapdoor is codified as an upright man with "cudgels," and that Tearcat claims to be a "ruffler" (a criminal of high rank, but below an upright man). She wants further proof, and checking if they "can cant" is the quickest and most dependable test of their criminal cultural status. Moll therefore challenges Trapdoor to a canting competition: "Come, you rogue, cant with me." Trapdoor accepts the invitation: "I'll have a bout, if she please" (188–91). So goes the match:

> *Trapdoor:* Ben more, shall you and I heave a booth, mill a ken, or nip a bung, and then we'll couch a hogshead under the ruffman's, and there you shall wap with me, and I'll niggle with you.
> *Moll:* Out, you damned impudent rascal!
> *Trapdoor:* Cut benar whids, and hold your fambles and your stamps.

Puzzled, because he cannot understand cant, Lord Noland inquires: Nay, nay, Moll, why art thou angry? what was his gibberish?

Moll responds by translating: Marry, this, my lord, says he: "Ben mort." good wench, "shall you and I heave a booth, mill a ken, or nip a bung?" Shall you and I rob a house, or cut a purse?

Omnes: Very good.

Moll: "And then we'll couch a hogshead under the ruffman's"; and then we'll lie under a hedge.

And Trapdoor affirms: That was my desire, captain, as 'tis fit a soldier should lie.

To which Moll adds: "And there you shall wap with me, and I'll niggle with you,"—and that's all.

But one of the gentry, Sir Beauteous Ganymede, is not satisfied. He inquires further: Nay, nay, Moll, what's that wap?

And Jack Dapper adds: Nay, teach me what niggling is; I'd fain be niggling.

To which Moll responds elusively: Wapping and niggling is all one, the rogue my man can tell you.

To which Trapdoor adds: 'Tis fadoodling, if it please you. (193–218)

Of course, by saying "fadoodling," which is a common nonsense word and not a cant term, Trapdoor is being elusive as well. He and Moll keep to themselves the secret that "wapping and niggling" means having sex. In this scene Moll simultaneously maintains her criminal solidarity with Trapdoor and Tearcat (by not revealing all that transpired between them) and her apparent solidarity with the members of the gentry (by translating for them).

The members of the gentry accompanying Moll are enthralled by the demonstration of the rogues's canting eloquence. Indeed, they are so amazed that Jack Dapper exclaims, "Zounds, I'll give a schoolmaster half-a-crown a week, and teach me this pedlar's French" (184–85). Despite the apparent negative implications of the term "pedlar's French" in his response— this term for cant was often used since the French were ridiculed by the English for their "immorality" (criminals were only thematically associated with the French)—Dapper is nonetheless seduced by cant's mysteriousness and high social value. He attempts to commodify cant so that he can purchase knowledge of it for himself. But knowledge of cant is not for sale, and Trapdoor keenly suspects that Dapper wants access to more than just the language. Accordingly, Trapdoor responds, "Do but stroll, sir, half a harvest with us, sir, and you shall gabble your bellyful" (186–87). Trapdoor suggests that Dapper's desire to learn cant is motivated by his desire to obtain firsthand knowledge of everything that cant signified. In other words, Dapper, who can be seen as symbolically representative of people like him, desires to become criminal. Trapdoor also points out that one must be a member of criminal culture to learn cant, that cant is an exclusive language. Finally, he emphasizes that an alternative lifestyle—that of criminal culture—is available to anyone willing to "stroll" transversally beyond the boundaries of their subjective territory and *with* the criminals, to walk on the wild side beyond the subjective and societal boundaries enforced by official culture. Unlike the gentry (the social class of which Dapper is a member), anyone could engage in the dynamic process of becoming criminal. Criminal culture, it seems, was not, or was hardly, discriminatory.

The type of canting competition between Moll and Trapdoor, which required deftness of wit and dissembling, was not unusual among members of criminal culture, which considered cant a skilled art form, like playing a musical instrument. It was an aesthetic that one crafted over time and only through experience as a criminal. Like that of minstrels, who needed to play music well, the criminals' livelihood and, to a lesser extent, their social status within the criminal community depended on their talent at canting. Dekker relates this understanding of cant when he discusses its etymology: "This word *canting* séemes to bee derived from the latine *verbe* (*canto*) which signifies in English, to sing, or to make a sound with words, thats to say to speake. And very aptly may *canting* take his derivation *a cantando*, from singing, because amongst these beggerly consorts that can play upon no better instruments, the language of *canting* is a kinde of musicke, and he that in such assemblies can *cant* best, is counted the best Musitian" (*Lanthorne* 179). However, cant was not only a "kinde of musicke" for criminal culture but was actually employed musically. In many of the texts in which cant is represented, it appears in lyrical form, especially in drinking songs, which function as bonding rituals for the criminals. Among the texts that include these songs are Robert Copland's *The Highway to the Spital-house* (1535–36), Rid's *Martin Markall, Beadle of Bridewell*, Dekker's *Lanthorne and Candle-Light* and *O per se O*, Jonson's *The Gypsies Metamorphos'd* (1621), Fletcher and Massinger's *Beggars Bush* (1641), Richard Brome's *A Jovial Crew: or, The Merry Beggars* (1641), and Dekker and Middleton's *The Roaring Girl*. For instance, after Moll's canting "bout" with Trapdoor, she entreats Tearcat: "Come, you rogue, sing with me."[15] Together they sing a drinking song in cant.

In the end Moll is convinced by her engagement with Trapdoor and Tearcat that they are authentic members of the criminal community: "Now I see that you are stalled to the rogue" (244–45). But Jack Dapper, who would have paid a high price to learn cant, is disillusioned by the alienation he experiences when exposed to the criminal solidarity expressed through and symbolized by Moll and Tearcat's singing of the song: "The grating of ten new cartwheels and the gruntling of five hundred hogs coming from Rumford market cannot make a worse noise than this canting language does in my ears" (236–39). For Dapper, cant is tantalizing but distressing, as would be the sound of "ten new cartwheels," which would have sounded unusually noisy to him. Cant also brings to his mind the image of "the gruntling of five hundred hogs." He associates cant with a large, unclean community that is also alternative acoustically as well as in speech and lifestyle. Bruce Smith writes, "As the inhabitants of a certain geographical space, a *speech* community also constitutes an *acoustic* community. Its identity is maintained not only by what its members *say* in common but what they *hear* in common."[16] Yet while Dapper *hears* the same sounds as the criminals within the same geographical space, they do not sound the same to him because he is not a member of their speech community. He relates the cant he hears to sounds he would register as noise within another, more familiar soundscape: that of Rumford Market. In doing so he also associates cant with abundance. To him, then, the rogue-vagabond community is so fantastic, offensive, and out of his reach—as ten new cartwheels and five hundred hogs—that its canting language is a "grating" reminder of the lack he feels when confronted with such an image. This community is more annoying or threatening to him than a multitude of hogs since it is not only gluttonous—supposedly like hogs (recall Trapdoor's comment about "gabbl[ing] your belllyful")—but, unlike hogs, capable of stealing from and harming the gentry. Therefore, Dapper's first and probably long-awaited encounter with cant culminates in his experience of it as "noise," not worth the price even if it were for sale.

This final reaction reveals that the irreconcilability of two or more realities or worlds ultimately overwhelms Dapper during this short episode. In Halliday's terms, because cant is an antilanguage, it "is the means of realization of a subjective reality: not merely expressing it, but actively creating and maintaining it" (172).[17] This "counter-reality" implies "a preoccupation with the definition and defense of identity through the ritual functioning of the [alternative] social hierarchy"; it implies "a special conception of information and of knowledge" that must effectively estrange outsiders even as it entices them. "This is where the secrecy comes in: the language is secret because the reality is secret" (172).[18] The canting song's lyrics are unintelligible to Dapper and his friends, but the feeling of camaraderie, solidarity, and secrecy that the singing of the song conveys— which alienates and disturbs Dapper—is so strong that later Lord Noland must inquire about it: "Moll, what was in that canting song?" (260). The alluring mystery of cant emphasized by Noland's question, which was probably a primary component of the play's popularity, is, in the end, only furthered and further fetishized by the play.

Like *The Roaring Girl*, Richard Brome's *A Jovial Crew* depicts the bilingualism shared by members of criminal culture and the fascination with cant shared by members of official culture. To the squire Oldrents, who owns the land on which a band of criminals are squatting, the Patrico (meaning gypsy or rogue priest in cant) says that his crew of rogues and vagabonds is bilingual, and that they will gladly speak English "if you [Oldrents] do rather choose / That we no word of canting use" (Brome 2.2.208–9). Brome portrays cant as a secondary or alternative language to English that can be learned and empowers those who understand it. Knowledge of cant makes one more adaptable and desirable in different social situations. In both criminal and official cultures, as we have just seen in *The Roaring Girl*, knowledge of cant increases what Pierre Bourdieu calls "social capital," which is any physical attribute, mode of behavior, acquired knowledge, or social or manual skill that works to determine one's position (respectable or otherwise) and therefore one's power within a particular social field, such as within a subcultural or mainstream group.[19]

In *A Jovial Crew* cant is not simply a linguistic, "*canting* commodity" (as Dekker puts it [*Lanthorne* 186]) sought after by those interested in boosting their social capital or accessing a clandestine culture. Here cant is represented as having a force of its own as a mechanism for a cryptic libertine society with the power to seduce new members away from the conventionality and piety of official culture. For instance, Randall, Oldrents's servant, informs Oldrents of his knowledge of cant: "I told you, sir, they would be gone tomorrow. / I understand their canting" (2.2.286–87). Randall learned cant while associating with the "rogues and beggars" (1.1.320) that dwell in the "old barn" (262–63) on Oldrents's property. His association with them, concretized by his proficiency in cant and his "merry [drinking] bouts with some of 'em" (300), caused him to not only "love 'em well" (1299), but to eventually become one of them, as a "player" in a performance they put on for Oldrents (5.1.394). In this case—possibly because of his lack of power, being only a servant in official culture, and his subsequent desire for power—Randall's association with criminal culture, concretized linguistically with cant, leads to his becoming criminal. But to what extent was cant really shared or shareable? As an expressive medium, how purposeful was it? These questions recall the crucial question asked by Middleton and Dekker's Lord Noland: "Moll, what was in that canting song?"

Sociolinguistic Innovation

Cant was an invented language, possessing what linguists consider the defining characteristics of both "natural" and "artificial" languages. A "natural language," as David Crystal puts it, is "a language used in ordinary human communication"; and an "artificial language" is "a language which has been invented to serve some particular purpose."[20] To make this argument (the terms of which I am not entirely comfortable with because of my own inclination to consider all or no languages "natural") I intend to demonstrate that cant, like all natural languages, was used in ordinary social interaction among members of criminal culture; and that cant, like all artificial languages, was invented for a particular purpose at a certain historical moment. Therefore cant was originally not the product of a slow linguistic evolution, although the grammar and vocabulary it borrowed, almost entirely from English, were evolutionary products, and its own neologistical vocabulary did expand over time. As I hope to establish through a dialectical and comparative analysis of cant's sociolinguistic features, like all artificial languages cant cannot be readily categorized as either a dialect, slang, jargon, pidgin, or creole, even though it possesses characteristics often ascribed to each of these language types.

Cant's sociolinguistic status—particularly if it was a natural-and-artificial language, which might mean, in other words, that it was some kind of highly and/or uniquely developed jargon—is crucial to our understanding of criminal culture and cant's own sociopolitical functionality. If, as I am asserting, cant was a standardized natural-and-artificial language within its own speech community, then criminal culture's members must have been creative and sophisticated enough to devise and implement such an exceptional multifunctional language. This enterprise would have required comprehension of the purposefulness of a common language for sociocultural distinction and consolidation. Moreover, this enterprise would reveal that there was much transversal power behind cant's initial development. For its originators to have pursued the realization of cant, they would have first had to conceptualize the alternative, deceptive, elusive, secret, anti-Christian, criminal society for which cant was indispensable. Such radical conceptualization, much less the ambitious pursuit of its realization, would have necessitated thought well beyond the official and subjective territories maintained by early modern England's state machinery. That cant's originators were willing to see the project through testifies to their own residence in transversal territory.

The following example of cant was initially recorded and translated by Harman in *A Caveat or Warening, For Commen Cursetors vulgarely called Vagabones* and was later reprinted by Dekker, together with other examples of cant, in *Lanthorne and Candle-Light*. Dekker's decision to include this example in his strikingly technical and detailed analysis of the grammar and etymology of cant is strong evidence for the language's enduring or increased stability and social status, as well as its salability in popular literature and stage plays.

A Canter in prose.

Stowe you beene Cofe: and cut benar whiddes and bing we to Rome vile, to nip a boung: so shall wee have lowre for the bowsing ken, and when we beng back to the Dewese a vile, we will filch some Duddes off the Ruffmans, or mill the Ken for a lagge of Dudes.

Thus in English.

Hold your peace good fellow: and speake better words and goe we to London, to cut a purse: so shall we have mony for the Ale-house, and when we come backe into the country, we will filch some clothes from the hedges, or rob the house for a bucke of clothes.[21]

From this representative passage, as well as from the many other examples of cant discussed throughout this chapter, it is clear that, like English, cant was an analytic language. This means that its grammar depended heavily on the use of word order and function rather than on the inflectional morphemes (prefixes, suffixes, infixes) of individual words, which is the case for synthetic languages such as Latin, Greek, and Arabic.[22] Cant had the syntactical and morphological structure of English, but most of its lexical words (those carrying meaning) were non-English. Apart from its use of English pronouns, conjunctions, adverbs, and some auxiliary verbs, cant words were usually neologisms, with no discernible etymology, and were therefore unique. Yet speakers of cant did use some English, French, and German nouns, verbs, and adjectives, and some Latin words.[23] These words were frequently contextually adapted such that their function or immediate meaning was unconventional.

According to the *OED*, whose definition agrees with that of most sociolinguists,[24] a dialect is "one of the subordinate forms or varieties of a language arising from local peculiarities of vocabulary, pronunciation, and idiom." It is a regional "variety of speech differing from the standard or literary language" of the culture in which it exists.[25] Although we have no way of discerning for certain whether English words used in cant speech were pronounced differently, we can compare the use of rhyming English words in canting verse, such as in drinking songs, to see if the rhymes are consistent. This type of examination, used to determine a language's regional specificity, is commonly employed by sociolinguists when analyzing a dead language. Consider the following examples in Richard Head and Francis Kirkman's *The English Rogue* (1665) and in Richard Brome's *A Jovial Crew*.

Head and Kirkman:

> To strawling Ken the Mort bings then,
>   To fetch loure for her *cheats;*
> Duds & Ruffe-peck, Rombold by Harman beck,
>   And won by Maunders *feats.*[26]

Brome:

> This is bene bowse; this is bene bowse;
>   Too little is my *skew.*
> I bowse no lage, but a whole gage
>   Of this I'll bowse to *you.*
> This bowse is better than rum bowse;
>   It sets the gan *a-giggling.*
> The autem *mort* finds better *sport*
>   In bowsing than in *niggling.*[27]

In addition to the lack of pronunciational difference suggested by these examples and the fact that cant was grammatically similar, if not identical, to English, we do know that cant was spoken in many of the socio-geographical spaces where dialects of English were predominant. The most obvious of these spaces were the thoroughfares, marketplaces, and public theaters of London and its suburbs. Although the London standard (the East Midlands dialect) was the dominant spoken language, cant was frequently spoken in these spaces since they were places where criminal activity was commonplace. Moreover, judicial records of rural East Midlands indicate the use of cant beyond the London vicinity. For instance, in 1581 Michael Hedge, who was arrested for disorderly conduct, admitted to Warwick magistrates that he "could cant";[28] and in Essex in 1590, according to the interviewing justice, Thomas Jackson, who was arrested for stealing hens, said that "concerning his Pedlar's French he will not make to me any account where he learned the same."[29] Another important sociogeographical example is the Kentish region, where a distinct variety of the Southern English dialect was the standard. This is the region where Harman was a justice of the peace, and thus where he conducted his research for *A Caveat or Warening, For Commen Cursetors vulgarely called Vagabones*. In this text he supplies a dictionary of one hundred and twenty-five words and a lengthy example of the criminals' "pedlars French or canting."[30] As Harman puts it, "Here I set before the good reader the lewd, lousy language of these loitering lusks and lazy lorels, wherewith they buy and sell the common people as they pass through the country."[31] To take a judicial example, in 1606 Stephen Christen, who was charged with burglary in Kent, was asked by the justices "whether he can cant and how long it was since he learned it." He replied that he could and had "learned it about some three years since."[32] These examples show that cant was spoken in the cities, towns, and country of both the Midlands region (London, Essex, Warwick) and the Southern region (West Saxon and Kentish districts). Hence cant was not regionally specific in either usage or derivation. It was not a dialect.

Thomas Pyles and John Algeo's definition of slang is the one generally accepted by sociolinguists: "Slang is a deliberately undignified form of speech whose use implies that the user is 'in' or especially knowledgeable about the subject of the slang term; it may be irresponsible language (such as a sexual or scatalogical taboo term) signaling that the speaker is not part of the Establishment, or it may be protective language that disguises unpleasant reality (such as *waste* for 'kill') or saves the user from fuller explanation (such as *dig you* for 'like, love, desire, sympathize with you')."[33] Another important characteristic of "slang" noted by Pyles and Algeo is its "changeability," its ephemeral nature (236). Like slang, cant was "speech whose use implies that the user is 'in,'" and it may at times have been "deliberately undignified," "irresponsible," "protective" of "unpleasant reality," or a means to avoid "fuller explanation," as in Dekker and Middleton's *The Roaring Girl* when Trapdoor proclaims in cant his sexual interest in Moll so that others present will not understand him ("There you shall wap [have sex] with me, and I'll niggle [have sex] with you").[34] Since cant was customarily and extensively used by criminals to communicate the goings-on of their everyday life, it must have been standardized and not short-lived. For instance, Head and Kirkman's 1665 canting dictionary, although much larger, is generally consistent with Harman's dictionary of 1567. In the earlier example given by Dekker, the speaker discusses, with some elaboration, criminal practices *and* other activities: "Bing we to Rome vile, to nip a boung: so shall wee have lowre for the bowsing ken, and when we beng back to the Dewese a vile." The speaker's obvious, functional employment of the then commonly used English word "filch" indicates that the speaker is not attempting to disguise the proposed criminal endeavor (which would have been considered an "unpleasant reality" by many people).[35] The speaker does not use cant as slang is typically used but rather as one would use any language when openly communicating with someone who speaks the same language.

Suzanne Romaine's understanding of jargon is consistent with that of most sociolinguists: "The term 'jargon' refers to a speech variety with a minimal linguistic system and great individual variation used for communicating in limited situations between speakers of different languages . . . while a pidgin has a certain degree of stability."[36] The most common alternative definition is given by Crystal, who states that "jargon" refers to "technical terms and expressions used by a group of specialists, which are not known or understood by the speech community as a whole."[37] The range in which cant was used, such as in Dekker's example (from pleasantries to travel and criminal plans in the future tense), shows that cant had neither a "minimal linguistic system" nor "great individual variation." Its linguistic system was elaborate inasmuch as it resembled the complex grammar of English. Although cant does resemble jargon in that it, too, was a specialized language of a trade, its "technical terms and expressions" were understood by the whole criminal cultural speech community, whose members learned cant from infancy—as Dekker puts it, "They study even from the Infancy, that is to say, from the very first houre"[38]—unless they were initiated into the community later in life. Jargons are not first languages learned from infancy. Most people in this community practiced the same overarching trade of deception and thievery, which benefited from the fact that cant was a specialized, secret language unintelligible to outsiders (but very possibly strategically sounding enough like English to have been further disguised because it was mistaken for English when overheard in crowded areas). Cant was the linguistic thread that wove together the cultural community of criminals; as a community language, it could not have experienced much "individual variation" and must have been standardized. For instance, in a letter dated 7 July 1585 from William Fletewoode, the Recorder of London, to Lord Burghley, Fletewoode reports on a school for criminals:

> One Wotton, a gentilman borne, and sometyme a marchauntt man of good credyte, who fallinge by tyme into decaye, kepte an Alehowse att Smarts Keye, neere Byllingesgate, and after, for some mysdemeanor beinge put downe . . . in the same Howse he procured all the Cuttpurses abowt this Cittie to repaire to his said howse. There was a schole howse sett upp to learne young boyes to cutt purses. There were hung up two devises, the one was a pockett, the other was a purse. The pocket had in yt certen cownters, and was hunge abowte with hawkes bells, and over the toppe did hannge a litle sacring bell; and he that could take owt a cownter without any noyse, was allowed to be a *publique Foyster:* and he that could take a peece of sylver owt of the purse without the noyse of any of the bells, he was adjudged a *judiciall Nypper.* Nota, that a Foister is a Pick-pockett, and a Nypper is termed a Pickpurse, or a Cutpurse.[39]

In the schoolhouse Fletewoode found poetry in cant "wrytten in a table," among which was the verse "Si spie, si non spie, Foyste, nyppe, lyfte, shave and spare not," for which he translates the cant terms: "*Foyste* is to cutt a pockett, *nyppe* is to cutt a purse, *lyft* is to robbe a shoppe or a gentilmans chamber, *shave* is to fylche a clooke, a sword, a sylver sponne or suche like."[40] This example establishes that cant was both a written and a spoken language. For this to have been the case, it must have experienced significant standardization. Indeed, Fletewoode implies that cant was taught at Wotton's school for criminals. Finally, it is important to note that cant would not have been a logical choice for communication "between speakers of different languages" since one would have had to speak English with considerable competence to be able to speak cant (recall that cant borrowed its grammar as well as its pronouns, conjunctions, adverbs, and some auxiliary verbs from English).[41] Therefore, cant cannot be categorized as a (typical) jargon. If cant is to be considered a jargon, as it is by Lee Beier[42] since it does meet at least one essential criterion for a jargon (it was a specialized language of a trade), it must have been a highly developed form of jargon or what I have been calling a natural-and-artificial language (which may be considered a unique or very rare form of jargon) invented by a dissident English-speaking population for professional *and* social purposes.

Dissident Cultural Functionality

To discover precisely what was in the canting song of *The Roaring Girl* that so fascinates Lord Noland and his pals, it is useful to look at some contemporary analyses of cant. In *The Description of England* Harrison comments on the history of the "trade" of roguery and vagabondage, which, generally speaking, means street crime more elaborate in practice than mugging and prostitution.[43] Such elaborate street crime included illegitimate and performative begging (without a license and/or while pretending to be poor and needy—like Trapdoor and Tearcat in *The Roaring Girl*), cut-pursing, and cony-catching, which was a sophisticated con (often scripted in detail) sometimes carrying over many days. "It is not yet full threescore years since this trade began," maintains Harrison, "but how it hath prospered since that time it is easy to judge, for they are now supposed, of one sex and another, to amount unto above 10,000 persons, as I have heard reported" (183–84). He then reports on the history of the language spoken by the criminals: "Moreover, in counterfeiting the Egyptian rogues, they have devised a language among themselves which they name 'canting' but other 'peddlers' French,' a speech compact thirty years since of English and a great number of odd words of their own devising, without all order or reason; and yet such is it as none but themselves are able to understand" (184). But there is a problem here. How can a language that is supposedly "without all order or reason" be spoken fluently by more than "10,000 persons"? The key to this history may turn on Harrison's use of the term "reason." To Harrison this language was reasonless simply because it was spoken by people who led alternative lives, without conventional "reason." Moreover, it was spoken by people who blatantly violated the official "order" of things.

Like Harrison and Harman (who claims that cant is a language "mingled without measure" [117]), Dekker insists, "I sée not that it ["cant"] is grounded upon any certaine rules" (*Lanthorne and Candle-Light* [1608],179). Also like Harman and Harrison, who hold that cant is a language that "none but [the criminals] themselves are able to understand" and therefore must have grammar or it would have been unintelligible to them, Dekker goes on to explain: "And no mervaile if it have none ["certaine rules"], for sithence both the *Father* of this new kinde of Learning, and the *children* that study to speake it after him, had beene from the beginning and stil are, the *Breeders* of a base disorder, in their living and in their *Manners:* how is it possible, they should observe any *Method* in their speech, and especially in such a Language, as serves but onely to utter discourses of villainies?" (179–80).[44] For Dekker, Harrison, and Harman it did not make sense that criminal culture could devise a structured language, although they all paradoxically claim that its members understood it and that criminal culture had a strict hierarchical structure. This apparent contradiction is primarily due to their shared assumption about the corrupt nature of members of this transgressive culture. This bizarre view of cant as being without rules and groundless is further evident in the previously mentioned fact that cant obviously borrows its grammatical structure from English (as in *The Roaring Girl*). Nevertheless, it was clear to them that cant's "*Method*," which was passed down from one generation of criminal culture to the next (from "*Father*" to the "*children*"), was incomprehensible to the average English citizen. It was also clear to them that criminal society was like a family, whose structure was very different from the official structure represented by the familial metaphors King James uses in his descriptions of monarchical rule. In *The Trve Lawe of free Monarchies* (1598) James maintains that the patriarchal monarch must care for his subjects like a father for his children to preserve order in the realm: "As the kindly father ought to foresee all inconuenients & dangers that may aryse towardes his children . . . [s]o ought the King towardes his people" (62). In contrast, writes Dekker, the patriarchal criminal and his children after him are "*Breeders* of a base disorder" who use cant to promote "discourses of villainies."

In *The Belman of London* Dekker supplies an explanation for cant's exclusivity and common unintelligibility when he asserts that "neither infidell nor Christian (that is honest) understandes it," and that cant is so complicated, "so crabbed," that "seven yeers study is little enough to reach the bottome of it, and to make it run off glib from the tongue" (147). Therefore one has to be both dishonest and learned to understand cant. Yet Dekker also asserts that cant is so well known and so widely understood by members of criminal culture or the criminal "nation" (his term) that "they know their owne nation when they meete, albeit they never sawe one another before" (147). According to Dekker, criminal culture constituted a subnation, with a language that meets Pierre Bourdieu's criterion for a "normalized language," which is one "capable of functioning outside the constraints and without the assistance of the situation, and is suitable for transmitting and decoding by any sender and receiver, who may know nothing of one another" (*Language and Symbolic Power* 44). Indeed, any criminal sender and receiver (like Moll and Trapdoor) could have shared secrets in cant. Both implicitly and explicitly Dekker portrays a criminal subnation, with a distinct culture, that was large enough to allow internal anonymity, dishonest enough to have a need for a secret language (a highly developed jargon or "antilanguage"), and devoted enough to invent, teach, learn, and standardize one. Criminal society normalized cant and thereby solidified its commitment to its own speech community and group identity. "In an antilanguage," as Hodge and Kress put it, "language exists primarily to create group identity and to assert group difference from a dominant group" (87). Unclear to Dekker and the other chroniclers of criminal culture, however, were the particulars and motivations behind cant's invention. These were persistent sources of concern for them.

In *The Belman of London* Dekker infers that cant is not an original language. It was not produced at the time of the Tower of Babel, when all languages supposedly originated: "The language which they [the criminals] speak is none of those which came in at the confusion of *Tongues*" (147). In *Lanthorne and Candle-Light* Dekker continues his discussion of the history of cant and its relationship to the Tower of Babel. He explains that the construction of a language corresponds to the empowerment of the people who speak it: "And in this manner did Men at the first make up nations: thus were words coynd into *Languages,* and out of those *Languages* have others béene molded since, onely by the mixture of nations, after kingdomes have béen subdued" (177). Nevertheless, cant developed without the requisite subduing of the English kingdom or current government. Does this mean that Dekker thought cant premonitory of England's fall or a (cultural) revolution or coup d'état? If so, was, say, *The Roaring Girl* meant to be instrumental? It seems that Dekker thought cant portentous of some form of major challenge to state power and official culture, especially when his statement is considered in light of his repeated emphasis on the dangerousness of the criminal population: "*More dangerous they are to a State, than a Civill Warre, because their villanies are more subtile and more enduring*" (*Belman,* 67).[45] Cant is unmistakably associated with resistance and rebellion.

Dekker provides another reason for cant's emergence, one more specific to criminal culture's needs: "As these people [the criminals] are strange both in names and in their conditions, so doe they speake a Language (proper only to themselves) called *canting,* which is more strange" (*Lanthorne,* 178). For Dekker it makes sense that these alternative ("strange") people should have an alternative means of expression, a language that is compatible with and complementary to their aesthetic ("proper only to themselves"). But criminal culture's need for a "strange" language extended well beyond the impetus to accommodate and maintain its strangeness, beyond basic issues of identity performance and substantiation. Criminal culture needed to ensure its members' loyalty and safety, and cant helped to accomplish this. As Dekker puts it:

> It was necessary, that a people (so fast increasing, and so daily practising new and strange *Villanies*), should borrow to themselves a spéech, we (so neere as they could) none but themsleves should understand: and for that cause was this Language, (which some call

Pedlers French,) Invented, to th'intent that (albeit any Spies should secretly steale into their companies to discover them) they might fréely utter their mindes one to another, yet avoide ye danger. The Language therefore of *canting,* they study even from the Infancy, that is to say, from the very first houre, that they take upon them the names of *Kinchin Coes,* til they are grown *Rufflers,* or *Upright men,* which are the highest in degrée amongst them. (179)

Like the English language for the bulk of England's populace, cant was learned and spoken by criminal culture's members from infancy ("from the very first houre") or else new members studied and learned it over time, either while associating with criminals or in covert criminal schools. (Recall that Dekker claims that "seven yeers study is little enough" to learn cant.) Contemporaries hold that the prisons, such as Newgate, Ludgate, Bridewell, The Fleet, The Clink, and The Counters (debtors' prisons), are schools for criminality.[46] For instance, in *The Fraternitye of Vacabondes* (1561), John Awdeley tells of criminals who have "taken degress in *Whittington* College," which was really Newgate; the latter having been built under former London mayor Richard Whittington.[47] In his *Defence of Conny catching. Or A Confvtation of those two iniurious Pamphlets published by R.G. [Robert Greene] against the practitioners of many Nimble-witted and mystical Sciences* (1592), Cuthbert Cunny-catcher writes: "I as desirous as hee [Plato] to search the deapth of those liberall Artes wherein I was a professour, lefte my study in *Whittington College,* & traced the country to grow famous in my facultie, so that I was so expert in the *Art of Cony-catching* by my continuall practise" (Cuthbert, 5).[48] Sir Alexander Wengrave in *The Roaring Girl* says that the "Counter" is a "university" where the scholars learn the "logic and rhetoric" of criminality (3.3.88–91). And John Taylor writes in his poem *The vertue of a Jayle, and necessitie of Hanging* (1630) that the jail is "an Vniuersitie of villany" (129).

In addition to the prisons, moreover, contemporaries hold that there are numerous underground criminal schools throughout the realm, especially in London, where cant is taught along with other criminal ideas and practices. For instance, in *The Belman of London* Dekker tells of a London *"Schoole of Beggers"* (101). And in *A Manifest Detection of Dice-play* (1552)

Gilbert Walker writes about "the college" for criminals, where, after "a good time of schooling," they learn the "craft" of thievery and "marvelous plenty of terms and strange language" (42, 49). Also recall Wotton's school for criminals, described in the letter from William Fletewoode, the Recorder of London, to Lord Burhgley. In this dissident alternative to the classical education in Greco-Roman art and literature, Christianity, and the London standard that was the conventional curriculum—allegedly designed for the purpose of enlightenment—criminal culture educated its members vocationally and culture-specifically in the arts of criminality and cant. Criminal culture's educational operation greatly undermined the punitive purpose of the prisons, the legal system, and official culture.

Thus, cant was invented so that members of criminal culture could communicate privately and securely while operating unlawfully within the physical and conceptual territory of official culture. In the words of Hodge and Kress: "Members of an antisociety do not use their language all the time. . . . [T]hey protect it, using it only when and where they feel secure. It is confined to their own domain, to a social space which is beyond the reach of the power which dominates public life, even though the rules of this antilanguage are formed out of those of the dominant language, created out of resistance to it" (69). In *Martin Markall, Beadle of Bridewell* Rid supports Dekker's explanation for the origin and purposes of cant. In the first part of this lengthy account of rogue-vagabond culture,[49] Rid critiques this culture and the state's treatment of it in a playful narrative response to Dekker's *Belman of London*. The criminals put the Bellman of London on trial because he "aimeth, tendeth to death and desolation, [and] subversion" of their criminal "state and fashion" (389). In his defense, the Bellman maintains that the "so great a swarming of loitering vagabonds and sturdy rogues" is potentially a "greater infection" than the plague, and that there is "no more hurtful a thing [than the criminal community] to a well-governed estate" (393). In this text, as in Dekker's, both criminal and official cultures are depicted as organized sociopolitical bodies, as states; the subnation/nation theme is very apparent. After the Bellman's speech, the trial is interrupted by the delivery of a letter from the "thrice-renowned Potentate, Don Purloiningo, Chief Governor of the Region of Thievingen" (395). The letter responds to a written complaint from his subjects, "the Gentlemen of the Ragged Order" of England's rogues and vagabonds (395). Don Purloiningo assures them that they are welcome in "Thievingen," a fictitious country of criminals, with a history and atmosphere similar to England's, that Rid created so that he could discuss indirectly the present situation of the criminal population in England. As Rid notes, Thievingen is even "fitting most directly for the latitude of Great Britain" (399). Thievingen is Rid's name for England's criminal subnation.

In their complaint, the criminals protest that state authorities have been cracking down on them: "That, whereas in all places we are daily persecuted by all sorts of officers, as marshals, beadles, sergeants, bailiffs, constables and such other officers, lying continually as spies to entrap and catch us poor souls as we are following our callings in markets, fairs, frays, throngs and assemblies, wherein heretofore we have lived reasonable well, though not with any great credit, yet void of suspicion or apprehension" (395). The criminals go on to explain that cant has not only lost much of its special practical purpose for them, but that it has actually become risky for them to speak it because the authorities have gained some knowledge of cant:

> And whereas our predecessors before, for the good of this commonwealth of ours, took great pains in devising a new speech or language, to the end we might utter our minds freely, and speak boldly without controlment one to another, which no doubt was a great help to us and our predecessors heretofore; yet such is the malice of some envious ill-willer of ours [the Bellman], that hath, we know not how, not only discovered our manners and fashions, but also this our language and speech, whereby we are oftentimes overheard, and taken and sent to prisons and tortures, and only by our own confessions, which we have uttered in this our language, and which we have trusted unto us boldly, as if we had been safe bolted in a castle or stronghold. (395)

This letter's prioritization of cant as one of criminal culture's most important features is complemented by a powerful statement made by Rid's Bellman: "According to the saying that you [the criminals] have among yourselves, if you can cant, you will never work: showing, that if they have been rogues so long that they can cant, they will never settle themselves to labour again" (394). In other words, to speak cant well is to be a good crook. Proficiency in cant enabled one fully to belong to criminal culture, to perpetrate elaborate crimes characteristic of this culture, and to achieve greater financial reward and social freedom than was typical of early modern England's legitimate working population. Through their establishment of an alternative culture and way of life, members of criminal culture transcended the social, cultural, and juridical constraints imposed on the populace by the sociopolitical conductors of state power and official culture. Even if the criminals were arrested and incarcerated, a term in prison was most likely an opportunity for (further) formal schooling in criminal methods and cant, as well as an opportunity to form promising criminal connections.

Essentially, any proficient speaker of cant, regardless of whether he or she had ever perpetrated a crime, was a verifiable member of criminal culture. Knowledge of cant was a privilege exclusive to criminal culture's members, and any member caught divulging or teaching cant to a person outside the criminal community was severely punished, if not killed. Dekker's Bellman in *O per se O* (1612) says, "For my better painting forth these monsters"—that is, so as to better record the ways of the criminals— "I once took one of them into my service" and inquired about cant:

Of him I desired some knowledge in their gibberish, but he swore he could not cant, yet his rogueship seeing himself used kindly by me, would now and then shoot out a word of canting, and being thereupon asked why with oaths he denied it before, he told me that they are sworn never to disclose their skill in canting to any householder, for, if they do, the other maunderers or rogues mill them (kill them), yet he for his part, he said, was never sworn, because he was a clapperdudgeon, that is to say, a beggar-born. (367)

Of course, whether the rogue was ever "sworn," which occurred when a person was "stalled" (initiated) into the criminal community, is merely a technicality and beside the point, which is that cant was very valuable to criminal culture, but only as long as it was kept private. This is affirmed by the period's judicial records, in which there are accounts of criminals who refused to disclose the extent of their knowledge of cant and where they acquired it. For example, according to the interviewing justice in Essex in 1590, Thomas Jackson, who was arrested for stealing hens, said that "concerning his Pedlar's French he will not make to me any account where he learned the same" (Essex Record Office, Q/SR 113/40a, quoted in Beier, 71). For this reason only people of high status in criminal culture's sociopolitical hierarchy, such as upright men, rufflers, and jackmen (conventionally and criminally educated rogues), could reveal cant; and even then they could reveal it only to another criminal member, such as a freshly stalled rogue. The centrality of cant in criminal culture—so vividly revealed by the texts discussed earlier and embodied in the slogan "If you can cant, you will never work"—is further illuminated by the significance of cant's role in criminal culture's stalling ritual, for which authorization to learn and speak cant was a decisive component.

This ceremony is colorfully represented by Harman, Dekker, and John Fletcher and Philip Massinger. According to these representations, cant is fundamental to both the stalling ritual and the subsequent libertine, communal lifestyle enjoyed by stalled rogues. Consider Harman's portrayal of the stalling ritual in his account of the life of an upright man:

> These upright-men will seldom or never want; for what is gotten by any mort, or doxy, if it please him, he doth command the same. And if he meet any beggar, whether he be sturdy or impotent, he will demand of him, whether ever he was stalled to the rogue or not. If he say he was, he will know of whom, and his name that stalled him. And if he be not learnedly able to show him the whole circumstance thereof, he will spoil him of his money. . . . Then doth this upright-man call for a gage of bouse, which is a quart pot of drink, and pours the same upon his peld pate, adding these words: "I, G.P., do stall thee, W.T., to the rogue, and that from henceforth it shall be lawful for thee to cant"—that is, to ask or beg—"for thy living in all places." (71–72)

As far as criminal culture was concerned, what is "lawful" is determined by upright men and not by the state; notwithstanding the state's laws against both begging without a license and traveling outside one's parish without a license, the stalled rogue was permitted to cant "in all places." Although it is implied by this passage that "to cant" means "to ask or beg," Harman makes it clear elsewhere in *A Caveat or Warening, For Commen Cursetors vulgarely called Vagabones* that he calls "canting" the language invented and spoken by a community of rogues and vagabonds.[50] Moreover, as we have seen, throughout the early modern period "beggar" was often used synonymously with "rogue" and "vagabond" to indicate a member of the criminal community.[51]

In *The Belman of London* Dekker also locates cant, as well as liquor, at the heart of the rogue initiation ceremony. This similarity, however, is not at all surprising since Dekker's representation is either loosely plagiarized from Harman or comparably informed by knowledge of a social event characteristic of the criminal community. Knowledge of this event may have been fairly popular in early modern England, just as it is popularly "known" in the United States today that street gangs often initiate new members "with beatings." In Dekker's account, the Bellman reports that he observed a criminal called "Captaine"—a functional name synonymous with "upright man" (recall that Moll is called "captain" by Trapdoor)—first ask a man who was attempting to pass as a rogue "if hee were stalled to the *Rogue* or no," and then inquired "by *Whom* he was *Stalled,* and *Where,* and *What manner of Complement* it was done" (82–83). Afterward the captain ordered the man "to bee stript" by the other rogues present:

> This done, the *Grand Signior* called for a *Gage* of *Bowse,* which belike signified a quart of drinke, for presently a pot of Ale being put into his hand, hee made the *yong Squire* kneele downe, and powring the full pot on his pate, uttered these wordes, I—doe stall thée—to the *Rogue,* by vertue of this soveraigne English liquor, so that henceforth it shall bee lawfull for thée to *Cant,* (that is to say) to be a *Vagabond* and *Beg,* and to speake that pedlers French, or that *Canting language,* which is to be found among none but *Beggers:* with that, the *Stalled Gentleman* rose, all the rest in the roome hanging upon him for joy, like so many dogges about a beare, and leaping about him with showtes like so many mad-men. (83)

Dekker's Bellman witnessed a festive and secret ceremony that facilitated the acceptance of the newly stalled rogue and promoted camaraderie among criminal culture's members. The new member is now considered, as the captain puts it, "a méere fresh-man" in their "Colledge" of criminality, where one learns "the *Rudiments of Roagarie*" (83–84). The captain's awareness of this ritual's dissident nature is exemplified by his ironic identification as "soveraigne English" of the liquor used to anoint the initiate. Regardless of the actual motivations and circumstances behind the criminal community's development, the Bellman relentlessly insists that its members were "open and professed foes to the *Republick*" (the state); and, according to the official view, which is also the Bellman's, they were enemies "to honesty, to civility, and to all humanity" (156). Dekker's account shows that the "*Canting language,* which is to be found among none but *Beggers,*" was an acknowledged language of dissidence and confederation.

Fletcher and Massinger affirm this understanding of cant. Their dramatic representation of the stalling ritual in their play *Beggars Bush* (first performed at court in 1622) also features cant and involves liquor. A nobleman named Hubert, disguised as a huntsman, appeals to a band of rogues: "May a poore huntsman, with a merry hart . . . Get leave to live amongst ye?" (3.2.92–94). A conversation ensues between him and two of the criminals, Clause and Higgen (the band's leader), in which Hubert is told: "Sir ere get your fredome" and "we take thee to us, Into our company" as long as "thou dar'st be true unto us?" To this Hubert answers affirmatively: "I, and obedient too." Then he is asked two additional crucial questions: "You can drink too?" and "And ye dare know a woman from a weathercock?" (Do you have sexual experience with women?) (3.2.128–41). After Hubert answers affirmatively to these, too, the initiation ceremony begins:

> *Gerrard:* Now sweare him.
> *Higgen:* I crowne thy nab, with a gage of benbouse,
>   And stall thee by the salmon into the clowes,
>   To mand on the pad, and strike all the cheates;
>   To mill from the Ruffmans, commission and slates,

Twang dell's i' the stromell; and let the Quire Cuffin:
And Herman Becks trine, and trine to the Ruffin.
Gerrard: Now interpret this unto him.
Higgen: I powre on thy pate a pot of good ale,
And by the Rogues oth a Rogue thee install:
To beg on the way, to rob all thou meetes;
To steale from the hedge, both the shirt and the sheetes:
And lye with thy wench in the straw till she twang,
Let the Constable, Iustice, and Divell go hang.
You are welcom Brother. (3.2.143–56)

In this account of the stalling ritual, knowledge of cant is not a prerequisite to initiation—Higgen must "interpret" for Hubert—but it is implied that the opportunity to learn cant is a key benefit of initiation. Inasmuch as *Beggars Bush* regularly pokes fun at the criminals even while primarily celebrating them (the play, after all, is a comedy), it is difficult to determine which of the prerequisites is most important to them and why. In a drinking song sung by "The Beggars" in Brome's *A Jovial Crew,* as in *The Belman of London,* consumption of ale is depicted as an act of rebellion against the state: "Here, safe in our skipper [barn], let's cly [take] off our peck [meat], / And bowse in *defiance* o'th' harman-beck [constable]" (Brome 57).[52] It seems that criminal culture valued excessive drinking because it was reckless and transgressive (like licentiousness), convivial, and indicative of the culture's irreverence toward and freedom from the constraints pervasive in conventional English society. Of course, criminal culture valued trustworthiness because it could not exist without it.

Most important to the present analysis, however, is the fact that the ritual is performed in cant. This suggests that by 1622 criminal culture's members' knowledge of cant, and thus cant's status within criminal culture, had greatly increased since Harman published his account in 1567. Furthermore (and more likely), since the play's intended audience was members of official culture, it suggests that popular knowledge of cant had substantially increased during the interim. I do not simply mean that more of official culture's members could speak or understand cant, although this might have been the case, but rather that the English populace was significantly more aware of cant's existence and sociocultural significance and consequently was much more interested in understanding cant's criminal-sociocultural functionality than ever before. This would explain Jonson's untranslated use of cant in his 1621 court masque *The Gypsies Metamorphos'd*. Whereas it is unlikely that the aristocratic and royal audiences of *The Gypsies Metamorphos'd* would have understood cant, it is certain that they would have wanted to know all about this influential popular fetish.

CHAPTER FOUR

Social Spatialization, Criminal Praxis, Transversal Movement

TO PROMOTE the hegemony of official culture and advance the state, early modern England's state machinery needed to construct, imbue, and regulate the populace's subjective territory: its range of conceptual and emotional experience. In conjunction, and by extension, it needed to rule the physical existence of the populace. I am primarily concerned with the populace's combined social and physical relationship to space. Like its conceptual territory, which was immanent, the populace's physical existence had spatiality, with each member living in a material world with sociospatial arrangements, demarcations, and sentiment. Specifically, each member had a prescribed sociospatial station or residence, indeed, a delimited and surveilled habitat, wherein he or she was expected to function in conformity with the interests of official culture. In order to govern with the greatest efficacy, the state machinery needed to keep people stationary or tracked, both socioeconomically and geographically. It is always the case that the infrastructural assemblages and sociopolitical conductors of official society and state power, especially their mechanisms for law enforcement, taxation, health care, and ideological inculcation (religious and educational structures), operate most efficiently when the citizenry are tractable, consistent, and ostensibly homogeneous in thought and action—in short, subjectified. To achieve the desired sociocultural compositionality, early modern England's state machinery endeavored, by means of moral and legal codes, to control the populace sociospatially not only by dictating behavior within particular places and spaces but also by re-stricting travel within the realm between places and spaces.

In this chapter I argue that early modern England's criminal culture of gypsies, rogues, vagabonds, beggars, cony-catchers, cutpurses, and prostitutes was defiantly and transversally mobile, nomadic, and expan-sive. It was transversal also in that its criminal practice was heterogeneous, discursive, elusive, and performative. Contemporaries understood crimi-nal culture's praxis, its customs and practical operations, in aesthetic terms as an innovative, often theatrical, artistic expression that was cultivated and demanded great skill, intelligence, and an immoral disposition. In effect, as I hope to demonstrate, criminal culture's sociospatial presence and articulation metamorphosed traditional spaces by altering people's re-lationships to them. Criminal culture's sociospatiality produced "differ-ential spaces" (sites of sociospatial contradiction), "wilderness effects" (ex-periences of alienation, adventure, or danger), and "discursive ruptures" (subversions or transversal movements) within fields of official spatializa-tion. Among these fields were England's public thoroughfares, market-places, localities for entertainment and recreation, and, more broadly, parishes, towns, and cities. These fields were officially spatialized insofar as they were purpose-built environments; conceptually and physically defined against the "out-of-field" (anything beyond a field's borders that is unknown or unseen but always present); socially, culturally, and polit-ically configured with a "place-image" (a prevalent conception of a place or space); and important to and monitored by the state machinery.[1]

Transspatial Incontinence

The legislation against unlawful travel within England's territory, as well as records of its enforcement, have been extensively documented by Frank Aydelotte, J. A. Sharpe, and A. L. Beier, respectively.[2] On the en-forcement of legislation against vagabondage, for example, Beier notes that "substantial numbers of reports survive in the State Papers, Domes-tic: from almost half the English counties, including details of 742 va-grants, for the [search] campaign of 1569–72; and from 39 of 52 English and Welsh shires, reporting nearly 25,000 arrests between 1631 and 1639."[3]

As was previously stated, I am interested in the sociopolitical implications of this legislation and its subversion and transcendence by members of criminal culture. I am most concerned with the representation of criminal culture's transversal sociospatial movement in the contemporary historiography and popular view. To illustrate the state's investment in sociospatial management, I want to discuss, as points of entrance, two noteworthy statutes. One is Henry VIII's 1531 "Proclamation . . . for punisshinge of vacabundes and sturdy beggars," and the other is the 20 June 1569 directive from the Privy Council to the London Aldermen that called for a large-scale search for rogues and vagabonds in London and its suburbs. These statutes are representative of early modern England's legislation against unlawful travel and vagabondage; as noted by Beier, their stipulations closely resemble the Acts of 1563, 1572, 1597, 1604, and 1631.

The 1531 statute exemplifies the state's concern with sociospatial constancy, which meant constancy of population, function, and place-image, that was to continue and, in fact, intensify throughout the early modern period. To protect the populace from the "contynuall theftes, mourdres, and other sundry haynous offenses and great enormities to the high displeasure of god" allegedly committed by vagabonds, the statute determined the quantitative space wherein a person could travel without a passport (one "hundred" miles), and called for the strict enforcement of this sociospatial delimitation. The statute reads:

> His highnes . . . commandeth all Iustices of the peas, maires, sheryffes, constables, bursholders, tethynge men, and other his mynysters [that] happen to fynde any vacabunde or myghty begger (be it man or woman) out of the hundred where he or she was borne, or out of the towne or place, where he or she last dwelled in, and continued by the space of thre yeres nexte before, and that vpon knowledge of the sayde proclamation, he or she hath not demaunded a Byllet to conuey them selfe to the sayde hundred or dwellynge place, and so be in theyr iourney thetherwarde, within the sayd two daies, that than the sayde Iustices and minysters and euery of them, shall cause the sayde vacubundes and beggars and euery of them, to be stripped naked, from the priuey partes of theyr bodies vpwarde

(men and women of great age of seke, and women with childe onely
excepte) and beinge so naked, to be bounden, and sharpely beaten
and skourged.[4]

To travel outside of one's parish required permission from the local justice
of the peace. If granted, one was issued a passport (a "Byllet"). When in
transit, one was expected to carry the passport at all times as proof of le-
gitimacy. As in the 1531 statute, state officials were ordered to inspect and
sign the passports of all travelers with whom they came in contact. People
caught traveling unlawfully, and therefore in violation of the sociogeographical enclosures, were harshly punished. Their sociospatial freedom
was completely abolished ("bounded"), however temporarily, and their
bodies marked ("sharpely beaten and skourged"). Through this discipli-
nary procedure, the state machinery demonstrated that the vagabonds
themselves as well as the ground they walk on are the property of the state,
that is, as long as the state machinery maintains control. After receiving
corporal punishment, convicted vagabonds were either sent back to their
place of birth or where they had last resided for a duration of three or
more years. Thus, the state must have considered three years the time it
customarily took for one to establish familiarity and relationships with
others within a given sociospatial habitat. In three years, it is implied, one
becomes well enough known by the community within which one lives
or associates that one's officially defined deleterious potential—for becoming criminal—is substantially diminished.

The 1567 ordinance highlights the drastic measures taken by state officials to ferret out and apprehend rogues and vagabonds. It also highlights
the subterfuge employed by members of criminal culture to facilitate their
sociospatial transgression:

First youe [the London Aldermen] shall secretlie accorde by way
of distribucion of your sellfes with the helpe of other inferior officers whom youe maie well trust, to cause a straight serch and good
stronge watche to be begon on sondaie at night abowte ix of the
clocke, which shall be the tenth of July, in every parishe and warde
of the Citie and the suburbes of the same within youre rule and
iurisdiccion and to continewe the same all that night, vntill foure of

the clocke in the after none of the nexte daie, and in that search and watch to apprehend all vacabonds, sturdy beggers comonlie called Roges, or Egiptians, and all other idle vagarant personnes havinge no masters nor any certainie howe or wherby to lyve, and theime cause to be imprisoned in stockes and suche like, and accordinge to the qualities of there faultes to procede againste theyme, as by the lawes ys ordered, and that with convenient severytye, so as thei may bee by punyshment forced to labor for theire lyvinge. And, as it is likly that youe haue in your former orders already remytted them whom youe haue not thought mete to retaine in work to departe to theire natyve countries.[5]

Like the 1531 statute, this one shows that the state took vagabondage very seriously and severely punished vagabonds who caused or constituted ruptures in fields of official spatialization. It also reveals the state's pursuit of sociospatial constancy and the mechanisms implemented to promote it. Displaced rogues, vagabonds, beggars, and gypsies were returned to their "natyve countries," which refers to the counties in which they were born. Either surreptitiously or blatantly, initiated members of criminal culture, such as those who had been "stalled to the rogue"[6] and people who were affiliated, if only symbolically, through their vagabondage, violated official mandates by "stray[ing] fare oute of theire righte waies." They often did this with the aid of counterfeit passports. The directive warns:

So are youe [the London Aldermen] to take good heed howe to aduoid the abuses of youre pasportes, by the which when the names only of the places to which thei are directed ar speciallie namyd, the said lewed persones craftelie spende theire tyme in passage, idellye, do stray fare oute of their righte waies, and doo in some places coullor theire goinge to the bathes for recouery of theire counterfeit sycknes, and thefore in the pasportes would be also named speciall townes beinge in theire right waies, by which thei shuld be chardged in theire pasportes to passe so as yf thei shall be founde oute of those highte waies thei may be newely and more sharplie punyshed, and in this cause allso the pasportes woolde be so discreatlie sealed, subscribed, and written, as thei shuld not easilie counterfait the same, which, as it ys reported, some of theime can readely doo, and do carry aboute with theim certaine counterfait seales of corporat townes and suche like to serve theire purposes in that behalfe; for the which before they shalbe dimissed due searche woulde be made. And after this searche made, which is intended to be made generall at one tyme throughe the whole Realme.[7]

Forging and selling state documents was one of criminal culture's most lucrative rackets. Beier concludes: "Counterfeit passports grew so common that the system became a nonsense. The Vagrancy Act of 1572 ordered that frauds be punished, and by 1580 JPs showed no surprise at discovering vagabonds with false papers."[8] As discussed in chapter 2, criminals who went by the functional name of "Jackman" (sometimes spelled "Jarkman," as Awdeley records) could "write and reade, and sometime speake latin," and "he vseth to make counterfaite licences which they call Gybes, and sets to Seales, in their [canting] language called Iarks."[9] Counterfeit passports were difficult to make. To create the ersatz seal, the forger had to engrave in wood the pattern of an authentic seal. To make the actual passport, the forger had to be literate in at least English, and ideally in Latin too, and capable of varying his or her handwriting. For instance, as reported in an Essex court record in 1581, Davy Bennett was regarded for his dexterity: "If he sees it in wax, he will lay it before him and carve it out in wood very perfectly," and "he writes in sundry hands."[10] There was a great demand for counterfeit passports. They were commodities manufactured by members of criminal culture and, presumably, sold to anyone. In *O per se O* (1612), a popular pamphlet about criminals, Thomas Dekker elaborates:

> They who are counterfeiters of passports are called [in cant] bene-fakers, that is to say, good makers. And these makers, like the Devil's hackney-men, lie lurking in every country, to send his messengers post to Hell. The best passports that ever I saw were made in S——shire, with the hand of one M. W. subscribed unto them. There was another excellent bene-faker about P——, a town in G——shire. In S——dwelt another, who took two shillings and sixpence (two bords and six wins, or two bords and a flag) for every passport that went out of his beggarly office; he counterfeited the seal of L. D.[11]

Clearly, as Beier emphasizes, counterfeit passports posed a "direct challenge to the state" and were "of great importance for vagabonds."[12] The challenge, however, lies less in the usurpation of authority than in the unlawful travel to which the counterfeit passports contributed. According to the period's personal, commercial, and state literature, criminal culture's members traversed England as they pleased or with little difficulty. This liberty allowed them to perpetrate crimes with greater anonymity and viability and to establish and expand criminal cultural networks. Not surprisingly, it also inspired becomings-criminal.

In *The Highway to the Spital-House* (1535–36) Robert Copland complains about vagabonds "Loitering and wandering from place to place, / And will not work," "For they do come as they were scattered sheep, / Wandering without, reason, rule, or guide," and "That all this land is with them infect."[13] This was written in the same decade that rogues, vagabonds, and gypsies were first recognized as a serious problem for the state. Although there were statutes enacted against vagabonds before 1531, such as the London Act of 1517, the 1531 statute was the first to consider vagabonds a real threat to official culture and state power. Indeed, it was issued with urgency. It declared that "vacabundes and beggars, haue of longe tyme encreased and daily dothe encrease in great and excessiue nombres, by the occasyon of ydelnes, mother and roote of all vices [and cause] contynuall theftes, mourdres, and other sundry haynous offenses and great enormities to the high displeasure of god, the inquietation and damage of his true and faithfull subiects, and to the disturbance of the hoole common weale of this his sayd realme."[14] During this decade the state also urgently issued its first statute against gypsies entitled "An Act concerning Egyptians" (1530). This act emphasizes the dangerousness of the "dyverse and many outlandysshe People callynge themselfes Egyptians [who] so many tymes by crafte and subtyltie had deceyved the People of theyr Money and also had comytted many and haynous Felonyes and Robberies."[15] As discussed in chapter 2, in 1533, according to Samuel Rid's *Martin Markall, Beadle of Bridewell* (1610), a "regiment" of "rogues" and "vagabonds," "calling themselves by the name of Egyptians," merged with another community of rogues and vagabonds called the "Quartern of Knaves;" and together they formed a "new-found government."[16] Moreover, says Rid, it was this confederation of rogues, vagabonds, and gypsies that invented the canting language spoken by criminals throughout the early modern period: "And first of all they think it fit to devise a certain kind of language, to the end their cozenings, knaveries, and villainies might not so easily be perceived and known in places where they come. And this their language they spun out of three other tongues, viz., Latin, English and Dutch— these three especially, notwithstanding some few words they borrowed of Spanish and French" (421).

I mention Rid's account, moreover, because of its apparent historical correlation with the fact that early modern England's state machinery officially pursued language standardization for the first time in 1535. Henry VIII prohibited the use of Welsh because a "great Discord Variance Debate Division Murmur and Sedition" had arisen since the Welsh people "have and do daily use a Speech nothing like, nor consonant to the natural Mother Tongue within this Realm."[17] Language variety challenged the state's quest for sociopolitical, nationalist uniformity, and unregulated travel by foreign speakers, speakers of obscure dialects, and the immoralist speakers of cant all contributed to vernacular multilingualism. Thus, during the 1530s the discursive ruptures in official sociospatiality effectuated by nomadic rogues, vagabonds, and gypsies were glaringly obvious and problematic. The transversal power of nomadism and criminality— a force capable of "infect[ing]" the "land" with idleness and immorality, constituting the "mother and roote of all vices," and precipitating the emergence of an alternative society with is own government and language—was for the first time a recognizable and imminent threat to the state.

But the state machinery's concerted efforts to suppress the emergent population of rogues and vagabonds were hardly successful. This is reflected throughout the early modern period. In addition to the repeated issuance of statutes against vagabondage, criminal culture's transversal movement was progressively represented in popularly marketed literary texts. In *The Fraternitye of Vacabondes* (1561) John Awdeley writes of "The Company of Cousoners and Shifters" and indicates that these "idle Vacabondes" peruse London's fields of official spatialization, including "Poules, or at Christes Hospital, & sometime at ye Royal exchaunge," looking for people to rob.[18] In *A Caveat or Warening, For Commen Curse-*

tors vulgarely called Vagabones (1567), Kentish justice of the peace Thomas Harman says that he calls "these vagabonds *cursitors* in the entitling of my book" because they are "runners or rangers about the country." To stress the importance of his project, which he says is "for the profit and benefit of my country . . . that the whole body of the realm may see and understand their lewd like and pernicious practices," he offers a rhetorical question: "Who is so ignorant by these days as knoweth not the meaning of a *vagabond?*"[19] According to Harman, vagabondage is of paramount concern to all honest English people. In *A Notable Discovery Coosnage* (1591) Robert Greene complains that cony-catchers are "a plague as ill as hell," that "such vipers are suffred to breed," and emphasizes the ubiquity of cony-catching: "This enormity is not onely in London, but now generally dispersed through all england, in euery shire, city, and town of any receipt, and many complaints are heard of their egregious cosenage."[20] In *The Belman of London* (1608) Dekker holds that the vagabond has complete sociospatial freedom: "The whole *Kingdome* is but his *Walke,* a whole Cittie is but his parish."[21] In the book's final section, entitled "The terrible extent of the evil," Dekker asserts that criminal infiltration is so widespread that there are "so many infected bodies being to bee found in every corner of the Land" (158). This view is supported by Samuel Rid, who, in *The Art of Juggling* (1612), attests to the pervasiveness of skilled and organized criminals: "The contagion of cheating is now grown so universal that they swarm in every quarter."[22] To give a last example, in "The Beggar" (1630) poet John Taylor underscores the vagabondage problem with a sarcastic declaration:

> In Court, Campe, City, Countrey, in the Ocean,
> A Begger is a right perpetuall motion,
> His great deuotion is in generall,
> He either prayes for all, or preyes on all.[23]

Like the statutes against vagabondage, criminal culture's chroniclers repeatedly stress the *everywhereness* of criminal culture. For them the highways, countrysides, towns, and cities of England are dangerous places; as Dekker puts it in *Lanthorne and Candle-Light* (1608), they have become "a *wildernesse*" where "*Monsters*" lurk, ready to prey on the innocent.[24] When supposedly civilized spaces are endowed with and are experienced as having wilderness or alien features and energy, they have become differential spaces. As a result, wilderness effects transpire. According to these writers, criminality was rampant, varied, fluid, proliferating, and ominous. Criminal culture was discursively disruptive and produced sites of sociospatial contradiction. This combined occurrence illuminated dissonance within and encompassed fields of official spatialization. Thus, the transversal movement made by rogues and vagabonds was translated within the resultant differential spaces. To be sure, this situation revealed official culture's lack of wholeness, the fact that its projected continuity, like the totalized state, can only ever be an illusion or fantasy. It showed that England's whole social world was fundamentally open and in flux. Following Henri Bergson, Gilles Deleuze posits an analogy that lends insight into this remarkable situation:

> It might be said that movement presupposes a difference of potential, and aims to fill it. If I consider parts or places abstractly—A and B—I cannot understand the movement which goes from one to the other. But imagine I am starving at A, and at B there is something to eat. When I have reached B and had something to eat, what has changed is not only my state, but the state of the whole which encompassed B, A, and all that was between them. When Achilles overtakes the tortoise, what changes is the state of the whole which encompassed the tortoise, Achilles, and the distance between the two. Movement always relates to a change.[25]

That vagabondage could occur, that there was sociospatial movement of this kind, indicates that there were differential relations, fluctuations, weaknesses, or gaps within the distribution of state power. The sociopolitical conductors of state power could not (and, incidentally, could never in any society) effectuate absolute hegemony or a hermetic system. There are always other preexisting forces circulating that preclude such fixity and purity. The early modern writers similarly understood vagabondage and criminal culture as forces of corruption.

Awdeley, Harman, Greene, Dekker, Rid, Middleton, and others who wrote about criminal culture not only claim that rogues and vagabonds are everywhere, and everywhere transgressive, but also that they are every-where infectious. Disease metaphors abound in descriptions of criminal culture, which was thought to be so corruptive and contagious that its chroniclers thought that their own and their readers' engagement with it, if only conceptually in written discourse, was likely to encourage crimi-nality since criminal culture created the potential for more transversal movement. For example, like the antitheatricalists discussed in the next chapter, who vehemently warned against exposure to the infectious wickedness of stage plays, Thomas Middleton writes in the "Epistle" to his *Black Book* (1604), "To all those that are truly virtuous, and can touch pitch [moral corruption] and yet never defile themselves, read the mis-chievous lives and pernicious practices of villains and yet be never the worse at the end of the book." He then speaks of criminal praxis as "the infectious bulks of craft, coz'nage and panderism, the three bloodhounds of a commonwealth."[26] Although Middleton entertains the possibility that his reader will become infected with the "pernicious" subject matter of his book, it is unclear whether he mentions this danger to entice or protect his reader. Either way, the fact that he suggests it at all—that criminality is so contagious or seductive that only the "truly virtuous" are immune to it—indicates that this might have been an issue of concern and was within the realm of possibility among his intended readership.

In *Lanthorne and Candle-Light* Dekker expresses similar concern: "Some perhaps wil say, that this lancing of the pestilent sores of a King-dome so openly, may infect those in it that are sound, and that in this our schoole, (where close abuses and grose villanies are but discovered and not punished) others that never before knew such evils, wil be now instructed (by the booke) to practise them."[27] According to Middleton, Dekker, and others, there are people who believe and are threatened by the possibility that criminality infects the minds of observers or those who have acquired some extended or "inside" knowledge of it. For criminality to be influen-tial in these ways it must infect certain places and spaces, conceptual and material, with the latter being the most recognizable. The material real-ization of criminal thought was a menacing actuality that variegated early modern England's fields of official spatialization. This was particularly the case for London and its suburbs. This region housed the chief governmental, educational, and religious leaders and institutions; it was the most densely populated and rapidly burgeoning area as well as the country's commercial, cultural, and socioeconomic center. For these reasons it was crucial that the state machinery diligently enforce its sociospatial prescriptions for London and its suburbs.

Places and Spaces of Influence

In this section I first want to establish with greater specificity this everywhereness of rogues and vagabonds by documenting references to actual places and spaces known for their criminal activity. Then I will briefly examine two notorious localities for criminality, St. Paul's Cathedral and Churchyard and the public theater, both of which were located in the London metropolitan area. By "public theater" I mean all the purpose-built commercial theaters in London and its suburbs that were open to public patronage, such as The Rose, The Globe, The Swan, The Fortune, and The Curtain. The dearth of popular literature about rogues and vagabonds in rural regions (beyond the East Midlands) to support the statutes and court records that document their activities in these regions precludes the kind of sophisticated literary-cultural treatment made possible by the diverse sources about rogues and vagabonds of London and its suburbs.[28] Thus, my focus throughout this section will be on the London metropolitan area.

The Elizabethan Act of 1566 against "Cutpurses or Pyckpurses" is singularly the strongest, most comprehensive state evidence for the existence, everywhereness, and transversality of criminal culture.[29] It explicitly refers to criminal culture's communal, cryptic, and parasitic nature by describing it as "a Brotherhed or Fraternitie of an Arte or Mysterie, to lyve idellye by the secrete Spoyle of the good and true Subjects of this Realme." It delineates criminal culture's blatant irreverence and transgression of all fields of official spatialization, from the popular ("in Fayres [and] Markettes . . . and at the tyme of doing of Execucion"), to the juridical ("at the Places and Courts of Justice") to the holy ("at Sermons and Preachings of the Woorde of God") to the royal ("the Princes Palace House"). It maintains that members of criminal culture commit crimes in these official localities without "feare or dreade of God, or any Lawe or Punyshment." In other words, it claims that they are deterritorialized from official and subjective territories (the official conceptualization and corresponding personal experience of each subject), and that they are resolute and comfortable with their occupation and lifestyle. It shows that the state machinery thought criminal culture a grave threat to state order, dangerous enough "that persons convicted of this crime shall be executed as felons without benefit of clergy." Indeed, this 1566 statute is so important and fascinating that it is worth quoting at length as a prelude to my brief tour of London's criminal infiltration.

> Where a certayne kynde of evill disposed persons commonly called Cutpurses or Pyckpurses, but in deede by the Lawes of this Lande very Fellons and Theeves, doo confeder togethers making among thenselves as it were a Brotherhed or Fraternitie of an Arte or Mysterie, to lyve idellye by the secrete Spoyle of the good and true Subjects of this Realme, and aswell at Sermons and Preachings of the Woorde of God, and in places and tyme of doing service and common Prayer in Churches Chappelles Closettes and Oratories, and not only there but also in the Princes Palace House, yea and presence, and at the Places and Courts of Justice, and at the tymes of Mynystracion of the Lawes in the same, and in Fayres Markettes and other Assemblies of People, yea and at the tyme of doing of Execucion of such as ben attaynted of anye Murder Felonye or other crymynall Cause ordeined chieflye for Terrour and Example of evill doers, do without respect or regarde of anye tyme place or person, or anye feare or dreade of God, or any Lawe or Punyshment, under the cloke of Honestie, by their owtwarde Apparell Countenance and Behaviour subtiltie privilye craftelye and felonyously take the Goodes of dyvers good and honest Subjects from their persons by cutting and pycking their Purses and other felonious Slaightes and Devices, to the utter undoing and impoverishment of many: Bee it therefore enacted by the aucthorite of this present Parliament,' &c., &c., to the effect that persons convicted of this crime shall be executed as felons without benefit of clergy.

Among the areas of London and its suburbs that were notorious for criminal activity are the districts of Spitalfields-Whitechapel, Newgate-Cripplegate, and Southwark and its Liberties.[30] Before discussing St. Paul's and the public theater, I am going to quickly survey the criminal place-imaging discursively manifested in the various texts that support the account of criminal culture given by the 1566 statute.

In *The Second Part of Conny-Catching* (1592), for instance, Robert Greene claims that cony-catchers' "chiefe walkes is Paules, Westminster, the exchange, Plaies, Bear-garden, running at Tilt, the L. Maiors day, any festiuall meetings, fraies, shootings, or great faires: to bee short, wheresoeuer is any extraordinary resort of people, there the nip [cutpurse] and the foist [pickpocket] haue fittest oportunity to shew their iugling agilitie."[31] He says that the criminals "haue a kind of corporation, as hauing Wardens of their company, and a hall. I remember their Hall was once about Bishopsgate, neere vnto Fishers folly, but because it was a noted place, they haue remooued it to Kent-street [in Southwark], and as far as I can learne, it is kept at one *Laurence Pickerings* house, one that hath beene, if he be not still, a notable Foist" (36). In *The Third Part of Conny-Catching* (1592) Greene writes, "Nowhere sooner then in this Cittie [London], where (I may say to you) are such a number of Connycatchers, Cossoners and such like, that a man can scarcely keep any thing from them, they haue so many reaches and sleights to beguile withall."[32] And in *A Notable Discovery of Coosnage* (1592) Greene explains, "The poore countrie farmer or Yeoman is the marke which they most of all shoote at, who they knowe comes not emptie to the Terme. . . . [A]fter dinner when the clients are come from Westminster hal and are at leasure to walke vp and downe Paules, Flet-stret, Holborne, the sttrond, and such common hanted places [in London], where these cosning companions attend onely to spie out a praie."[33] Greene portrays an organized community of criminals who hold regular meetings in a "Hall," perpetrate crimes wherever people assemble or a throng gathers, and take advantage of the naive, such as "the poore countrie farmer or Yeoman." Like animal predators in the wild, members of criminal culture preyed on the vulnerable. But unlike animal predators, they spared the lives of their victims (mugging-murders were rare). Apparently, by unlawfully feeding on but not permanently harming their inhabitants, criminal culture wanted to capitalize on officially constructed sociospatial assemblages without destroying them.

In *The Black Dog of Newgate* (1596) Luke Hutton interviews a cony-catcher named Zawny about the "infinite number of this sect and company of cony-catchers."[34] Zawny tells many stories of their devious crimes, sometimes against other criminals, and stresses their ubiquity. For instance, he explains: "At term-time, these fellows H. and S. [both cony-catchers] have had great booties by their practices in this art . . . [at] Westminster Hall," where they con both the cutpurses and their victims (287). While this text holds that the criminals stole from each other, most accounts of criminal culture do not. But, as was discussed in the previous chapter, almost all speak of localized sociopolitical hierarchy and organization. In *The Belman of London* Dekker writes, "For that purpose therefore, (as if a whole kingdome were theirs) they [the criminal leaders] allot such countries to this Band of *Foists,* such townes to those, and such a City to so many *Nips:* whereupon some of these *Boote-halers* are called *Termers,* and they ply Westminster Hall"; he names the following as hotbeds for criminal activity: "*Cheapside, East-cheape,* the *Shambles,* both *Fishstreetes,* the *Stockes,* and ye *Borough* in Southwarke."[35] In Lo Barry's play *Ram-Alley* (1611), named after the actual street in Whitefriars that was notorious for its crime, rogues and prostitutes are said to operate in the "Suburbs," where they must "scapt so many searches" by state officials. One rogue in particular, Captaine Face, is identified by where he operates when a prostitute named Taffata orders him: "Sir get you gonne, You swaggering cheating Turne-bull-streete roague."[36] In Middleton and Dekker's *The Roaring Girl* (1612) upright man Trapdoor exclaims: "As every throng is sure of a pickpocket; as sure as a whore is of the clients all Michaelmas term, and of the pox after the term."[37] Like Greene, these writers indicate a discursive criminal network that determined ("allot[ed]") its own territorialization of London and its suburbs.

This brings us to St. Paul's Cathedral and Churchyard, which were among the most criminally territorialized fields of official spatialization. In *The Art of Juggling,* Rid writes about a notorious cony-catcher: "This Cuthbert is esteemed of some and thought to be a witch of others; he is accounted a conjurer, but commonly called a wise man, and are able of themselves to tell you where anything that is stolen is, as to build Paul's steeple up again."[38] Built during the twelfth and thirteenth centuries, Paul's was spatialized, first of all, for the purposes of the church. Throughout the early modern period divine services were held daily within the cathedral, and occasionally at Paul's Cross in the Churchyard. Paul's was the largest cathedral in England and one of the largest in Europe, with its steeple ascending 489 feet. The Churchyard was also very large, covering twelve and a half acres. In addition to its religious function, Paul's was a hugely popular marketplace and locality for professional, recreational, and social assembly. It was the heart of London. By the late sixteenth century Paul's suffered from structural wear and tear; its steeple, which was struck by lightning in 1561, was dilapidated. Yet despite Paul's longtime official spatialization, Rid associates Paul's with criminality and heresy. He claims that Cuthbert participated in heretical practices, such as witchcraft and conjuring. Rid also asserts that Cuthbert (who may stand for cony-catchers in general) has in his possession the parts missing from the steeple. This assertion points metaphorically to the wear and tear Rid thought crime has inflicted on Paul's. That Rid thought the crimes committed there were contradictory to the design and spirit of Paul's, that they converted Paul's into differential space, is accentuated by the farfetched nature of this assertion. If tongue in cheek, it may have been meant to emphasize hyperbolically the criminals' prevalence. At 489 feet, the spire was inaccessible (without scaffolding); moreover, it was composed of commonplace building materials and was therefore of little value on the black market.[39] For criminals to have stolen parts of the steeple, they would have needed to have had either complete control of Paul's, which would have required control of London's municipality, or supernatural powers. Either way, Rid thought criminal culture a very powerful force.

Gilbert Walker's *A Manifest Detection of Dice-play* (1552) consists of a dialogue between two friends, M and R, in which M informs R of the methods by which he was conned by a band of cony-catchers. R was lured into the scheme by a man he met at Paul's: "Happily as I roamed me in the church of Paul's now twenty days ago . . . there walked up and down by me in the body of the church a gentleman, fair dressed in silks, gold, and jewels, with three or four servants in gay liveries."[40] After an elaborate con job that took several days to complete, R found himself forty pounds poorer. Essentially R was befriended by the man he met at Paul's; he was invited to stay at the man's house and play cards with his friends, and after several days of winning he was cheated out of all his money. In his response, M associates Paul's with crime; he tells R that cons "betide every day" and "so soon as ye began your declaration of the first acquaintance in Paul's, I felt aforehand the hooks were laid to pick your purse withal" (33–34). M goes on to explain various criminal operations. For example, about cutpurses and pickpockets he says:

> Their craft, of all others, requireth most sleight, and hath marvelous plenty of terms and strange language; and therefore no man can attain to be a workman thereat, till he hath had a good time of schooling, and by that means do not only know each other well. . . . Some two or three hath Paul's Church in charge; other hath Westminster Hall in term-time; divers Cheapside with the flesh and fish shambles; some the Borough and bear-baiting; some the Court; and part follow markets and fairs in the country with pedlars' foot-packs; and generally to all places of assembly. Some of them are certainly 'pointed, as it were, by their wardens to keep the haunt, with commission but a short while, and to interchange their places as order shall be made, to avoid suspicion. (48–49)

With much detail M repeatedly stresses the criminals's organization, competence, and everywhereness, insisting they are no match for the average citizen: "Lo, how gentle lambs are led to the slaughter-man's fold! How soon reckless youth falleth in snare of crafty dealing!" (30). As we have seen, throughout the early modern period this same image of criminal culture was upheld in personal, popular, commercial, and state literature, where Paul's is consistently mentioned as one of criminal culture's principal haunts, usually as a key sociospatial component to criminal culture's manifestation. But Paul's is also described as the center of London society's public life. Hence criminal culture's territorialization of Paul's situates criminal culture at this epicenter, amid the hustle and bustle of London's official culture, as an alternative, shadow culture, one that is everywhere felt and present but barely discernible.

Like Rid and Walker, Greene writes about criminal culture's disruption of Paul's place-image and official spatialization. In *The Second Part of Conny-Catching* he says that Paul's is a tourist attraction, especially during term time, when people come to London from all over England to have their cases heard in court, and every tourist is a likely victim of crime if he or she visits Paul's. According to Greene, church services at Paul's attracted both the pious and the sinful, but the sinful came not for redemption but only to steal from the pious:

> In Paules (especially in the tearme time) between x. and xi., then is their howers, and there they [the criminals] walke, and perhaps, if there be great presse, strike a stroke in the middle walke, but that is vppon some plaine man that stands gazing about, hauing neuer seene the Church before, but their chiefest time is at diuine seruice, when men deuoutly giuen do go vp to heare either a sermon, or els the harmony of the Queere [choir] and the Organes: there the nip, and the foist as deuoutly as if he were som zealous person, standeth soberly, with his eies eleuated to heauen, when his hand is either on the purse or in the pocket, surueying euery corner of it for coyne, then when the seruice is done, & the people prese away, he thrusteth amidst the throng, and there worketh his villanie.[41]

In *The Black Book* Middleton's Lucifer, who is on earth surveying the workings of his minions, gives a comparable impression of Paul's: "I walked in Paul's to see fashions, to dive into villainous meetings, pernicious plots, black humours and a million of mischiefs which are bred in that cathedral womb and born within less than forty weeks after. But some may object, and say, 'What? Doth the Devil walk in Paul's then?' Why not, sir, as well as a sergeant, or a ruffian, or a murderer?[42] For Middleton's Lucifer Paul's is a potpourri of sociality open to anyone, criminal or otherwise; it is the antithesis of sacred space.

Moreover, Paul's is repeatedly represented as a principal locality for criminal cultural congregation as well as criminal practice.[43] In *The Third Part of Cony-Catching* Greene writes: "A CREW of these wicked companions being one day met togither in Pauls Church, (as that is a vsuall place of their assembly, both to determine on their driftes, as also to speede of manie a bootie) seeing no likelihood of a good afternoone, so they tearme it either forenoone or after, when ought is to be done: some dispersed themselues to the plaies, other to the bowling Allies, and not past two or three stayed in the Church."[44] Criminals are again depicted as having community and organization and, consequently, deliberate and unfettered access into all public sociospatialities (all social spaces, including particular ones: places). By convening and committing crimes in these spatialized areas, the criminals transformed them into contradictory sites where their own public behavior was privately enacted and the public liberties of their victims were threatened and circumscribed, if not rendered illusory.

Here is how John Earle characterizes Paul's in his remarkable account of contemporary London entitled *Micro-cosmography* (1628):

> The whole world's map, which you may here discern in its perfectest motion, justling and turning; . . . and were the steeple not sanctified, nothing liker Babel. The noise in it is like that of bees, a strange hum, mixed of walking tongues and feet; it is a kind of still roar or loud whisper. It is a great exchange of all discourse, and no business whatsoever but is here striving and afoot. It is the snyod of all parties politic, jointed and laid together, in most serious position, and they are not half so busy at the parliament. . . . It is the general mint of all famous lies. . . . All inventions are emptied here, and not a few pockets! The best sign of a temple in it is, that it is the thieves' sanctuary, which rob more safely in a crowd than in a wilderness."[45]

Ironically, according to Earle, Paul's is most like a temple not because it is a place to worship God but because it is a sanctuary for thieves. Its intended Christian function was radically undermined, almost inverted, by criminal infestation. For the criminals it was familiar space and a haven for criminal activity and congregation; at Paul's criminals could avoid the unpredictability of London at large, their "wilderness." But for people who were not members of criminal culture and were aware of the coexistence of criminal and official culture, aware that criminals were everywhere stalking their prey, Paul's embodied much of the danger and unknown associated with the wilderness. It signified the bestial or evil worlds beyond the boundaries of civilization. These people, like John Earle, were wilderness effected. As a result of the prevalence of criminality, for them many fields of official spatialization were lacking security and largely out-of-field. In addition to Paul's, the most significant was the public theater. As I discuss in the next chapter, the theater was a serious and persistent problem for many people. This was particularly true for certain intellectual and religious communities of Oxford, Cambridge, and London. Zealously committed to abolishing the public theater, they wanted to protect people from the corruptive power of what they believed was the Devil's institution. Indeed, the steady proliferation of vehement antitheatricalist discourse throughout the period is indisputable evidence of wilderness effectuation.[46]

In the literature discussed thus far, we have seen that the public theater is typically listed among the sociospatialities most infiltrated by members of criminal culture. Recall that in *The Second Part of Cony-Catching* Greene says that among the "chiefe walkes" of cony-catchers are "Plaies."[47] He also maintains that "at Plaies, the nip standeth there leaning like some mannerly gentleman against the doore as men go in, and there finding talke with some of his companions, spieth what euery man hath in his purse, & wher in what place" (32). And in *The Belman of London* Dekker says that some criminals "haunt Playhouses only and the Bearegarden."[48] To give an example from a text not about rogues and vagabonds, in his travel diary *Itinerarium* (1598) Paul Hentzner recounts: "While we were at the show, one of our company, Tobias Salander, doctor of physic, had his pocket picked of his purse with nine crowns *du soleil,* which without doubt was cleverly taken from him by an Englishman who always kept very close to him that the doctor did not in the least perceive it."[49]

As at Paul's, criminals regularly operated at the public theater, but their relationship to the theater was very different and more complicated. Whereas Paul's was quintessential differential space, rife with sociospatial contradictions of cultural and ideological import, the public theater was a consistent, commercial *interactive space* designated for entertainment. Popularly known for its fashionable, festive, and ribald atmosphere, early modern England's public theater's place-image was fairly constant and predictable. Nevertheless the public theater was a tremendous source and vehicle for transversal power. It was a primary, transversal influence *on* criminal culture. Criminals experienced the public theater, witnessed the theatricality staged, and were part of the public theater's scene and ambience. As I shall demonstrate, descriptions of criminal praxis indicate that the theatricality presented at the public theater had a major impact on the criminals. Furthermore, the terminology used by criminal culture's chroniclers to describe its criminal operations is almost always theatrical. Yet evidence suggests that the theater was also significantly influenced *by* criminal culture. There seems to have been a symbiotic relationship between the infectious, transversal power manifested *as* and *through* both the public theater and criminal culture. The most explicit similarity, and apparently the most important, was that they both implemented, among other common theatrics, the naturalistic form of impersonation fundamental to early modern England's public theater. Naturalistic impersonation (where a person appears and acts like another person, say, of a different class or gender), as opposed to the allegorical representation characteristic of the earlier mystery and morality plays, was unprecedented in the history of institutionalized theater in England. It was the characteristic of the public theater most condemned by the period's antitheatrical moralists.

The most obvious example of the criminals' naturalistic theatricality was their impersonation of gypsies. As analyzed in chapter 2,[50] there were many statutes against and much discourse about rogues and vagabonds pretending to be gypsies or Egyptians (these terms were used synonymously during the period). Evidence in personal, popular, commercial, and state literature indicates that rogues and vagabonds did, in fact, disguise themselves and act "like" gypsies; that is, they acted like most people thought gypsies acted or should act based on stereotypes of gypsies either imported from the continent, where "gypsies" were a more prevalent phenomenon, or in effect constructed of their own English gypsy-criminal tradition. Nevertheless, this identity construction and/or impersonation was only one of many forms of theatricality, including naturalistic impersonation, employed by early modern England's rogues and vagabonds.

Theatrical Methods and the Rise of a Criminal Aesthetic

Long before the first purpose-built public theater opened in 1567 (The Red Lion), in Robert Copland's poetic work *The Highway to the Spital-*

House, which contains a dialogue between Copland and the porter of a spital house, the porter comments on the deception perpetrated by beggars: "For they do wear soldiers' clothing, / And so, begging, deceive folk over all, / For they be vagabonds most in general."[51] According to popular, commercial, and state literature, criminals naturalistically impersonated sick, crazy, and needy people.[52] As discussed in Chapter 2, Harman, Dekker, Rid, and others report that criminal culture had functional names for, among other criminal occupational types, those who specialized in certain impersonations. For instance, in order to arouse sympathy when begging or after having been caught stealing, criminals called "abrammen" performed madness. As Harman notes, "These abram-men be those that feign themselves to have been mad, and have been kept either in Bethlem or in some other prison a good time, and not one amongst twenty that ever came in prison for any such cause."[53] For the same reasons, other criminals called "counterfeit cranks" feigned sickness. Harman writes, "These that do counterfeit the crank be young knaves and young harlots, that deeply dissemble the falling sickness [epilepsy]. For the crank in their [canting] language is the falling evil" (85).[54] The extensive concern over these naturalistic impersonations in both state and commercial literature suggests that they were effective in destabilizing the social order.

The criminals's naturalistic impersonations, however, were not limited to that of needy people. Like actors on the stage, they also impersonated people of different classes and genders. For example, in *Lanthorne and Candle-Light* Dekker discusses the cross-class dressing of gypsy criminals: "The [gypsy] women as ridiculously attire themselves, and (like one that plaies the Roague on a stage) weare rages, and patched filthy mantles upermost, when the under garments are hansome and in fashion."[55] In this account, the gypsies's impersonations are explicitly compared to that actors of the public theater. To cite another example, in his poem "A Whore" (1630) John Taylor comments on the gender indeterminacy of the cross-gender dressed prostitute:

> Shee's all compact of mirth, all *Meretrix,*
> And with finall teaching she will soone decline
> *Mulier* into the Gender Masculine,

By her Attire, or which sex she should be,
She seemes the *doubtfull Gender* vnto me,
To either side her habit seemes to leane,
And may be taken for the *piscene*. [56]

This comment recalls the anxiety over gender indeterminacy that pervades the antitransvestismist discourse that was characteristic of the period's antitheatricalist polemics. In the next chapter I will discuss in detail the antitheatricalist and antitransvestismist discourse. The following quotation from antitheatrical moralist Stephen Gosson's *Playes Confuted in Fiue Actions* (1582) is representative:

Plays are no Images of trueth, because sometime they hādle such thinges as neuer were, sometime they runne vpon truethes, but make them seeme longer, or shorter, or greater, or lesse than they were. . . . The profe is euident, the consequęt is necessarie, that in Stage Playes for a boy to put on the attyre, the gesture, the passions of a woman; for a meane person to take vpon him the title of a Prince with counterfeit porte, and traine, is by outwarde signes to shewe them selues otherwise then they are, and so with in the compasse of a lye, which by *Aristotles* iudgement is naught of it selfe and to be fledde.[57]

In both material and conceptual terms, criminal culture's chroniclers continually link criminals to the actors and theatricality of the public theater. For them there is a definite parallelism, and probably very real social connections, between criminals and actors and between criminal and theatrical praxis. At the very least, both use deception to further their own ends.

In *The Life and Death of Gamaliel Ratsey a famous thief, of England, Executed at Bedford the 26 of March last past* (1605) and *Ratseis Ghost. Or the Second Part of his madde Prankes and Robberies* (1605), the workings—beyond impersonation—of the notorious criminal Gamaliel Ratsey are regularly compared to those of actors in the public theater. For example, the author writes: "But everie day hee [Gamaliel Ratsey] had new inventions to obtaine his purposes: and as often as fashions alter, so often did he alter his Stratagems, studying as much how to compasse a poore mans purse, as Players doe, to win a full audience."[58] Just as actors continually employed new techniques to sway the audience's emotions and conceptualization of the actions and ideas presented, to wholly captivate the audience, Ratsey manipulated his victims daily with newfangled stratagems. For instance, on separate occasions he pretended to be a lawyer, a scholar, and a conjurer to con people who identify themselves as such. Ratsey was considered a highly talented criminal.

In *The Belman of London,* just as the audience would observe unnoticed the criminal congregation at the Boar's Head Tavern in a staged production of *1 Henry 4,* Dekker's Bellman recalls his observance of a clandestine criminal gathering: "Shee [the female proprietor of the country cottage] told mee I should be a *Spectator* of the comedy in hand, and a private gallery behold all the Actors, upon condition I would sit quietly and say nothing; And for that purpose was I convaied into an upper loft where (unseene) I might (through a wodden lattice that had the prospect of the dyning roome) both see and heare all that was to be done or spoken."[59] The Bellman describes the criminals in theatrical terms for no other reason than that he perceives them as fantastic in comparison to common people; they inspire wonderment like the public theater. "I know you wonder," says the Bellman to his readers, "and have longing thoughts to know what *Generation* this is, that lived in this hospitable familiarity . . . they are a people for whom the world cares not, neither care they for the world; they are all freeman . . . great travellers they are, and yet never from home [because their home is everywhere]; poore they are, and yet have their dyet from the best mens tables" (80–81). Like the notorious Ratsey, whose alternative way of life made a familiar concept (life) unfamiliar, exciting, and marketable in popular pamphlets and ballads, the unfamiliar congregation of criminals both alienated and entertained the Bellman. He imagines himself a "*Spectator*" at the theater; this theatricalized account undoubtedly contributed to the salability and success of *The Belman of London*, which went through four editions the first year and many more after that.[60]

The view that the everyday life of the criminals was theatrical and positively debauched is supported by many texts. In his poem "A Thiefe" (1630) John Taylor maintains:

Whores and *Thieues* . . . are like Acters, in this wauering age,
They enter all vpon the worlds great Stage:
Some gaine applause, and some doe act amisse,
And *exit* from the scaffold with a hisse.[61]

According to Taylor, unlike the common people on the "worlds great Stage," criminals, like actors, are performers who seek acclaim. Put differently, the criminals need to perform well not only to gain acceptance from their peers—and perhaps an infamous popular reputation—but also to avoid punishment from the law. This connection between actors and criminals is maintained by the Act for the Punishment of Vagabonds (1572), which categorizes actors ("players")—as well as sturdy beggars, tinkers, and bearwards—as rogues and vagabonds, and is literalized in such plays as Middleton's *Hengist, King of Kent* (1604–6) and *It's a Mad World, My Masters* (1617–20) and Richard Brome's *A Jovial Crew: or, The Merry Beggars* (1641), all of which feature either vagabonds or confidence tricksters as players. In *A Jovial Crew,* for instance, Squire Oldrents inquires, "But is there a play to be expected, and acted by beggars?" To which Justice Clack responds, "That is to say, by vagabonds; that is to say, by strolling / players. They are upon their purgation. If they can present / anything to please you, they may escape the law."[62] If the rogues and vagabonds—who are by definition "strolling players" in the context of this play—can perform effectively, which is to say, practice their criminality successfully, then they can "escape the law." Thus, like the art of acting, criminal praxis is understood qualitatively and in aesthetic terms. Like institutionalized theater, albeit less ephemeral because it was real life and thus with more immediate real-life consequences, it was an avenue out of living within social norms.

Transversally connected to the theater, criminal culture's praxis was an elaborate form of artistic expression similar to the theatrical practices associated with the public theater. In addition to their use of naturalistic impersonation, like the actors on the public stage, criminals scripted or planned role-playing when perpetrating certain cons. For example, as Robert Greene describes it in *A Notable Discovery of Coosnage* (1591), the "crossbiting law," (sometimes called the "sacking law") requires one criminal to pretend to be a prostitute and another her husband.[63] When she is with a client, the fake husband bursts in, threatens violence, and accepts compensation for the wrong done to his honor or demands money in exchange for not informing the client's wife that her husband is an adulterer. Rather than further elucidate this or other cons, as this has already been done by Frank Aydelotte, I want to focus on the fact that criminal culture's chroniclers openly and repeatedly acknowledge and extol criminals for their theatrical and rhetorical skills. In describing criminal praxis, contemporary writers frequently situate their accounts of cons and other practices within an overarching discourse on the development and value of a criminal aesthetic.[64] While criminal praxis emerges in this discourse as artistically creative and worthy of recognition, it is also treated in comparable terms as a technical discipline that is both rational and logical, like that of an applied science.

In *A Manifest Detection of Dice-play* (1552), speaker M provides a historical account of the criminal practice of cheating at dice and how it became an art form and a science: "And to speak all at once, like as all good and liberal sciences had a rude beginning, and by the industry of good men, being augmented by little and by little, at last grew to a just perfection; so this detestable privy robbery, from a few and deceitful rules is in few years grown to the body of an art, and hath his peculiar terms, and thereof as great a multitude applied to it, as hath grammar or logic, or any other of the approved sciences."[65] M maintains that cheaters learn their trade in criminal "schools" (36) and adds that to be "skilful" at cheating requires "four or five years practice" (41). As discussed in chapters 2 and 3, members of criminal culture set up criminal schools—either in prisons, taverns, inns, or other public sites—where criminals learned the canting language as well as criminal methods and customs. For instance, on cheating Dekker's *The Belman of London* is consistent with Walker's *A Manifest Detection of Dice-play:* "One notable pollicy is (as a *Rule*) set downe in this *Schoole* of *cheating,* and that is a *Cheator never discovereth the secrets of his Art to any.*"[66] But cheating at dice was only one aspect of criminal culture's multifaceted art form, which, as John Awdeley stresses in *The Fraternitye of Vacabondes,* involved "devices *Deceptio visus, Deceptio tactus, et Deceptio Auditus.*"[67]

Rhetorical wherewithal—the ability to manipulate with logic and eloquence—was crucial to the perpetration of many cons; it was necessary to influence the victims's minds, as though the latter were under the sway of "Spirits." Awdeley maintains: "You must also have your words of Art, certain strange words, that it may not only breed the more admiration to the people, but to lead away the eye from espying the manner of your conveyance, while you may induce the mind to conceive and suppose that you deal with Spirits."[68] Like Awdeley, in *A Notable Discovery of Coosnage* Greene celebrates the criminals' use of logic and rhetorical innovativeness:

> Sée Gentlemen what great logicians these cony-catchers be, that haue such rethoricall perswasions to induce the poor countrie man to his confusion, and what varietie of villany they haue to strip the poore farmer of his money. . . . If I shoulde spend many shéets in deciphering their [the criminals's] shifts, it were friuelous, in that they be many, and ful of variety, for euery day they inuent new tricks, and such queint deuises as are secret, yet passing dangerous, that if a man had *Argus* eyes, he could scant prie into the bottom of their practises. Thus for the benefit of my countrey I haue briefly discouered the law of Cony-catching.[69]

In another work by Greene entitled *The Third Part of Conny-Catching* (1592), he tells of an incredible feat accomplished by a "coosening companion, who would need trie his cunning in this new inuented art, and how by his knauery (at one instant) he beguiled half a dozen and more."[70] As Nightingale does in Jonson's play *Bartholomew Fair* (1614), the cozener distracts a crowd with a witty ballad. During the performance he alludes to cutpurses so that the crowd will check its purses. Meanwhile, his cronies, who are scattered among the crowd, watch for the location of the purses, and then, at the cozener's signal, surreptitiously rob them in an "instant." This sort of recollection of the incredible feats of criminals is typical of the period's literature about criminal culture.

In Greene's *A Disputation between a Hee-Conny-Catcher and a Shee-Conny-Catcher* (1592), which consists of a dialogue between a male criminal named Lawrence and a female criminal named Nan, the importance of rhetorical cunning and reason are also highlighted as essential to the cony-catcher. Lawrence declares:

I and beshrow me, but you reason quaintly, yet wil I proue your wittes are not so ripe as ours, nor so readie to reach into the subtilties of kinde cousonage, and though you appropriate to your selfe the excellencie of Conny-catching, and that you doo with more Art than we men do, because of your painted flatteries and sugred words, that you florish rethorically like nettes to catch fooles, yet will I manifest with a merry instance, a feate done by a Foyst, that exceeded any that euer was done by any mad wench in England.[71]

Again a "feate" is applauded, and reason is privileged, in this case over the "mad[ness]" Lawrence attributes to female criminals. In *The Defense of Conny-Catching* (1592), its alleged author, Cuthbert Cony-catcher, similarly emphasizes the importance of linguistic competence and wit: "Hee that cannot dissemble cannot liue, and men put their sonnes now a dayes Apprentices, not to learne trades and occupations, but craftes and mysteries."[72] This view is further supported by John Taylor in his poem "A Bawd" (1630): "A *Bawd* is a *Logician*, which is perceiued by her subtill and circumuenting speeches, doubtfull and ambiguous Apothegmes, double significations, intricate, witty, and cunning equiuocations, (like a skilfull Fencer that casts his eye vpon a mans foot, and hits him a knocke on the pate) so She, by going the further about, comes the neerer home, and by casting out the *Lure*, makes the *Tassell Gentle* come to her fist."[73] Taylor claims that bawds, like the cozening ballad singer described by Greene, distract their victims in order to take advantage of them. But in the case of bawds, as we have seen in the two previously quoted passages about cony-catchers, the bawd's criminal stratagems depend on logic. The bawd confuses and orchestrates her victims with convoluted but cogent rhetoric; her machinations surpass the mental abilities of the average person, as though "Spirits" are at work (as Awdeley would have it).

Of course, for many cons and other criminal practices rhetorical ingenuity and finesse would not ensure success. The ideal criminal had to be both rhetorically and manually skilled. The expertise of the cutpurse, for example, is lauded in Middleton's *Black Book* (1604): "Your deepconceited cutpurse, who by the dexterity of his knife will draw out the money and make a flame-coloured purse show like the bottomless pit."[74]

Moreover, as explained by Autolycus in Shakespeare's *Winter's Tale*, criminals's needed sensory as well as manual adroitness: "I understand the business, I hear it. To have an open ear, a quick eye, and a nimble hand, is necessary for a cut-purse; a good nose is requisite also, to smell out work for the other senses. I see this is the time that the unjust man doth thrive."[75] Clearly, Autolycus is quite skilled himself, for the rustics (the characters Clown and Shepherd) succumb to his rhetoric and gladly give him money: "He seems to be of great authority," states Clown, "close with him, give him gold; and though authority be a stubborn bear, yet he is oft led by the nose with gold: show the inside of your purse to the outside of his hand" (4.4.802–5).

The importance of these kinds of sensory perception, rhetorical puissance, and dexterity is also recognized by Antonio in James Shirley's play *The Sisters* (1642). Concerning the band of criminals, presently disguised as mathematicians, Antonio asserts:

What nation have we here?
Fortune flingers? . . .
Her [Paulina's] house is open for these mountebanks,
Cheaters, and tumblers, that can foist and flatter
My lady gewgaw.[76]

Antonio is skeptical of the criminals' disguise and thinks that they will use their fancy rhetoric to manipulate and con Paulina; he correctly suspects that they are really "knaves that stroll the country, / And live by picking worms out of fools' fingers" (383). Unfortunately, his instincts and skepticism do not prevent even him from being robbed, for his pockets are sneakily picked as he delivers these lines.

In conjunction with the consistent, explicit focus on the rhetorical, logical, and manual ingenuity of the criminals in the literature about criminal culture, there is a consistent, implicit reference to the foolishness of their victims. Criminal culture's chroniclers esteem the criminals as one might scholars; they praise their mastery of language, logic, and reason. Even if only suggestively, in doing so they put down the average person as intellectually inferior. All of the chroniclers were highly educated, and many of them, such as Greene, Middleton, and Dekker, were also poets and playwrights. Indeed, in many respects the chroniclers treat the criminals as peers. They revere them for their expertise in rhetorical activities similar to those in which they themselves regularly engaged. Like the criminals, as commercial writers the chroniclers used language to appeal to and manipulate the sensibilities of their audiences. However intentionally, they revealed, obscured, or created "truths."

To be sure, the malleability of "truths" exploited by the criminals, and possibly by those who wrote about them, illuminates the fact that all historiography is necessarily both actual and imaginary. The literary representation of criminal culture is itself a differential space where the actual and the imaginary simultaneously collide and coalesce. In reading this representation, we must take into consideration, if not allow ourselves to be liberated by, the conceptual space made possible by historiography's actual and imaginary elements, especially since it is often difficult, if not impossible, to discern between the two. On the one hand, the abundance of state documents that support the largely uniform depiction of criminal culture presented by the various forms of its literary representation work to carve out actual space within criminal culture's historiography. On the other hand, all of our means of exploring criminal culture are highly mediated through time, language, and personal bias (ours and that of the chroniclers). Much of the mediation is also through literary texts of genres (plays, ballads, and popular pamphlets) that are, because of their fictive qualities, of questionable historical reliability. This mediation encourages the production of imaginary components of our own study of criminal culture. Just as its early modern chroniclers were forced, and probably capitalized on the opportunity, to extrapolate at times because of their limited access to this exclusive and clandestine culture, historical difference, both sociocultural and spatiotemporal, forces us to extrapolate on the available information. Therefore, this analytical tour of early modern England's criminal culture must be, among other things, a transversal venture into differential conceptual spaces.

CHAPTER FIVE

Antitheatrical Discourse, Transversal Theater, Criminal Intervention

IN THE PRECEDING CHAPTERS we have seen the many ways by which transversal power manifested *as* and *through* early modern England's emergent criminal culture of gypsies, rogues, vagabonds, beggars, cony-catchers, cutpurses, and prostitutes. Criminal culture's transversal movement occurred in various modes, including countercultural ritual, language innovation, theatrical expression, radical sociospatialization, and criminal practice. Its representation in the period's personal, popular, commercial, and state literature reveals official culture's commodification and fetishization of criminal culture. This representation also shows the ways in which criminal culture influenced the conceptual space of official culture's members, disrupted the borders of their subjective territories, and inspired their becomings-other-social-identities. Consequently, in conjunction with stimulating alternative ways of thinking and living, criminal culture's transversal movement gave rise to a criminal aesthetic. As we have seen, criminality is consistently described by its contemporary chroniclers as both an art and a science. In effect, a new genre of literature emerged specifically about criminals. Crucial to this sociohistorical phenomenon (as discussed in the previous chapter) was the presence of the public theater.[1] The goal of this chapter is to provide a better comprehension of the public theater's role as a sociopolitical conductor, particularly as it functioned in many respects independent of but at the same time influenced the criminal culture that was philosophically, socially, and professionally connected to it.

Recent work on early modern England's public theater has been pre-occupied with the politics of the drama.[2] Central to this preoccupation is whether particular plays were either critical, subversive, or supportive of the government and the official systems of belief. This is usually deter-mined through an analysis of the plays, especially how the play texts might have been interpreted during the period, and by measuring responses to them by the Lord Mayor and Aldermen of the City of London, the Mas-ter of the Revels, the Privy Council, the monarch, and members of the court. While this chapter is also interested in political issues related to the public theater, it is for the most part not concerned with *the drama,* the actual plays and their plots which were performed, but with *the the-ater,* the mode of theatrical presentation and the general experience it characteristically inspired. Put differently, I am primarily concerned with the conceptual and material influence of the form in which the drama was presented (the theater) on the social world in which the public theater op-erated rather than with any surreptitiously articulated or openly stated in-tentions that informed the public theater and its drama.

I want to conduct a "transversal poetics" of the public theater: an investigative-expansive analysis, operating according to transversal theory, that pursues comprehension of the relationships between things, especially the ironic (dis)connections, rather than an absolute meaning or an absolute cause, both of which transversal theory considers fantasies. In the pres-ent study of early modern England's criminal culture, we have seen how a transversal poetics situates rather than totalizes or reduces the subject matter under investigation. Among other sociocultural associations re-vealed, my use of the investigative-expansive mode led to the uncovering of important links between criminal culture and the nature, methods, and presence of the public theater that are the focus of this final chapter. In the case at hand, the investigative-expansive approach has led me to examine the sociopolitical role of the theater by evaluating responses to it in the pe-riod's high-profile antitheatrical debate and in other discourses, like those on the criminalized London fashion of female-to-male transvestism, which do not concentrate on or deal explicitly with any aspect of the public the-ater. Through this examination, I discovered a significant contradiction, the implications of which I hope to explain by the end of this chapter.

The contradiction is epitomized by three passages that would be familiar to anyone reading today's studies on cross-dressing and homoeroticism in early modern England. Published over a thirty-two-year period, the passages are drawn from three representative antitheatricalist polemics: cultural chronicler Phillip Stubbes's *Anatomie of Abuses* (1583), renowned Oxford scholar John Rainoldes's *Overthrow of Stage-Playes* (1600), and Cambridge scholar John Greene's *Refutation of the Apology for Actors* (1615). The remarkable similarity between the passages of Stubbes and Greene, though Greene probably plagiarized from Stubbes, indicates the enduring topicality and pertinence of their assertions. In other words, the fact that Greene thought Stubbes's censure accurate and worth repeating shows that the issues had not changed. Rainoldes's assertions, similar to theirs thematically and structurally, helps put their logic into perspective. According to Stubbes, "Than, these goodly pageants being done, euery mate sorts to his mate, euery one bringes another homeward of their way verye freendly, and in their secret conclaues (couertly) they play *the Sodomits,* or worse. And these be the fruits of plays and Enterluds for the most part."[3] For Rainoldes stage plays must be "cutt off " "sooner" than later because they are "the means and occasions whereby men are transformed into dogges, the sooner, to cutt off all incitementes to that beastlie filthines, or rather more than beastlie."[4] According to Greene, "Then these goodly pageants being done, euery one sorteth to his mate, each bring another home-ward of their way: then begin they to repeate the lasciuious acts and speeches they haue heard, and thereby infect their minde with wicked passions, so that in their secret conclaues they play the *Sodomite,* or worse. And these for the most part are the fruits of Plays."[5] The use of "or worse" and "or rather more than beastlie" in these passages is problematic and warrants investigation because these phrases suggest a transcendence of the assertion, pervasive in these and all early modern antitheatrical tracts, that social identity is predetermined and fixed within a God-ordained hierarchy. The "or worse" and "or rather more than beastlie," allegedly produced by the *seeing* and *hearing* of "lasciuious acts and speeches" that "infect their minde with wicked passions," point to the dangerous possibility of other immoral, heretical, or supernatural supplements, in effect signifying one or more possible practices or identities alternative to those identifiable and nameable. The question remains: What was it about the public theater that propelled these learned thinkers and devoted moralists to transgress conceptually the Christian ideology that they purportedly represent?

Early modern England's controversial public theater was an exceptional cultural apparatus whose experience in English history exemplifies the phenomenon of transversality about which we have seen so much evidence in the historiography of the period's criminal culture. The historically and socially contingent phenomenon of transversal power, although apparent to some degree in the goings-on and remains of most societies, developed with increasing magnitude in association with the emergence of the public theater (from 1567 to 1642). The public theater was a composite of everything commonly and ominously associated with it. It was bacchanalia, criminality, the Devil, the unspeakable, the unthinkable, "or worse." The public theater's revolutionary otherworldliness made it a sociopolitical conductor that both exemplified the potentialities of transversality and functioned as a public gateway between subjective and transversal territories. I hope to show that this new public institution, with its strange mode of theatrical presentation (its sensational mise-en-scène, naturalistic impersonations, resonant acoustics, and incontinent ambiance), was truly a *transversal theater,* and that its conceptual and material influence, its affective presence, is evident in the period's popular, scholarly, religious, antitheatricalist, and antitransvestismist literature.[6] In turn, I want to show how this literature further emphasizes the performative and philosophical similarities and connections between the public theater and criminal culture.

The period's literature about the public theater and transvestism reveals that transversal power jetted forth from the state structure's faultlines *as* and *through* theater such that everyone exposed to the public theater's efflorescing reach, including its most fervent enemies, was infected with transversal thought. Moreover, the literature also reveals that the practice of female-to-male transvestism on the streets, like the performance of gypsyism discussed in chapter 2, is evidence that the theater's power extended beyond its own spatiotemporal domain. Surprisingly, however, it is not the official concepts of state thought (negation, essentialism, normality, constancy, homogeneity, and eternality) that primarily underlie this literature's heavily religious and pragmatic rhetoric, as Stephen Greenblatt, Jean Howard, and Laura Levine have argued.[7] Instead, what surfaces under the pressure of investigative-expansive analysis and dialectical scrutiny are the chief concepts of transversal thought (heterogeneity, mutability, performance, nomadism, expansion, and indeterminacy), and consequently the curious allegiance of this literature to the transversal power that fueled the very activities that it so vehemently censured.

Transversal Conduction, Intellectual Infection

The present analysis takes as its premise the reality of the theatrical threat that is not considered by Greenblatt and not taken seriously by Levine and Howard. This may be why these critics do not analyze in detail the antitheatricalist claim that the transformative power of the theater, as the stimulator and orchestrator of becomings, supersedes one's ability to construct or maintain one's own identity. According to my reading of the antitheatrical tracts, the power that flows within and from the medium of the public theater not only supersedes free will but actually *forces* and *determines* the becomings of the players, the audience, and beyond. It therefore supersedes the indispensable power of the state machinery to determine and control the subject's place in the sociopolitical hierarchy. Whereas the readings of Greenblatt, Howard, and Levine adhere to and superimpose state theories of singular and binary structures, the antitheatrical tracts clearly surpass these parameters. Contrary to the dogma of the state structures that they purportedly represent, the tracts suggest multiplicities of identities and becomings, both known and unknown, that extend well beyond the individual, social, or natural world. Ironically, what emerges in the antitheatrical tracts and the discourses concerned with the perniciousness of transvestism (discussed in the next section) is a transversal model that reflects the praxis of criminal culture. Against the grain of the official Christian order, this model exposes the possibility of multiple and contradictory determinative agencies beyond the God-Devil paradigm.

One such agency was the public theater. Especially endowed with transversal power, the theater—an ideational conductor with its own wizardry—caused the ironic reformulation (from state thought to transversal thought) of the antitheatricalist and antitransvestismist moralists's arguments. Thus, it caused a transformation of their conceptual territory. It is my hypothesis that the intellectual venture of the antitheatricalists and antitransvestismists into the transversal theater's uncharted conceptual territory—their intense contemplation of the wondrous operations and social impact of the public theater—led them to become infected with transversal thought. As a result, like Harman and Dekker writing poetically about criminal culture's sexual practices (discussed in chapter 2), they transgressively conceptualized outside the boundaries of their designated subjectified localities within official territory and resided, to a significant extent, in transversal territory. Not surprisingly, for much the same reasons that the state outlawed association with gypsies (discussed in chapter 2), it is precisely residence in the public theater, where one *experiences* (*sees, hears,* and *feels*) representations of alternative ideologies, lives, and worlds, that the antitheatricalists most adamantly warn against.

Jean-Jacques Rousseau, a later antitheatricalist, echoes a key assumption of the early modern antitheatricalists when he theorizes that "residence implies consent: to inhabit the territory is to submit to the sovereign."[8] Greene's *Refutation of the Apology for Actors* (1615) rebuts Thomas Heywood's *Apology for Actors* (1612) with a striking account of "a Christian woman [who] went into the Theater to behold the plaies." According to Greene, "She entered in well and sound, but she returned and came forth possessed of the Diuell. Wherevpon certaine Godly brethren demanded Sathan how he durst be so bould, as to enter into her a Christian. Whereto he answered, that *hee found her in his owne house,* and therefore took possession of her as his own."[9] The "well and sound" Christian, exposed to a virulent iconoclastic force, was "enter[ed]" and "possessed of the Diuell." If the church is the house of God, the public theater is the Devil's "*owne house*": it's "Sathans Synagogue."[10] Like the church, the Devil's theater has its pulpits, priests, ceremonies, and congregations. Greene insists that "God hath set his holy Word and Ministers to instruct vs in the way of Life: the Diuell instituted Plaies and Actors to seduce vs into the way of Death" (60). Sovereignty in the public theater resides with the "Plaies and Actors" or, through them, with "the Diuell." The audience inhabits the theater on its own accord, and therefore consents to its sovereign, whether consciously or not. The theater's sovereign reigns over its own dissident space, a sociospace replete with criminals as well (discussed in chapter 4), within the state's material domain.

Like the other antitheatricalists, Greene chiefly discusses the proficiency with which the actual performance of stage plays (the theater) rather than the explicit representational usage of spells and incantations in play texts (the drama) adulterates the characters of its spectators as well as the characters of its actors. According to Greene, despite the apparent stability of one's moral and social identity, to be an actor or a spectator is thus to subject one's self to the weird, furtive, pestilent "Word" that is theater (the "Plaies"). As Marshall McLuhan says, "The medium is the massage"; it does something to you.[11] But what makes the theater the "Word" of "the Diuell" or "the way of Death" and not something else? When confronted with transversal power, it is common for people to attribute it to something familiar, such as the idea of the Devil, so that it will be easier for them to relate to and compartmentalize safely within their own subjective territory. The Devil, the chosen scapegoat in the case at hand, was already the official culture's proxy for everything oppositional; it was the all-encompassing negative component within the state's binary system of thought. But if the theater was not the Devil's apparatus, from where did it come? Whose interests did it serve?

About the emergent public theater Stephen Orgel writes, "All at once, theater was with an institution, a property, a corporation. It was real in the way that 'real estate' is real; it was a location, a building, a possession—an established and visible part of society."[12] A number of public theaters were erected by entrepreneurs in the Liberties, an area just outside the jurisdiction of the City of London.[13] Among them were The Red Lion , the first purpose-built public theater, which opened in 1567, and the more famous establishment called The Theater, which was opened in 1576 by James Burbage. The entrepreneurs chose the liberties to avoid or dissuade antagonism and regulation from the civic authorities and Privy Council, who, as Richard Dutton and Janet Clare respectively document, saw the public theater as a threat to the peace and moral order of English society.[14] Steven Mullaney historicizes the emergence of the public theater in a tradition of cultural and geographical marginality upon which, he claims, its drama capitalized: "Effectively banished from the city by increasingly strict regulations, popular drama translated the terms of its exile to its advantage."[15] He further argues: "The marginality of Elizabethan drama was not, however, merely a literary affair. Ambivalence, paradox, and cultural contradiction were not new to the margins of the city," which had been the domain of brothels, gaming houses, lazarets, and monasteries, "and the liberty or license popular drama gained when it moved out into the Liberties had long existed there" (31). Especially important to the present analysis is Mullaney's observation that the public theater's mise-en-scène was different from that of the private playhouses within the city. The "private playhouses" did not "redefine the place or power of their audience within the theater to the degree characteristic of the public stage. Spectators took an active part in the plays presented [in "private playhouses"] . . . voicing their own objections, comments, quips, and quiddities as the drama unfolded," whereas in the public theaters the division between spectator and theatrical presentation was much more concrete (53). The specialty of the public theater's theatricality is further delineated by Martin Butler, who explains that this novel institution had theatrical "roots" that were "first and foremost diverse: it inherited the sophisticated experiments of the courtly and academic stages, but also a vast spectrum of types of popular performance." It had a "quite extraordinary range of social and cultural reference," a "multi-dimensional character," and audiences that were socially and economically heterogeneous.[16] The public theater was infused with assorted constitutive faculties that made it radically different from other early modern forms of theater.

In addition to those mentioned by Mullaney and Butler, the public theater's theatricality was also different from that of traveling theater companies and the court masque. Although traveling theater companies might very well have been transversally inspired, as their nomadism might indicate, the scarcity of primary sources precludes a detailed investigation here. Unlike the public theater, the court masque was produced and performed by and for aristocracy and state officials; it was an exclusive affair designed to entertain, reflect, and consolidate its privileged audience. As Matthew Wikander has shown, the state's involvement in the public theater was minimal by comparison; it was primarily regulatory through scant censorship of potentially seditious plays and King James's preemption of several acting companies.[17] In his monograph on the relationships between the public theater and the burgeoning market society, Jean-Christophe Agnew argues that the court masque was constructed in contradistinction to other forms of theater, particularly the public theater. "More than any thing else," maintains Agnew, "the dramatic conventions of the masque expressed the court's contempt for the players [of public stage plays] and, by the same measure, the world the players represented. Elite masquers never doubled, nor did they impersonate in any naturalistic sense."[18] It is particularly significant that the masquers neither doubled nor impersonated naturalistically, since these were the tactics characteristic of the public theater that were most feared by the antitheatricalists. Hence, these tactics, shared (as we have seen in chapters 2 and 4) by members of criminal culture, who performed everything from epilepsy to aristocratic status, are critical to our understanding of the ways by which the public theater was transversally empowered and connected to criminal culture.

An Investigative Expansion

At this juncture, in a characteristically investigative-expansive move, I want to shift this analysis's focus briefly to consider a major factor that I think contributed to this transversal empowerment, one that had been largely overlooked by scholars researching the early modern English public theater until the recent publication of Bruce Smith's book *The Acoustic World of Early Modern England*. The architectural structures that housed the public theater, the buildings we refer to today as theaters, were (as they are today) acoustic instruments themselves. Taking the Globe Theater (1599) as an example, Smith explains:

As a device for propagating sound, the 1599 Globe was extraordinarily efficient. In its tubular shape it approximated the shape of the human vocal tract. In a theater, as in the human body, production of sound requires three things: (1) an energy source, (2) something that vibrates in response to that energy, and (3) something that propagates those vibrations into ambient space. In the case of the

human body, the energy source is the lungs, the vibrator is the larynx, and the propagator is the throat, mouth, and sinuses. If the
structure of the Globe is imagined as the vocal tract, the energy
source was either lungs (for vocal sounds and wind instruments) or
arms and hands (for plucked and bowed instruments, drums, and
sound effects). The vibrator was the stage. The propagator was the
architectural surround. In the production of "theatrical" sound, the
building itself functions as the larynx, mouth, and sinuses do in the
production of purely vocal sound: they give the sound its harmonic
profile and influence its volume.[19]

One major difference, however, between the theaters during the early
modern period and those today is how the audience must have related to
them. As was mentioned earlier, purpose-built public theaters were new
to London and were possibly as exciting for their patrons as high-tech
theme parks are for many of us today. As Smith puts it, "The multiple cultures of early modern England may have shared with us the biological materiality of hearing, but their protocols of listening could be remarkably
different from ours. . . . Through all the variables, cultural as well as individual, one thing is certain: sound is inescapable." (8). Thus, occupation of
space within a public theater was extraordinary for acoustic reasons as well.[20]

Each theater's acoustics were different inasmuch as the substance and
architecture of each was different. They were comprised of combinations
of wood, plaster, thatch, mortar, and air, with or without ceilings or
canopies, and were either circular (The Globe), square (The Fortune), or
rectangular (The Blackfriars) in shape, yet the audiences were almost always horse-shoed around the stage. Every acoustic instrument, like the
vocal apparatus of every person, has unique frequencies that overlay any
fundamental note (wave-motion vibration, such as middle C) made by the
instrument. This distinguishes the sound of that instrument from the
sound of all others. Smith's succinct definition of sound is helpful here:

Sound is a periodic displacement of molecules in the air. Now closer
together, now farther apart, the molecules set up a sound wave that
takes a certain number of microseconds to complete a cycle. The
number of times per second a vibration pattern repeats itself con-

stitutes its frequency. That much is a matter of time. But the wave also takes place in space: the vibration exerts pressure on the air molecules, and the greater that pressure happens to be, the greater the displacement of air molecules. The degree of the molecules' displacement constitutes that sound wave's amplitude. (7–8)

Thus, the vocal apparatuses of the actors and audience and the musical instruments used during performances, operating in space and time, all contributed to harmonic variations on any fundamental note produced. Each member of the audience experienced incorporation and assimilation into the acoustic instrument of the theater, both through his or her own sound effects (cheers, claps) as well as by just being present. By occupying space within the public theater, and thereby producing, absorbing, and reflecting sound waves with their bodies, the audience members became functioning components of that theater's acoustic structure and, one might add, were therefore influenced by the molecular changes within that space.

Building on Smith's findings, my point here is that should resonance have occurred between audience members and any of the sounds produced in the space, a profound natural connection would have been achieved. That is, if an audience member or members and a sound-producing source or sources share the same fundamental frequency, then vibration is mutually induced (resonance). Of course, the effects of resonance, like those of any sound for a hearer, might be very different for the respective participants; material structures, including people, might expand, transform, or collapse because of the vibration. Sound waves effect physical changes that, by extension, cause psychological changes. Hence, the *experience* in the public theater involved *seeing, hearing,* and *feeling;* it was psychophysiological in unprecedented ways.

Transversal Theater

Indeed, the public theater actualized something new, mysterious, exciting, experimental, and transcendent. In Mullaney's words, "In the broad chronicle of literary history, the theater of Marlowe and Shakespeare is a brief and flaring thing, something of an aesthetic fluke, an oddity, an anomaly."²¹ Agnew concurs: "For the brief moment of Elizabethan and Jacobean rule, English theater enjoyed a deliberate, if delicate, extraterritorial status: a marginal existence in which the potent possibilities of marginality were explored in unprecedented depth and with extraordinary imagination."²² Yet the transversality of the public theater came from no place in particular, was not self-serving or prejudicial, and served no particular purpose. It arose when people transcended state power or when state power failed to invent sufficient numbers of scapegoats, criminals, and nomads for the purpose of consolidating its body politic; in other words, when state power allowed or was unable to prevent people and ideas from running amok and rupturing established certainties. Transversal power conducted the public theater and the public theater became a conductor for transversal power. Transversal conduction occurred through performance, during reception of performance, and by thinking about performance. Instead of reflecting or affirming a "sensibly" ordered society, this transversal theater exposed and advanced a contingent, arbitrary, deceptive, fluid society. Never before in England's history had fictions and realities been shown to be so similar and relativistic. Never before had the blurring between fictions and realities been so easy, attractive, and lucrative. The public theater transmitted the novel idea that anything goes: the world is negotiable, performative, manipulable—an idea upon which, as we have seen, criminal culture capitalized.

In *The Schoole of Abuse* (1579), a work almost certainly commissioned by London authorities,²³ moralist and onetime playwright Stephan Gosson compares poetry to "the cuppes of Circes," insisting that stage plays have the power to "turne reasonable creatures into brute beastes."²⁴ This is because humans, although "reasonable creatures," are "so weake that we are drawne with every thread, so light that we are blown away with every blast, so unsteady that we slip in every ground, neither peyse our bodyes against the winde . . . nor use any witte to garde our owne persons, nor shewe our selves willing to shunne our owne harmes, running most greedily to those places where wee are soonest overthrowne" (33–34). The dangerous "places" to which this passage refers are the theaters. For Gosson, as for Greene, public theaters constitute precisely the environment in which "our selves" will be "blown away" and "overthrowne." He argues that "theaters" are like "Pandoraes boxe; lift upp the Lidde, out flyes the Devil; shut it fast; it cannot hurt us" (34). Oxford scholar John Rainoldes reports the seductive means by which he thinks stage plays persuade people to violate moral standards: "Can wise men bee perswaded that there is no wantonnesse in the players partes, when experience sheweth (as wise men haue observed) that *men are made adulterers and enemies of all chastitie by coming to such plays? that senses are mooved, affections are delighted, heartes though strong and constant are vanquished by such players? that an effeminate stage-player, while hee faineth love, imprinteth wounds of love?*" [25] For Rainoldes, like Greene and Gosson, the theater corrupts even "wise men"; it can vanquish "heartes though strong and constant" and "imprinteth wounds of love."

In another work entitled *Playes Confuted in Five Actions* (1582) Gosson argues that "*Stage Plaies are not to be suffred in a Christian comon weale*" because they "are the doctrine and inuention of the Deuill."[26] He concludes his argument with a representative ("daily bred by plaies") account of a stage play so moving that it compelled its audience to imitate automatically what it saw on the stage: "When Bacchus rose up, tenderly lifting Ariadne from her seate, no small store of curtesie passing betwene them, the beholders rose up, every man stoode on tippe toe, and seemed to hover over the play. When they sware, the company sware, when they departed to bedde; the company presently was set on fire, they that were married posted home to their wives; they that were single, vowed very solemly, to be wedded" (G5). For Gosson this account illustrates the typical proficiency with which the Devil captivates and governs people through the theater. In this case, the end result of marriage cannot be justified and is, in fact, invalidated by the impious motivation (lust) with which the stage play conducted "they that were single . . . to be wedded." As Gosson emphasizes, "If this ["Carnall delight"] be not gouerned by the rule of Gods word, we are presently caried beyond our selues" (F3v). So, according to Gosson, Greene, and Rainoldes, if the performance is convincingly naturalistic, the spectators will lose control of their moral sensibility and blindly become what they see on the stage. If nothing else, as was the case for most victims of criminal culture's own theatricality, the spectators will be conned into believing what they see, hear, and feel.

The actors's bewitchment and corruption, since they regularly play "immoral" parts, was also considered an inevitability of their occupation. Greene speaks for many when he asserts, "The form that consists in the Actors, is the parts they play."[27] This view of the actor's character or body being determined or possessed by that of each character he plays suggests that his original identity or anatomical structure ("form") was not absolute. In his defense of stage plays, *An Apology for Actors* (1612), Heywood gives an exemplary account of the idea that, beyond the stage illusion, an actor actually becomes the character he plays. The actor embodies and personalizes the traits of the character, which he did not possess prior to playing the role. On behalf of actors, Heywood declares that "Julius Caesar himselfe for his pleasure became an actor, being in shape, state, voyce, judgement, and all other occurents, exterior and interior, excellent."[28] Heywood then paradoxically recounts an incident that occurred during a performance of *Hercules Furens,* when Caesar, playing Hercules, actually kills the actor playing Hercules's enemy, whom he was only meant to feign to kill: "Although he was, as our tragedians use, but seemingly to kill him by some false imagined wound, yet was Caesar so extremely carried away with the violence of his practised fury, and by the perfect shape of the madnesse of Hercules, to which he had fashioned all his active spirits, that he slew him dead at his foot, and after swoong him, *terque quaterque* (as the poet says) about his head" (45). There is no concept of an immutable identity in this description. Caesar, who was once "exterior and interior, excellent," is transformed into a killer by the theater's magical power. His role-playing overpowered his ability to self-fashion for the purpose of role-playing. In his response to Heywood, Greene claims that Heywood's "example indeed greatly doth make against" stage plays rather than defends them.[29] In regard to Caesar's behavior, Greene says: "For it's not vnlikely but a Player might doe the like now, as often they haue done" (28). Hence, at the very least Greene views identity as changeable and capable of being "fashioned" (as Heywood says) by role-playing, but not in the same senses described by Greenblatt in his groundbreaking study *Renaissance Self-Fashioning: From More to Shakespeare.*

For Greenblatt this self-fashioning "involves submission to an absolute power or authority situated at least partially outside the self—God, a sa-

cred book, an institution such as church, court, colonial, or military ad-
ministration." In the case at hand, it would involve submission to the
Devil or the transversal theater, but only if the self in question was already
familiar with these powers. Greenblatt also says that "self-fashioning is
achieved in relation to something perceived as alien, strange, or hostile,"
and that "self-fashioning always involves some experience of threat, some
effacement or undermining, some loss of self."[30] Greenblatt's argument
takes for granted the existence of an integral self that can be lost, and he
treats "the self" as an exclusive, self-evident category.[31] He says almost
nothing about the profound connectedness between any self and its environment. The antitheatricalists, on the other hand, imagine a process of
identity construction and reconstruction that is not necessarily self-
conscious. Specifically, they imagine a multiplicity of arbitrary becomings
of selves rather than the self-(conscious)-fashioning of an already existent,
singular self (as Greenblatt would have it). They see identity becomings,
albeit mysteriously profound, as informed or determined by context, appearance, performance, an "unholy" supernatural force, at once directly
related to the soul and diametrical to their God. Typically, identity becomings are partly conscious endeavors, such as those, perhaps, of actors,
witches, transvestites, and gypsy-criminals, but they never actually or completely occur on purpose. People do not consciously submit to identity
becomings but are infected by them. (As Gosson says of the theater's audience, "They that came honest to a play, may depart infected.")[32] Like an
infectious disease, identity becomings are an antirational, inspirational
contagion. They are the virus of the Devil—"or worse."

The antitheatricalists were attempting to self-fashion themselves (in
Greenblattian terms) with their polemics against the theater. They define
themselves in opposition to the theater, in the names of God, the church,
and state power ("the Commonwealth") and against "something perceived as alien, strange, or hostile" (the public theater and the Devil). In
doing so, they ironically experience "some loss" of a previously constructed "self." This loss is evinced by their contradictory logic, their in-
consistent performance, and their argument for a fixed social identity. As
it turns out, theirs is really an argument for the *fixing* of social identity that
takes for granted the possibility of identity (re)construction in opposition

to the identity desired by the state machinery and official culture. In other words, for the antitheatricalists to argue that identities or "our selves" are "turne[d]," "blown away" and "overthrowne" (Gosson), "possessed" and "seduce[d]" (Greene), "*made*" and "*vanquished*" (Rainoldes), or "carried away" and "fashioned" (non-antitheatricalist Heywood) by the theater is to presuppose the possibility of identity becomings and negate the idea of a singular, absolute identity. This is not to say that their argument undermines or deconstructs itself with this antipodal presupposition but rather that their argument was sneakily undermined, deconstructed, or reconstructed by the contagious subject matter that obsessed them. Because of the antitheatricalists' proximity to the public theater, like the chroniclers of criminal culture they, too, were infected with transversal power. Their own identity reconstruction had begun. But they were not the only ones to get swept away by and into the current of transversality.

Nomadic Transversality

The antitheatricalists cite numerous examples of identity transformation as their main evidence for the wickedness of stage plays. Their identification of the public theater as *the* problem (second only to the Devil, of course) suggests that the transversal power so threatening to official territory privileged this institution as its most significant operative space. Nevertheless, as accurate as this inference is, it implies considerable circumscription of the theater's transversal power. This inference thus makes little sense unless it is analyzed in light of the theater's expanding reach outside its own material space. Therefore, a more complete understanding of the theater reveals that the antitheatricalists were correct to measure the theater's influence according to certain patterns of conduct noticeable on the outside and distinctly associated with the theater. These include many forms of criminality, such as transvestism, sexual immorality, and skulduggery; and, from our historical perspective, the constant attacks against the theater. The transversal theater communicated to the public the nature of social identities as naturelessness, as performance, as becomings. It communicated the simple fact that identity is (merely) performed. In effect, to a traceable extent, the transversality of the public theater spread and territorialized nomadically well beyond the theater's walls. Indeed, Gosson complains that little was done to prevent the transformed actors and spectators from "infecting the rest" of the social body.[33]

Naturally the areas most intensely affected were the Bankside suburb of Southwark and its Liberties, where most early modern theaters were located. This is why (as Beier, McMullan, Mullaney, and I have documented), long before the closing of the public theaters in 1642, they fittingly gained "the most venerable reputation as a resort for criminality."[34] Southwark and its Liberties were notorious for their itinerant and resident masterless men, actors, rogues, bawds, prostitutes, and other social dissidents, all of whom were subject to vagrancy laws.[35] Theater owners, such as Philip Henslowe, were often also the owners of Southwark's brothels and taverns. Vagabonds, cony-catchers, cutpurses, beggars, and prostitutes (male, female, cross-dressed, whatever) commonly operated within and near the theaters. By extension, as we have seen in the previous chapter, their operations were theater too. Recall that in the popular literature of such prominent Elizabethan and Jacobean writers as Robert Greene and Thomas Dekker criminal conduct is described in the language of the theater. For instance, in *The Belman of London* (1608) Dekker refers to certain collaborative criminal practices as "comedies" and to the criminals involved as "Actors." He also speaks of the "ubiquity of the cut-purse" that "haunt Playhouses" of such suburbs as "Southwarke."[36]

Southwark and its Liberties were spaces of transversality where radical identity becomings transpired, social demarcations were blasted, and where change and its myriad possibilities were triggered and conducted by the transversal theater. The suburb proved so provocative that it also became a battlefield during such demonstrations as the Shrove Tuesday riot of 1617, when a throng of London moralists attempted to demolish a public theater and its neighboring brothels.[37] Yet transversal power did not stop at Southwark's borders. Most strikingly, in addition or subsidiary to criminal praxis, it infected London *as* and *through* the fashion of female-to-male transvestism, which meant not just cross-dressing but also the impersonation of the masculine gender in the "naturalistic sense" characteristic of the public theater.[38]

Transvestism, Effeminacy

In regard to the controversial popularity of the fashion, Puritan preacher Thomas Adams (1615) refers derogatorily to female-to-male transvestites as "both he and shee" and says, "For if they had no more euident distinction of sexe, then they have to shape, they would be all man, or rather all woman." He predicts that *"Hic mulier* will shortly bee good latine."[39] By 1620, when the term "hic mulier" had become a sobriquet for the cross-dressed woman, the contention over the fashion climaxed. Shortly before the publication of the famous polemical pamphlets *Hic Mulier: or, the Man-Woman* and *Haec-Vir: or, the Womanish-Man* (1620), which respectively attack and defend female-to-male transvestism, John Chamberlain commented twice in his letters on what had become a sociopolitical crisis. This crisis was motivated less by fears of emasculation and effeminization of both man and the state than by fears of the becomings-man and transversal thought of the female-to-male transvestite. This is because the very idea, not to mention the reality, of women transforming themselves into men threatened a fundamental principle of the state's overall system of dominance. The principal that God created woman to serve man (Gen. 2:20) directly informed the subjective territories of early modern men and women. Accordingly, Chamberlain indicates not only that condemnation of female-to-male transvestism "rings continually" from the pulpits but that even King James took action against it by demanding stricter sumptuary legislation, prohibiting transvestism of gender and class status, and requiring the unified denunciation of female-to-male transvestism in church services.[40]

When preacher John Williams connects the female-to-male transvestism problem with the public theater in his *Sermon of Apparell* (1619), he signals that transversal thought had become so infectious by this time that it extended far beyond "Sathans Synagogue," beyond the unruly streets of London, and into God's house. He states that God "diuided male and female, but the deuill hath ioyn'd them, that *mulier formosa,* is now become *mulier monstrosa superne.*" He further argues that these people "halfe male, and halfe female" should not be permitted "to enter

Gods house, as if it were a Play-house."[41] Like *Hic Mulier,* which sees transvestite women as "the gilt durt, which imbroders Play-houses,"[42] Williams sees the "Play-house" as the source of and place for female-to-male transvestism. Yet the theater's role in the proliferation of transvestism was not so clear for everyone: regardless of whether one was for or against transvestism or the theater, the theater was permitted to operate for another twenty-one years. Likewise, transvestite women continued to roam the city unlawfully, but now in much greater numbers than when the fashion began during the public theater's first decade.

In *The Description of England* (1587) William Harrison recalls, "I haue met with some of these trulles [prostitutes] in London so disguised, that it hath passed my skill to diserne whether they were men or women."[43] Four years earlier Stubbes remarked on both the gender indiscernability of the transvestite that Harrison speaks of and the already apparent subversive, transformative power of both female-to-male and cross-class transvestism:

> There is such a confuse mingle mangle of apparell in Ailgna [England], and such preposterous excesse therof, as every one is permitted to flaunt it out, in what apparell he lust himselfe, or can get by anie kind of meanes. So that it is verie hard to knowe, who is noble, who is worshipfull, who is a gentlemen, who is not.

> Apparell was giuen vs as a signe distinctiue to discern betwixt sex and sex, & therefor one to weare the Apparel of another sex is to participate with the same, and to adulterate the verities of his own kinde. Wherefore these Women may not improperly be called *Hermaphroditi,* that is, Monsters of bothe kindes, half women, half men.[44]

Howard rightly points out that the first passage implies that "fixed hierarchies within the social order are no longer stable and no longer reliably marked visually," but she still maintains that Stubbes also "evokes the feudal notion of identity as determined by the estate or social position to which one has been born," and that he sees social identity as "preordained and fixed."[45] Howard focuses on Stubbes's and the other moralists' ideological desire for fixity. Instead of recognizing that this desire is only a fantasy whose very articulation demonstrates their belief in identity becomings, she somehow slips into accepting their desire as a belief in fixity as true, real, present. Contrary to Howard's reading, Stubbes claims that transvestism, realized "by anie kind of meanes," obfuscates class distinctions, alters sexual-gender identity, and produces "Monsters of both kindes." Even "*Proteus,* that Monster," he laments, "could neuer chaunge him self into so many fourmes & shapes as these women doo."[46] For Stubbes transvestism (a form of social appearance and performance) can change people previously gendered female into people who are "half women, half men," but a transvestite woman still cannot "become" entirely a man: "If they could as wel chaunge their sex; & put on the kinde of man, as they can weare apparel assigned onely to man, I think they would as verely become men" (73). Could this transformation have been a real possibility for Stubbes, as his logic suggests, but not one he chose to communicate frankly? The thought that women could physically transform themselves into men, or back into men (as Greenblatt claims a wide range of people thought possible), could be frightening for a man enjoying the social privileges exclusive to the male gender. Similarly, it could be frightening for an upper-class person to imagine or learn that his or her "peers" may have come from other socioeconomic positions.

Thirty-seven years later *Hic Mulier* and *Haec-Vir* (1620) seek to resolve the then widespread cultural anxiety over the unfixing and denaturalizing of social identity spurred by the transversal theater. *Hic Mulier* reverberates with fear as it asserts the standard dogma. Yet, like its antitheatricalist cohorts, it also exudes evidence of transversal thought. The tract protests that "since the dais of *Adam* women were never so Masculine; Masculine in their genders and whole generations, from the Mother to the youngest daughter; Masculine in number, from one to multitudes; Masculine in Case, even from the head to the foot . . . for (without redresse) they were, are, and will be still most Masculine, most mankinde, and most monstrous."[47] If "multitudes" of women are "Masculine in their genders," regardless of whether "genders" here refers to anatomical or behavioral difference, then women cannot also be fixed in their feminine identity. In her study of the period's female-to-male transvestism, Linda

Woodbridge nonetheless concludes that *Hic Mulier*'s "author firmly believes that women have a fixed nature."[48] To prove this she cites the following: women are "crownes of natures worke, the compliments of mens excellencies, and Seminaries of propagation"; they "maintaine the world, support mankinde," are "modest," and "gentle."[49] While these quotations do reflect the then dominant view of femininity, they do not substantiate Woodbridge's conclusion. Like Greenblatt, Howard, and Levine, Woodbridge does not explore the moralists's contradictory assertions about fixity and mutability of identity in relation to their assertions about the infectious power of female-to-male transvestism and the theater. Moreover, she does not consider the theatrically determined connection between the transvestite fashion and the process of becomings-others. As these critics exemplify, the residual power of the early modern transversal theater, still stirring in written media, necessarily encounters much resistance (however inadvertently) from even the most unassuming mechanisms of today's official culture. Given more exposure, more conductors through which it can influence today's forms of subjective territory, there is no telling what becomings will result from the revitalized transversal theater. But if history is any indication of what this revitalization has in store for us, then we need to examine in greater depth the results of the early modern theater's transversality.

Hic Mulier maintains that the female-to-male transvestism fashion is indiscriminate and virulent: "It is an infection that emulates the plague, and throws it selfe amongst women of all degrees."[50] It has the power to make a "man" out of the lowest-class prostitute, and infect a woman (of any "degrees") with whom she-he comes in contact. It causes women "to lose all the charmes of womens naturall perfections" and is therefore "base, in respect it offends man in the example, and God in the most vnnaturall vse; Barbarous, in that it is exorbitant from Nature, and an *Antithesis* to kinde; going astray (with ill-fauoured affection) both in attire, in speech, in manners, and (it is to be feared) in whole courses and stories of their actions" (B3, B1). Like the antitheatrical tracts, *Hic Mulier* alludes indirectly to the unspeakable or the unknown. What is the especially "feared" dissidence existing in the "whole courses and stories of their actions"? According to *Hic Mulier*, if it is lesbianism or any unorthodox expression of the female gender, then female-to-male transvestism seeks to marginalize or obviate conventional masculinity and/or the biologically male. In any case, when *Hic Mulier* complains that transvestite women are "going astray (with ill-fauoured affection) both in attire, in speech, in manners," thereby abandoning the characteristically feminine, *it* speaks to a crucial factor: without the feminine there can be no masculine, since these terms exist, as binary oppositions, in codependency. The extended threat of this identity decomposition is that without the masculine there can be no patriarchal state. *Hic Mulier* nevertheless moves beyond the masculine-feminine binary structure by finally claiming that transvestite women are "so much man in all things, that they are neither men, nor women, but iust good for nothing" (B2). But if "they are neither men, nor women," what are they? As *Hic Mulier* sees it, they could be anything; they can "mould their bodies to euery deformed fashion" (B1).

To violate sumptuary law, as *Hic Mulier* and Stubbes argue, was to upset the order of things by blurring the distinction between performance and reality, rich and poor, man and woman. In essence, it blurs the distinction between the optical proof of an allegedly fixed social hierarchy and the monarchical-patriarchal-biblical ideology behind it. Contagiously ("by example"), just as the observance of stage plays caused the audience to perform or become alternative identities, sumptuary violation caused more folks to do the same. In his antitheatrical tract *A Mirrour of Monsters* (1588), William Rankins identifies such identity manipulation as among "the manifold vices, and spotted enormities, that can be caused by infectious sight of Playes."[51] Transversal power is thus transmitted visually: seeing is infectious and instigates becomings. It is also transmitted aurally and physically in the theater *as* and *through* sound waves and resonance. When exposed to the transversal power of the transvestism fashion, people encounter the idea of theater and are infected with the theatrical concept of limitless becomings.

In *Haec-Vir,* which is in the form of a dialogue, the character Hic Mulier responds to the accusations made in *Hic Mulier.* Hic Mulier disputes the idea that their "deformities is most iniurous to Nature, or most effeminine to good men, in the notoriousnes of the example."[52] Forty-four years after the emergence of the transversal theater, Hic Mulier holds firmly to the new and revolutionary idea that people were *designed* to change: "For what is the world, but a very shop or ware-house of change? . . . Nature to euery thing she hath created, hath giuen a singular delight in change" (B1). Hic Mulier delineates identity becomings or self-constructing as affirmative, as naturally willful: "But to man, both these and all things else, to alter, frame and fashion, according as his will and delight shall rule him" (B1). This is perhaps the first time in English history that such a radical statement was made. Hic Mulier refuses to be "dependant on Custome" and laments that female-to-male transvestism is still "a Stranger to the curiositie of the present times, and an enemie to Custome" (B2). This view anticipates Judith Butler's conclusion that the transvestite "effectively mocks both the expressive model of gender and the notion of a true gender identity."[53] Although *Haec-Vir* ends with a plea that if men would be more masculine, women would be more feminine (which, as Woodbridge notes, could be interpreted as "tongue-in-cheek"),[54] "the fact remains," as Howard opines, "that through the discussion of women's dress emerged a strong and subversive reading of the conventionality of the whole gender system."[55]

Effeminacy, Sodomy

The issues at hand, however, relate to much more than mere "reading." Viewed in conjunction with the abundance of correlative evidence already disclosed, it becomes apparent that the antitheatricalists and antitransvestismists affirmed that transvestism, whether performed in the streets or on the stage, was an expression of the theater's transversal power. This is most brashly articulated in their accusations regarding the causal connectedness of the theater to male homosexuality, homoeroticism, or, as Valerie Traub qualifies it, "sodomy or buggery."[56] Indeed, as in the passages by Stubbes and Greene quoted in the introductory section of this chapter, contemporaries frequently use the word "sodomy" or a derivative when writing about the public theater. This is what led Alan Bray and Bruce Smith respectively to declare that "the Elizabethan and Jacobean theater acquired a reputation for [male] homosexuality."[57] But recent work by these and other critics reveals that early modern usage of the term "sodomy" always refers to more than sexual relations between men, albeit only implicitly at times. As Bray explains, "Elizabethan 'sodomy' differed from our contemporary idea of 'homosexuality'. . . . It covered more hazily a whole range of sexual acts, of which sexual acts between people of the same sex were only a part."[58] Donald Mager addresses and supplements this range with some nonsexual meanings, asserting that the word "sodomy" was a "discursive site . . . which in rapid order seems to allude to adultery, clerical sexual indulgence, necrophilia, prostitution, homosexuality, revenge, murder, and atheism."[59] However discursive, Bray privileges the sexual currency of "sodomy," noting that "it was not only a sexual crime. It was also a political and a religious crime and it was this that explains most clearly why it was regarded with such dread."[60] That sodomy was both a political and religious crime explains why the antitheatrical tracts explicitly link it to the theater as an iconoclastic force of social change. Of course, for the transversal theater sodomy or homosexuality, like transvestism and criminality, was simply a result of becomings.

For the antitheatricalists the theater instigates a series of identity becomings that directly affront official culture. These becomings begin, for the men, with becomings-woman. Any movement away from traditional masculinity is becomings-woman, such as through dressing or acting like a "woman" or simply not acting like a "man" (like Shakespeare's Henry VI). This becoming does not require compatibility with traditional femininity but must constitute a digression from the official masculinity embodied in the state machinery.[61] In 1587, when Harrison complains, "Thus it is now come to pass, that women are become men, and men transformed into monsters," he associates the female-to-male transvestism fashion with male-to-female transvestism, either on the stage or in the street, or both. He supplicates: "I praie God that in this behalfe our sinne be not like vnto that of Sodoma and Gomorha."[62] For Harrison the theatrical practice of transvestism is capable of transforming social identity and turning people like himself ("our") into "monsters" that practice the "sinne" of male homosexuality ("like vnto that of Sodoma and Gomorha"). In 1579, when Gosson declares that theaters "effeminate the minde as prickes vnto vice," he refers to the homoerotic desire, the "inordinate lust," that he understands stage plays to actively inspire among the male members of the audience (recall the homoerotic epilogue in *As You Like It*).[63] To substantiate his argument against male-to-female transvestism in the theater (1600), Rainoldes reports that Cyprian wrote of a "stage-player who made boyes effeminate by instructing them how to play the women," warning, "If you can, ought you beware of beautifull boyes transformed into women by putting on their rainment, their feature, lookes and facions."[64] Once "effeminate[d]" or "transformed into women," he insists, "those monsters of nature, which *burning in their lust one toward an other, men with men worke filthines,* are as infamous, as *Sodome:* not the doers onelie, but the sufferers also."[65] Jonathan Goldberg notes that in Renaissance literature "effeminacy was more easily associated with, and was a charge more often made about, men who displayed excessive attention to women than taken as an indication of same-sex attraction."[66] But Rainoldes's use of the term, which is representative of the antitheatrical tracts, refers explicitly to homosexuality (*"men with men"*).

In 1633, nine years before the mandatory closing of the public theaters, the antitheatrical attacks culminated in William Prynne's grandiose tirade *Histrio-mastix: The Player's Scourge or Actor's Tragedy.* As Levine points out, Prynne cites "long lists of precedents for the notion that sodomites titillate themselves by dressing their boys in women's clothing," seeing the theater as "always a pretext for male homosexuality."[67] For instance, Prynne compares actors to incubi and associates homosexuality with emasculation, both of gender and anatomy, when he claims that incubi "clothed their Galli, Succubi, Ganymedes and Cynadi in woman's attire, whose virilities they did oft-time dissect [castrate], to make them more effeminate, transforming them as neere might be into women, both in apparell, gesture, speech, behavior."[68] For Prynne, like the other antitheatricalists, playing a character (in "apparell, gesture, speech, behavior") leads to becoming that character. Yet Prynne adjusts this paradigm by stating that an identity impersonator is actually an alternative identity and not just a simulator or shifter of identities: "He who puts on a woman's rayment though it be but once, is doubtless *a putter on of woman's apparel*" (180). Obviously infected with transversal thought, Prynne argues that once people are turned on to the theatrical practice of transvestism, there is no turning back: they are now performers, and the more parts they play, "though it be but once," the more diversified their identities become, or the more identities they have. The case of the notorious criminal Gamaliel Ratsey (discussed in chapter 4), who regularly impersonated different social identities "as Players doe," illustrates Prynne's assertion.[69] Social identities are therefore subject to theater; and because theater, as a conceptual conductor of transversality, is boundless, so must be social identities.

Transversal Thought "or worse"

At this point, in light of Prynne, I want to return to the "or worse" and "or rather more than beastlie" in the passages by Stubbes, Rainoldes, and Greene. Like the other moralists discussed in this chapter, all three maintain that identity impersonation causes the impersonator to become the impersonated identity and the observer to embark on the process of becomings (to "repeate" it, as Greene says, "and thereby infect their minde"). They recognize that the public theater, teeming with naturalistic impersonations, collapses traditional sexual, gender, moral, class, and anatomical differentiations by forcing and determining identity becomings. By extension, they posit all social categories, such as "man" and "woman," as constructs that must be performed *to be*. They suggest that the body (with or without a vagina) only matters inasmuch as it is a point of departure for becomings. They even consider the potentialities for becomings and what becomings have to offer. But when they do this by employing the supplementary phrases "or worse" and "or rather more than beastlie" as the vanishing points of resolution to their own dialectical crises, Stubbes, Rainoldes, and Greene epitomize the ways by which transversal power undermined the antitheatricalists's efforts to fashion themselves. Their use of these phrases not only reveals symptomatically that they were infected with transversal thought but that they radically transcended official territory. In doing so they themselves became promulgators of the miraculous, destabilizing, and liberating unknowability that energized and radiated from the transversal theater. They illustrate the revolutionary power of the transversal conductor from which they desperately sought refuge.

To further explain their transcendence of official territory, I want to turn to Jacques Derrida's theory of "supplementarity," which maintains that language, as a finite system, excludes hermeneutic totalization. Rather than the field being inexhaustible or too large, it is missing a center, origin, or destination which could ground the play of signifying substitutions. Therefore, any sign used to replace the center is, in fact, a supplement to the absent center. As Derrida puts it, this "movement of signification adds something, which results in the fact that there is always more."[70] The rhetoric of Stubbes, Rainoldes, and Greene thus attempts to signify the central antitheatricalist fear but ends up becoming a play of substitutions that results in this rhetoric itself becoming a supplement to the absent central fear. What absent central fear are the antitheatricalists trying to ground? It is fear that, after a cancerous progression along a continuum of immorality, the "evil" ideas and becomings excited by transvestism and stage plays will eventually manifest themselves in unmentionable or unimaginable forms. The play of substitutions is evident in their progression from "the *Sodomite*" and "that beastlie filthines" to the supplementary expressions "or worse" and "or rather more than beastlie." When the moralists speak of sodomy, their meaning can be grounded in both the Bible, English sodomy law, and the extensive currency of the word. (Recall that it referred to "adultery, clerical sexual indulgence, necrophilia, prostitution, homosexuality, revenge, murder, and atheism.")[71] When they speak of "beastlie filthines," some indication of their meaning is given by their claims that transvestism and stage plays have the power to "turne reasonable creatures into brute beastes" (Gosson) and that they are "the means and occasions whereby men are transformed into dogges" (Rainoldes). It is implied that becomings-animal is a likely result of transversal thought. But when they speak of things "worse" than sodomy and "more than beastlie" without providing examples or explanation, their meaning is elusive. Their discourse exceeds the ordinary, the "reasonable," the natural. It enters transversal territory.

Thus, for the antitheatricalists the supplements "or worse" and "or rather more than beastlie" signify one or more unthinkable or unspeakable yet possible alternative practices or identities. These are positioned on an infinite scale of transgressive practices or identities somewhere after those that are "sodomitical" and "beastlie." As Derrida says, the supplements suggest that there are "always more" ("or worse," or possibly even better—if "rather" means "preferably") sexual-gender practices, identities, becomings, mechanisms, and purposes. Their open-endedness undermines the idea of a fixed or stable sexual orientation, gender identity, or social order. They call into question all binary oppositions and therefore undermine state thought. The supplements "or worse" and "or rather more than beastlie" indicate multiplicities of alternative perspectives, energies, realities, and universes. Hence the transversal theater—looming, evolving, and spreading heterogeneous multiplicities (ideational, symbolical, and material)—determined the process of becomings that forced Stubbes, Rainoldes, Greene, and the other moralists to think beyond the limitations and impositions of state thought and state power. Once infected with transversal thought, as with Prynne's "*putter on of woman's apparel,*" the moralists must always be transversal thinkers. Like actors and criminals, they must always undergo becomings. They must forever problematize the sociopolitical conductors that so established their raison d'être. Their experience is exemplary of how transversal power forever constitutes a *real* threat to all organizational social structures.

Transversalism and Immoralism

The causal relationship between early modern England's public theater and criminal culture was one of reciprocity, with each informing the other. Transversality was realized by criminal culture through theatricality and, contemporaneously, the emergent public theater realized transversality together and separately from criminal culture. The transversal power of both criminal culture and the public theater affected official culture in many ways, the most significant of which we have seen in the populace's criminal becomings; the fetishization of the gypsy sign; the creation of a commercially successful genre of literature about criminal culture; the intervention of a criminal language; the sociocultural transformation of traditional public spaces; the spread of the female-to-male transvestism fashion; and the transversal thought of the antitheatricalists and antitransvestismists. Furthermore, the ironic contradictions and transversal ideas expressed by the antitheatricalists and antitransvestismists reflect aspects of criminal culture's transversality that were central to the plays, pamphlets, and poems devoted to this culture. In fact, based on all of the literature I have discussed, it is clear that transversal power was most evident in transgressions of the church's ideology and corresponding official territory: the dominant properties of a society's interiority that work to coalesce overlap among the respective subjective territories of the society's members.

Criminal culture's ideology, aesthetic, and praxis (its "Art and Mystery") was predicated on an alternative, quasi-religious philosophy that negated and problematized the official systems of belief. As a result, criminal culture brilliantly personified the "immoralist" concept coined three hundred years later by Friedrich Nietzsche. "Fundamentally," says Nietzsche, "my term *immoralist* involves two negations. For one, I negate a type of man that has so far been considered supreme: the good, the benevolent, the beneficent. And then I negate a type of morality that has become prevalent and predominant as morality itself—the morality of decadence or, more concretely, *Christian* morality."[72] For Nietzsche all moral impositions are decadent inasmuch as they necessarily, by definition, corrupt the inherent purity of immoralism. Christianity, being among the most truculent, oppressive, and dogmatic of moral imposers, is mendacity par excellence. Criminal culture, on the other hand, was an immoralist culture with a motley population of wrongdoers and anti-Christians who unabashedly reaped the benefits of official culture's Christian benevolence and morality. Recall that members of criminal culture would feign impoverishment, sickness, or physical disability so that they would be given alms by the parishes (parishes were required by state law to give alms to the legitimately needy).[73]

Despite its flagrant exploitation of official culture, it was specifically the transversality of criminal culture's immoralist subversion of the conceptual boundaries drawn and supported by the state machinery that most contributed to its mass appeal. For instance, as Gamini Salgado observes, "If the desire for entertainment drew the common people to the gypsies, their association with witchcraft and sorcery was an even more powerful magnet." This is so because "beneath the pieties of official Christianity there lay in Elizabethan life a deep vein of belief in demons and spirits, witches and their families. The gypsy fortune teller tapped this vein with great skill and subtlety."[74] Witchcraft was transversal and England's witch craze reached its height during the Elizabethan and Jacobean periods. Yet, while it is irrefutable that criminal culture capitalized on popular beliefs, superstitions, and fascinations, historiographical evidence does not suggest that there were actual social or professional relations between witches and members of criminal culture.[75] Criminal culture became a transversal gateway for the popular imagination.

Moreover, the fetishized criminal culture was not the antithesis of official culture and its Christianity. On both personal and sociocultural levels, it is criminal culture's conceptual and material nomadism, best exemplified by its transient parasitism, promiscuity, and theatricality, that made it so transversal. Whereas every transversal movement made by members of criminal culture caused at least a microsubversion, criminal culture's occupation of transversal territory and its general transversality, like the public theater's, depended more on its parasitic adjacency and tangentiality than on its resistance to official culture. Coexistence and difference were crucial. Criminal culture manifested socioculturally, from the standpoint of official culture, what Derrida calls "différance."[76] It was different virtually and in actuality from official culture, and its mysterious, fluid stature caused the ineluctable deferral and obfuscation of explanation, identification, and placement. Criminal culture's transversal power resists interpretation, such as through the exceptional endowment and subsequent objective agency of the gypsy sign and its absent referent. It highlighted morality's multidimensionality as it exposed, through its abundant use of disguise and theatricality, the arbitrariness and performativity of social identity.

Let us recall once more the dialogue between Rachel and Meriel in Brome's play *A Jovial Crew,* who declare that their criminal community is "th'only happy people in a nation" and "the only free men of a commonwealth; free above scot-free; that observe no law, obey no governor, use no religion, but what they draw from their own ancient custom, or constitute themselves, yet are no rebels."[77] Frapolo, the chief criminal in Shirley's play *The Sisters,* also comments on the issue of religion: "I have thought," he says to his followers, "and you shall be no pagans, Jews, nor Christians. . . . But every man shall be of all religions."[78] The criminals "constitute[d] themselves," being neither "pagans, Jews, nor Christians" but rather of "no" or "all" religions, and therefore not subscribing to any one religion in particular. Criminal culture inspired multiplicities of alternatives to conventionality and its Christian grounding. It was the resounding motivation for becomings-criminal.

CHAPTER ONE

1. I first introduced my "transversal theory" in my article "The Devil's House, 'or worse': Transversal Power and Antitheatrical Discourse in Early Modern England," *Theatre Journal* 49: 2 (May 1997): 143–67. See also Bryan Reynolds and Joseph Fitzpatrick, "The Transversality of Michel de Certeau: Foucault's Panoptic Discourse and the Cartographic Impulse," *Diacritics* 29:3 (Fall 1999): 63–80; Bryan Reynolds, "'What is the city but the people?': Transversal Performance and Radical Politics in Shakespeare's *Coriolanus* and Brecht's *Coriolan*," in *Shakespeare Without Class: Misappropriations of Cultural Capital,* ed. Bryan Reynolds and Donald Hedrick (New York: St. Martin's Press, 2000): 107–32; Bryan Reynolds and Joseph Fitzpatrick, "Venetian Ideology or Transversal Power?: Iago's Motives and the Means by Which Othello Falls," in *Critical Essays on* Othello, ed. Philip Kolin (New York: Garland, 2001); and Bryan Reynolds and D. J. Hopkins, "The Making of Authorships: Transversal Navigation in the Wake of *Hamlet,* Robert Wilson, Wolfgang Wiens, and Shakespace," in *Shakespeare After Mass Media,* ed. Richard Burt (New York: Palgrave/St. Martin's, 2001).

2. See, for instance, Francis Ford Coppola's *The Godfather,* parts I (1972), II (1974), and III (1990); John Huston's *Prizzi's Honor* (1985); Jonathan Demme's *Married to the Mob* (1988); and Martin Scorsese's *GoodFellas* (1990).

3. Consider biographies and novels such as Peter Maas's *The Valachi Papers* (1968), Nicolas Pileggi's *Wiseguy: Life in a Mafia Family* (1985), John Cummings's *Goombata: The Improbable Rise and Fall of John Gotti and His Gang* (1990), and Mario Puzo's *The Last Don* (1996); or songs such as Paper Lace's "The Night Chicago Died" (1974), Bob Dylan's "Joey" (about Joseph Gallo [1975]), and Bruce Springsteen's "Atlantic City" (1982).

4. For an interesting discussion of the job of the historian, see Hayden White,

Tropics of Discourse: Essays in Cultural Criticism (Baltimore: Johns Hopkins University Press, 1978), especially the chapter entitled "The Historical Text as Literary Artifact." 81–100.

5. Frederic Jameson, *The Political Unconscious: Narrative as a Socially Symbolic Act* (Ithaca: Cornell University Press, 1981), 82.

6. James Intriligator and I introduced this concept in a paper entitled "Transversal Power: Molecules, Jesus Christ, The Greatful Dead, and Beyond" presented at the Manifesto Conference at Harvard University on May 9, 1998.

7. For an intriguing comparison of the "mythological" presences of Santa Claus and Shakespeare that is theoretically related to The Smithereens' comparison cited here, see Michael Bristol, "Shakespeare: The Myth," in David Scott Kasten ed., *A Companion to Shakespeare* (Oxford: Blackwell, 1999), 489–502.

8. An earlier version of much of this section was published in my article "The Devil's House, 'or worse': Transversal Power and Antitheatrical Discourse in Early Modern England," *Theatre Journal* 49:2 (May 1997), 143–67.

9. For an in depth discussion on Ideological State Apparatuses, see Louis Althusser's "Ideology and Ideological State Apparatuses (Notes Towards an Investigation)" in his *Lenin and Philosophy and Other Essays* (New York: Monthly Review Press, 1971). For Althusser "every State Apparatus, whether Repressive or Ideological, 'functions' both by violence and by ideology," but "the (Repressive) State Apparatus functions massively and predominantly *by repression* (including physical repression), while functioning secondarily by ideology," and "the Ideological State Apparatuses function massively and predominantly *by ideology*" (145). Whereas this paradigm is useful to a discussion on the sociopolitical situation of early modern England, it is ultimately inadequate because the repressive aspect of all the state apparatuses was rarely primary and never constituted, as Althusser asserts, a cohesive or singular repressive state apparatus that was "secured by its unified and centralized organization" (149); neither Queen Elizabeth nor King James possessed a professional army.

10. In *The Elizabethan World Picture* (New York: Random House, 1945), E. M. W. Tillyard holds that despite the many differences between factions of the church, such as the Puritans, and the courts of James and Elizabeth, all were "more united by a common theological bond than they were divided by ethical disagreements" (4). Carl Bridenbaugh upholds Tillyard's conclusion in his *Vexed and Troubled Englishmen, 1590–1642* (Oxford: Oxford University Press, 1976); his analysis of a variety of Elizabethan and Jacobean texts leads him to emphatically assert, "Indeed, Church and commonwealth did constitute society" (274). In his *Shakespeare, the King's Playwright: Theater in the Stuart Court, 1603–1613* (New Haven: Yale University Press, 1995), Alvin Kernan subscribes to the view that "authority" in early modern England's "Leviathan state" was "centralized" dyadically, "with the king as head of church and state" (1–2). Throughout his book *The Emergence of a Nation*

State: The Commonwealth of England, 1529–1660 (London: Longman, 1984), Alan G. R. Smith describes an often fractured and conflicted government comprised of church officials, parliaments, crowns, and courts—all nonetheless contributing to the establishment of a largely unified "nation-state."

11. In his *Critique of Pure Reason* Immanuel Kant sums up his position as follows: "If, therefore, Space (and Time also) were not a mere form of your intuition, which contains conditions *à priori,* under which alone things can become external objects for you, and without which subjective conditions the objects are in themselves nothing, you could not construct any synthetical proposition whatsoever regarding external objects. It is therefore not merely possible or probable, but indubitably certain, that Space and Time, as the necessary conditions of all our external and internal experience, are merely subjective conditions of all our intuitions, in relation to which all objects are therefore mere phenomena, and not things in themselves, presented to us in this particular manner" (trans. J. M. D. Meiklejohn [Buffalo, N.Y.: Prometheus Books, 1990], 39).

12. See Henri Lefebvre, *The Production of Space,* trans. Donald Nicholson-Smith (Oxford: Blackwell, 1993), especially the introductory chapter entitled "Plan of the Present Work," 1–67.

13. My understanding of "hegemony" matches that of Raymond Williams, who succinctly defines the concept as "an integral form of class rule" within a society "which exists not only in political and economic institutions and relationships but also in active forms of experience and consciousness" (*Keywords: A Vocabulary of Culture and Society* [New York: Oxford University Press, 1983], 145). For instance, in addition to the overall hegemonic society promoted by the state machinery, there are usually sub-societies, such as those of a university or a criminal organization, which are also hegemonic. See also the chapter entitled "Hegemony" in Raymond Williams, *Marxism and Literature* (New York: Oxford University Press, 1977): 108–14.

14. Pierre Bourdieu, *Language and Symbolic Power,* ed. John B. Thompson (Cambridge, Mass.: Harvard University Press, 1991), 170.

15. Benedict Anderson, *Imagined Communities: Reflections on the Origin and Spread of Nationalism* (London: Verso, 1983). Like Anderson, I see the nation or nation-state as an imagined community that is both inherently limited and sovereign:

It is *imagined* because the members of even the smallest nation will never know most of their fellow members, meet them, or even hear of them, yet in the minds of each lives the image of their communion. . . . In fact, all communities larger than primordial villages of face-to-face contact (and perhaps even these) are imagined. Communities are to be distinguished, not by their falsity/genuineness, but by the style in which they are imagined. . . . The nation is imagined as *limited* because even the largest of them, encompassing perhaps a billion living human beings, has finite, if elastic, boundaries, beyond which lie other nations. No nation imagines itself coterminous with mankind. . . . It is imagined as *sovereign* because . . . nations dream of being free, and, if under God, directly so. The gage and emblem of this freedom is the sovereign state. Finally, it is imagined as a *community,* because, regardless of the actual inequality and exploitation that may prevail in each, the nation is always conceived as a deep, horizontal comradeship. (15–16)

16. André Glucksmann, *Master Thinkers,* trans. Brian Pearce (New York: Harper & Row, 1980), 112.

17. *Certain Sermons or Homilies (1547) and A Homily against Disobedience and Wilful Rebellion (1570): A Critical Edition,* ed. Ronald B. Bond (Toronto: University of Toronto Press, 1987), 161.

18. For a discussion of the subversion/containment paradigm as well as critical employments of this paradigm by new historicists, see Jonathan Dollimore, *Sexual Dissidence: Augustine to Wilde, Freud to Foucault* (Oxford: Clarendon Press, 1991), 81–91; Michael D. Bristol, *Shakespeare's America, America's Shakespeare* (London: Routledge, 1990), 189–211; Alan Sinfield, *Cultural Politics–Queer Reading* (London: Routledge, 1994), 21–39; and Louis Montrose, "Professing the Renaissance: The Poetics and Politics of Culture," in *The New Historicism, ed.* Aram H. Veeser (New York: Routledge, 1989), 20–24. See also Jean E. Howard and Marion F. O'Connor, "Introduction" (1–17); Walter Cohen, "Political Criticism of Shakespeare" (18–46); and Don E. Wayne, "Power, Politics, and the Shakespearean Text: Recent Criticism in England and the United States" (47–67)—all in Jean E. Howard and Marion F. O'Connor, eds., *Shakespeare Reproduced: The Text in History and Ideology* (New York: Methuen, 1987)

19. Terry Eagleton, *William Shakespeare* (New York: Basil Blackwell, 1986), 2. In addition to the conceptual influence of the practices of transvestism of gender and class on and off the public stage, I am thinking of the huge conceptual influence of Puritan radicals and belief in the occult. On the Puritan influence, see Christopher Hill, *The World Turned Upside Down: Radical Ideas During the English Revolution* (London: Penguin, 1975) and his *Intellectual Origins of the English Revolution* (Oxford: Clarendon Press, 1980); and Patrick Collinson, *The Elizabethan Puritan Movement* (Oxford: Clarendon Press, 1990). On the influence of the occult, see Alan Macfarlane, *Witchcraft in Tudor and Stuart England: A Regional and Comparative Study* (London: Routledge, 1970); Christina Larner, *Witchcraft and Religion: The Politics of Popular Belief* (Oxford: Blackwell, 1984); and Sydney Anglo, *The Damned Art* (Boston: Routledge, 1977).

For a political discussion of *Macbeth,* see Bryan Reynolds, "The Terrorism of Macbeth and Charles Manson: Reading Cultural Construction in Polanski and Shakespeare," *Upstart Crow* 13 (1993), 109–27; Alan Sinfield, *"Macbeth:* History, Ideology, and Intellectuals," in his *Faultlines: Cultural Materialism and the Politics of Dissident Reading* (Berkeley: University of California Press, 1992), 95–108; Stephen Greenblatt, "Shakespeare Bewitched," in *New Historical Literary Study: Essays on Reproducing Texts, Representing History,* ed. Jeffrey N. Cox and Larry J. Reynolds (Princeton: Princeton University Press, 1993), 108–35; and Alvin Kernan, "The Politics of Madness and Demonism" in his *Shakespeare, the King's Playwright,* 71–89.

20. Félix Guattari, *Molecular Revolution: Psychiatry and Politics* (New York: Penguin Books, 1984). In the section on "Institutional Psychotherapy" Guattari writes: "Transversality in the group is a dimension opposite and complementary to the structures that generate pyramidal hierarchization and sterile ways of transmitting messages. Transversality is the unconscious source of action in the group, going beyond the objective laws on which it is based, carrying the group's desire" (22). For more on Guattari's understanding of transversality, see his collection of essays (1965–70) entitled *Psychanalyse transversalité* (Paris: Maspero, 1972).

21. Guattari, *Molecular Revolution,* 26.

22. Gilles Deleuze, *Negotiations, 1972–1990,* trans. Martin Joughin (New York : Columbia University Press, 1995), 25.

23. Glucksmann, *Master Thinkers,* 106.

24. Ernesto Laclau, ed. *New Reflections on the Revolution of Our Time* (London: Verso, 1990), 79 (see also pp. 5–17); and Slavoj Zizek, "Beyond Discourse-Analysis," in Laclau, *New Reflections,* 252.

25. Slavoj Žižek, *The Sublime Object of Ideology* (London: Verso, 1989), 5.

26. Laclau, *New Reflections,* 79.

27. For more on becoming, see Gilles Deleuze and Félix Guattari, *A Thousand Plateaus: Capitalism and Schizophrenia,* trans. Brian Massumi (Minneapolis: University of Minnesota press, 1987, especially the chapter "Becoming-Intense, Becoming-Animal, Becoming-Imperceptible . . ." (232–309); see also the chapter "Becoming a Woman" (233–35) in Guattari's *Molecular Revolution.* Identity becoming is rarely a singular, one-dimensional process, that is, when a person becomes directly something else that is specific and readily identifiable. For this reason I follow Deleuze and Guattari by pluralizing the term "becoming" (as in "identity becomings" and "becomings-child") when speaking generally about a teleological category or direction for becoming rather than an ontological destination.

28. For substantiation and discussion of the importance of these binaries, see Ian Archer, *The Pursuit of Stability: Social Relations in Elizabethan London* (Cambridge: Cambridge University Press, 1991), where he discusses the "binary polarities that historians of ideas see as characteristic of the age" (205); Michael D. Bristol, *Carnival and Theater: Plebeian Culture and the Structure of Authority in Renaissance England* (New York: Routledge, Chapman and Hall, 1989); Rebecca C. Bushnell, *Tragedies of Tyrants: Political Thought and Theater in the English Renaissance* (Ithaca, N.Y.: Cornell University Press, 1990); Jonathan Dollimore, *Radical Tragedy: Religion, Ideology and Power in the Drama of Shakespeare and His Con-*

temporaries (Chicago: University of Chicago Press, 1984), especially the introductory chapter "Contexts" (3–28); David Scott Kastan and Peter Stallybrass, "Introduction: Staging the Renaissance," in *Staging the Renaissance: Reinterpretations of Elizabethan and Jacobean Drama,* ed. Scott Kastan and Peter Stallybrass (New York: Routledge, 1991); and Tillyard, *The Elizabethan World Picture.*

29. One should acknowledge, however, that these characteristics are also likely to be appropriated by the state under the conditions of global capitalism, with its self-serving interest in breaking down boundaries, hierarchies, and stabilities (sometimes of the identity and power of the nation-state itself), as Fredric Jameson and others have characterized the situation for the logic of postmodernism at the present historical juncture.

30. These include Frank Aydelotte, *Elizabethan Rogues and Vagabonds,* Oxford Historical and Literary Studies, 1 (Oxford: Oxford University Press, 1913); A. L. Beier, *Masterless Men: The Vagrancy Problem in England, 1560–1640* (London: Methuen, 1985); James Crabb, *The Gipsies' Advocate: or Observations on the Origin, Character, Manners, and Habits, of the English Gipsies* (London: Mills, Jowett, and Mills, 1832); Charles G. Leland, *The English Gipsies and Their Language* (New York: Hurd and Houghton, 1873); John L. McMullan, *The Canting Crew: London's Criminal Underworld, 1550–1700* (New Brunswick, N.J.: Rutgers University Press, 1984); Judith Okely, *The Traveler-Gypsies* (Cambridge: Cambridge University Press, 1983); Gamini Salgado, *The Elizabethan Underworld* (London: J. M. Dent, 1977); T. W. Thompson, "Gleanings from Constables' Accounts and Other Sources," *Journal of the Gypsy Lore Society* (3rd ser.), 7, no. 1 (1928): 30–47; Brian Vesey-Fitzgerald, *Gypsies of Britain: An Introduction to Their History* (Newton Abbott, England: David and Charles, 1973); Eric Otto Winstedt, "Early British Gypsies," *Journal of the Gypsy Lore Society* (n.s.), 7, no. 1 (1913–14): 5–36.

CHAPTER TWO

1. My understanding of fetishism is largely derived from the work of Jean Baudrillard, although I do not wholly subscribe to his view. In "Fetishism and Ideology: The Semiological Reduction" (in *For a Critique of the Political Economy of the Sign,* trans. Charles Levin [St. Louis, Mo.: Telos Press, 1981]), Baudrillard writes:

> If fetishism exists it is thus not a fetishism of the signified, a fetishism of substances and values (called ideological), which the fetish object would incarnate for the alienated subject. Behind this reinterpretation (which is truly ideological) it is a *fetishism of the signifier.* That is to say that the subject is trapped in the factitious, differential, systematized aspect of the object. It is not the passion (whether of objects or subjects) for substances that speaks in fetishism, it is the *passion for the code,* which, by governing both objects and subjects, and by subordinating them to itself, delivers them up to abstract manipulation. . . . Thus, fetishism is actually attached to the sign ob-

ject, the object eviscerated of its substance and history, and reduced to the state of marking a difference, epitomizing a whole system of differences. (92–93)

It is important to note that Baudrillard's use of the term "signified" incorporates what I mean by the term "referent." That is, he uses the term "signified" to refer to the concept behind the signifier, but he also uses it to refer to the actual, material object to which the "signifier" refers. My view of fetishism differs significantly from Baudrillard's in that, like Pierre Bourdieu, I am inclined to emphasize the correspondence and connectedness between social and symbolic systems, while Baudrillard disassociates the symbolic from the social. Baudrillard's claim that fetishism achieves a state of abstraction and commutability within a closed system of exchange and codification "separated out from the process of real labor" and "eviscerated of its substance and history" denies but cannot erase the social mechanisms that produced and reproduce the socially and historically conditioned human participation and hermeneutic code on which all fetishism necessarily depends. See Bourdieu, *The Field of Cultural Production,* ed. Randal Johnson (New York: Columbia University Press, 1993), especially chapters 1–3 and 5.

2. Baudrillard, *For a Critique of the Political Economy of the Sign,* 155–56.

3. Lefebvre, cited in Baudrillard, *For a Critique of the Political Economy of the Sign,* 155.

4. See Marshall McLuhan and Quentin Fiore, *The Medium Is the Massage* (New York: Bantam Books, 1967).

5. I am using the Windsor version because it is the longest, most complete, and most authentic. Throughout this study I use editions with early modern spelling and syntax because my analysis of the language that the criminals used (especially in the next chapter) is largely concerned with grammar, sentence structure, and phonetics. Ben Jonson, *Masque of Gypsies, In the Burley, Belvoir, and Windsor Versions,* ed. W. W. Greg (London: Oxford University Press, 1952).

6. England's first act specifically against "people callynge themselfes Egyptians" (the term "gypsy" is a diminutive of "Egyptian") was passed in 1530. This act is quoted at length in Salgado, *The Elizabethan Underworld,* 152. I discuss the legislation against gypsies in detail later in this chapter.

7. Stephen Orgel, *Ben Jonson: The Complete Masques* (New Haven: Yale University Press, 1969), 30. The letter from John Chamberlain to Sir Dudley Carleton is quoted at length in Stephen Orgel, *The Jonsonian Masque* (Cambridge, Mass.: Harvard University Press, 1965), 70.

8. Orgel, *The Jonsonian Masque,* 100.

9. Richard Dutton, *Ben Jonson* (Cambridge: Cambridge University Press, 1983), 18. This explanation is the subject of Dale B. J. Randall's excellent book *Jonson's Gypsies Unmasked: Background and Theme of* "The Gypsies Metamorphos'd" (Durham: Duke University Press, 1975).

10. Jacques Derrida, "Signature, Event, Context," in *Limited, Inc.,* ed.Gerald Graff and trans. Samuel Weber and Jeffrey Mehlman (Evanston, Ill.: Northwestern University Press, 1988), 18.

11. Judith Butler, *Bodies That Matter* (New York: Routledge, 1993), 226–27.

12. Friedrich Nietzsche, *On the Genealogy of Morals,* trans. Walter Kaufman (New York: Vintage Books, 1989), 77.

13. Butler, *Bodies That Matter,* 223.

14. The plot to Jonson's *The Gypsies Metamorphos'd* runs as follows: Enter a group of gypsies consisting of five children, who say nothing for the duration of the masque, and eight adult males, who begin dancing, singing, and boasting about the particulars of their "nation" (125, 133). Using the language generally attributed to rogue-vagabond culture, the gypsies brag, with much fervor and detail, about their criminal exploits, such as their "angling of purses" and "true legier-demaine," as well as their merry, debauched lifestyle (129). They ask the audience of their "fine play" to remain in their "places," adding, "Be not frighted with our fashion" or "tawney faces" (131, 125). Their "Captaine" then notices that there is a "kinge" present—"Iames" is in the audience—and they immediately change their tune from vainglory to cajolery, without allowing their charisma to dwindle (136–37). They tell James, Prince Charles, the Lord Chamberlain, the Lord Keeper, and others their fortunes, which are all pleasant and complimentary. Afterward four male rustics enter and are instantly enamored of the gypsies, for whom they generously supply "wenches" since the gypsies are all male (157). The gypsies so impress the rustics with song, dance, and repartee that the rustics think them "learnd men all." The rustics and their wenches are so preoccupied with the gypsies that the gypsies easily "plucke" their purses (163). When the gypsies admit to stealing their purses, the rustics' admiration for them only intensifies, increasing as the gypsies relate the story of their meeting place, " the Deuills Arse" (175). The rustics now not only wish that they had more money for the gypsies to steal but desperately want to become gypsies themselves. For instance, rustic Pvp says to the gypsies, "I haue a terrible grudging now vpon mee to be one of your companie. . . . I would binde my selfe to him [your Captaine], bodie and soule, either for one and twentie yeares, or as many liues as he would" (183). At the masque's conclusion, the gypsies exhibit more of their "skill" in disguise and theatricality and "like Lordes to appeare" and "become newe men" (fine gentlemen); as newfangled "true men," they dance and sing for the audience, with almost every lyric profusely professing the eminence of King James (189).

15. Thomas Harman, *A Caveat or Warening, For Commen Cursetors vulgarely called Vagabones* (1567) in A. V. Judges ed., *The Elizabethan Underworld. A Collection of Tudor and Early Stuart Tracts and Ballads* (London: E. P. Dutton, 1930), 64. Beier also accepts as fact that Harman was a Kentish justice of the peace (see, e.g., *Masterless Men,* 160–61), and I've come across no evidence to suggest otherwise.

16. William Harrison, *The Description of England* (1587), ed. Georges Edelen (Ithaca, N.Y.: Cornell University Press, 1968), 184.

17. Aydelotte, *Elizabethan Rogues and Vagabonds*, 19.

18. In *Jonson's Gypsies Unmasked* Randall suggests that Jonson was able to represent the gypsies with so much accuracy because he "may have encountered English and Scottish gypsies personally during his four-hundred-mile walking tour to Scotland in 1618 and 1619 (when he certainly met country and village folk something like those he put in the gypsy masque)" (56).

19. Jonson, *The Gypsies Metamorphos'd*, 121.

20. John Awdeley, *The Fraternitye of Vacabondes* (1561), ed. Edward Viles and F. J. Furnivall, Early English Text Society, extra series, 9 (1869) (Millwood, N.Y.: Kraus Reprint, 1988); Thomas Harman, *A Caveat or Warening, For Commen Cursetors vulgarely called Vagabones* (1567), and Samuel Rid, *Martin Markall, Beadle of Bridewell: His Defense and Answers to the Bellman of London* (1610) both in *The Elizabethan Underworld: A Collection of Tudor and Early Stuart Tracts and Ballads*, ed. A. V. Judges (London: E. P. Dutton, 1930); William Harrison, *The Description of England* (1587), ed. Georges Edelen (Ithaca, N.Y.: Cornell University Press, 1968); and Thomas Dekker, The Belman of London *and* Lanthorne and Candle-Light (1608) *and* The Gull's Horn-Book (1609) (London: J. M. Dent, 1904).

21. Awdeley:

An *Vpright Man.* An Vpright Man is one that goeth wyth the trunchion of a staffe, which staffe they cal a Filtchman. This man is of so much authority that meeting with any of his profession he may cal them to accompt [account], & command a share or snap vnto him selfe, of al that they haue gained by their trade in one moneth. . . . He may also command any of their women, which they cal Doxies, to serue his turne. He hath ye chiefe place at any market walke, & other assemblies, & is not of any to be controled. (4)

A *Iack Man.* A Iarkeman is he that can write and reade, and sometime speake latin. He vseth to make counterfaite licences which they call "Gybes," and sets to Seales, in their language called Iarkes. (5)

A *Kintchin Mortes.* A Kintchin Mortes is a Gyrle; she is brought at her full age to the Vpryght Man to be broken, and so she is called a Doxy, vntil she comes to ye honor of an Altham. (5)

Dekker:

An *Upright-man* is a sturdy *big bonde knave,* that never walkes but (like a *Commander*) with a short troncheon in his hand, which hee cals his *Filchman.* At Markets, *Fayres* & other meetings his voice amongst *Beggers* is of the same sound that a Constables is of, it is not to be controld. He is frée of all the shiers in England, but never stayes in any place long; the reason is, his profession is to be idle, which being looked into, he knowes is punishable, and therefore to avoid the whip, he wanders. (90, 91)

A *Jack-man*. And because no common wealth can stand without some *Learning* in it, Therefore are there some in this *Schoole of Beggers,* that practise writing and *Reading,* and those are called *Jackmen:* yea the *Jackman* is so cunning sometimes that he can speake Latine. (101)

A *Rogue* is knowne to all men by his name, but not to all men by his conditions; no puritane can discemble more than he, for he will speake in a lamentable tune and crawle along the stréetes, (supporting his body by a staffe) as if there were not life enough in him to put strength into his legs. (94)

These *Doxyes* will for good victuals or a small peice of money, prostitute there bodies to servingmen if they can get into any convenient corner about their maisters houses, & to ploughmen in barnes, haylofts or stables: they are common pick-pockets, familiars (with the baser sorts of cut-purses), and oftentimes secret murtherers of those infants which are begotten of their bodies. (104)

The one exception to this list, which should be mentioned because of its importance to our understanding of the distribution of power among members of criminal culture, is Jonson's use of the term "Captain" instead of "Upright Man" as the title of his criminal leader in *The Gypsies Metamorphos'd.* However, this cannot be considered an exception to a rule. In a letter dated "the last of August 1559," the Lord-Lieutenant of Dorsetshire, Lord Mountjoy, wrote to the Privy Council for instructions on what to do with a large number of "people naming themselves Egiptians" who had recently been apprehended in his county. In response, Queen Elizabeth said that "some sharpe example and executiō shuld be made uppō a good nōber of them," and that no favor was to be shown to those "such as have frō there youth of long tyme hanted this lewd lyffe nor to such as be yᵉ pincipall captens and ryngledars of the cōpany" (*State Papers—Domestic—Elizabeth,* vol. 7., 137–38). Here, as in Jonson's masque, "captens" is used to signify leaders or heavies among the gypsies. Yet in Thomas Middleton's pamphlet about criminal culture entitled *The Black Book* (1604), which does not mention gypsies, the narrator speaks of "copper-captains" ("copper" being a generic term for coinage), those rogues in charge of stealing purses in such thoroughfares as Pauls's Walk (ed. G. B. Shand, in *The Collected Works of Thomas Middleton,* ed. Gary Taylor [Oxford: Clarendon Press, 2002, line 67). In Middleton and Dekker's play *The Roaring Girl* (1611), which is one of several popular texts about the notorious London criminal personality Mary Frith (a female-to-male transvestite, a rogue, a prostitute, and the ringleader of a gang of thieves), the words "Captaine" and "Upright Man" are used to denote the same or a similar position in the criminal sociopolitical hierarchy. Mary Frith appears as "Captaine Moll cutpurse" and Trapdoor as an "Upright Man," and there is no mention of gypsies (*Drama of the English Renaissance II: The Stuart Period,* ed. Russell A. Fraser and Norman Rabkin [New York: Macmillan, 1976]). I say "similar" because "Upright Man" is also used in this text, but only when referring to someone gendered male (e.g., at 5.1.156). In Shakespeare's *Two Gentleman of Verona* (1594), in which gypsies are not mentioned, the leader of the outlaws is referred to as "captain" (ed. Clifford Leech [London: Methuen, 1986], 4.1.65; 5.3.2). Hence "Captain" and "Upright Man" are used synonymously, or at least similarly, in representations of rogue-vagabond and gypsy culture. With its confluence of critical signifiers and signifieds, Jonson's use of "Captaine"—as well as the other functional names listed earlier, though they represent only a few of the numerous types cataloged—demonstrates the gypsy-rogue-vagabond cultural and semantic conflation in *The Gypsies Metamorphos'd;* the same terminology generally attributed to rogues and vagabonds is comfortably attributed to gypsies.

22. Jonson, *The Gypsies Metamorphos'd,* 123.

23. The primary source for this translation is the dictionary of cant in Harman's *A Caveat or Warening, For Commen Cursetors vulgarely called Vagabones.*

24. Jonson, The Gypsies Metamorphos'd, 157. Harman, *A Caveat or Warening,* 115; Dekker, *Lanthorne and Candle-Light,* 184; Richard Head and Francis Kirkman, *The English Rogue* (1665) (London: George Routledge & Sons, 1928), 32.

25. Thomas Middleton, *More Dissemblers Besides Women,* ed. John Jowett, in *The Collected Works of Thomas Middleton,* 4.2.58–59; 4.2.213.

26. Aydelotte, *Elizabethan Rogues and Vagabonds,* 18.

27. Okely, *The Traveller-Gypsies,* 8. Okely keenly elaborates on this problematic reasoning:

The Gypsiologists make the same mistakes as the nineteenth-century anthropologists in the general study of languages and racial distribution. Some believed in the notion of a united Indo-European race with a 'real' language of which many European and Asian forms were considered to be mere fragmentations. Similarly, Gypsy language and the "original culture" have been located as things once intact in India. It is assumed that Gypsies existed in India many centuries at as a "pure" group or separate society with language, customs and genetic structure hermetically sealed, until some "mysterious event" caused their departure from their mythical homeland. From then on they are said to have been "corrupted" in the course of migration and during contact with non-Gypsies. Thus any custom which seems strange to the Gorgio [non-Gypsy] observer is explained not in terms of its contemporary meaning to the group, but according to some "survival" from mythical ancient Indian days, or even the contemporary caste system. Any cultural similarity between Gypsy and Gorgio is explained away and denigrated as "contamination." . . . Paradoxically, there is very little evidence that Indian origin had been indicated or used by Gypsies until it was first given to them by Gorgio scholars (see Vesey-Fitzgerald 1973:16). Even today the title "Romany" is not generally interpreted at the local level as of Indian origin. The most frequent explanation which I was given by Gypsies was: "We're Romanies 'cos we always roam." (9–10, 12)

Okely concludes that there is not sufficient evidence, based on language or culture, for the gypsies' spatial or genealogical Indian origin, but that some linguistic forms, creole or pidgin, related to Sanskrit, and some Asian customs may have been transported or appropriated by people operating or traveling along the trade routes between East and West. In his book *Gypsies of Britain: An Introduction to Their History* (Newton Abbott, England: David & Charles, 1973), Brian Vesey-Fitzgerald does "not deny the Indian origin of the Gypsies" (11), insisting that "any attempt to establish the original home of the Gypsies by reference to their language is bound to fail, for the very simple reason that we have no knowledge of the dialects of India at the time the Gypsies left" (4).

28. To provide an example discussed in the next chapter, in Thomas Dekker's *O per se O* (1612), which is the sequel to his *Belman of London,* the Bellman recounts: "I once took one of them [members of criminal culture] into my service. . . . Of him I desired some knowledge in their gibberish, but he swore he could not cant, yet his rogueship seeing himself used kindly by me, would now and then shoot out a word of canting, and being thereupon asked why with oaths he denied it before, he told me that they are sworn never to disclose their skill in canting to any householder, for, if they do, the other maunderers or rogues mill them (kill them)" (*The Elizabethan Underworld,* ed. A. V. Judges [New York: E. P. Dutton, 1930], 367).

29. Beier, *Masterless Men,* 60.

30. Rid, *Martin Markall, Beadle of Bridewell,* 407.

31. Ibid., 420–21.

32. In his book *The English Gipsies and Their Language* (New York: Hurd & Houghton, 1873), Charles Leland records a Romany ("gypsy") language used in nineteenth-century England that he claims is entirely distinct from cant except for a few words. The language he records is structurally similar to English and cant in that it is an analytic language whose grammar depends heavily on the use of word order and function. Like cant it includes numerous English words, albeit mostly conjunctions, pronouns, and prepositions. Consider the following example provided by Leland:

"Savo's tute's rye?" putched a ryas mush of a Rommany chal. "I've dui ryas," pooked the Rommany chal: "Duvel's the yeck an' beng's the waver. Mandy kairs booti for the beng till I've lelled my yeckora habben, an' pallers mi Duvel pauli ajaw."

Translation:

"Who is your master?" asked a gentleman's servant of a Gypsy. "I've two masters," said the Gypsy: "God is the one, and the devil is the other. I work for the devil till I have got my dinner (one-o'clock food), and after that follow the Lord." (236)

Since there are similarities among many (but not all) of the languages spoken by gypsies throughout the world (they use some of the same words), some scholars have tried to concretize linguistically a connection between them and distinguish gypsies from other nomadic peoples. Hence the totalizing referent "Romany." But because their languages always include words from many different languages, sometimes the same languages, this is an extremely difficult argument to make (see Okely, *The Traveller-Gypsies,* 8–13). The language recorded by Leland may have been brought to England after the early modern period, it may be the language that cant developed into, or some combination of both.

33. T. W. Thompson, "Gleanings from Constables' Accounts and Other Sources," *Journal of the Gypsy Lore Society,* 3rd ser., 7, no. 1 (1928):30–48, 43. Idem, "Gypsy Marriage in England," *Journal of the Gypsy Lore Society,* 3rd ser., 5, no. 1(1927): 9–37; and "Gypsy Marriage in England," *Journal of the Gypsy Lore Society,* 3rd ser., 6, no. 4 (1927): 101–29, 151–82.

34. Two excellent books by Gypsiologists who, like Thompson, spent considerable time with England's gypsies are George Borrow's *The Romany Rye* (1837) (rpt. London: Dent, 1969) and John Sampson's *The Wind on the Heath* (London: Chatto and Windus, 1930).

35. Gamini Salgado, *The Elizabethan Underworld* (London: J. M. Dent, 1977), 152; Aydelotte, *Elizabethan Rogues and Vagabonds,* 116.

36. Aydelotte, *Elizabethan Rogues and Vagabonds,* 116.

37. Consider Robin Hood's representation within the magical world of the medieval Robin Hood ballads, such as "A Gest of Robyn Hode," "Robin Hood and the Monk," "Robin Hood's Death," and "Robin and Maid Marian," as well as his representation in such early modern plays by Anthony Munday (and Henry Chettle) as *The Downfall of Robert, Earl of Huntington* (1598) and *The Death of Robert, Earl of Huntington* (1598), in which he is depicted "positively" to the extent that he has the king's approval and friendship. If Cock Lorel aligned himself or had been aligned with the state like Robin Hood, perhaps there would be movies made about him today too.

38. Beier, *Masterless Men,* 60–61.

39. Salgado, *The Elizabethan Underworld,* 157.

40. McMullan, *The Canting Crew,* 96.

41. In *Jonson's Gypsies Unmasked* Randall also resists the evidence for "intermingling" between early modern England's gypsies and rogues and vagabonds: "One cannot imagine that there really was much intermingling between genuine gypsies and English rogues. Most gypsies are endogamous and have always felt quite removed from *Gorgios*" (51). It is interesting that he rationalizes this conclusion by anachronistically referring to the endogamy and feelings of present-day gypsies.

42. In the most thoroughly researched study of the history of gypsies in Eng-

land, Henry T. Crofton concludes: "The date of the first appearance of Gypsies in England is unknown" (5). Crofton points out that the first mention of gypsies in Great Britain is in Scotland's state papers: "1505, Apr.22. Item to the Egyptianis be the Kingis command, vij lib," and the earliest mention of gypsies in England is of a gypsy woman who practices palmistry in Thomas More's *A Dyalog of Syr Thomas More, knyght* (1514) ("Early Annals of the Gypsies in England," *Journal of the Gypsy Lore Society,* Third Series, 1, no. 1 (1888): 5–24.

43. See Eric Lott, *Love and Theft: Blackface Minstrelsy and the American Working Class* (New York: Oxford University Press, 1993).

44. Aydelotte, *Elizabethan Rogues and Vagabonds,* 18.

45. Beier, *Masterless Men,* 58.

46. For instance, Okely (*The Traveller-Gypsies,* 156) maintains:

My evidence suggests that the general prohibition against marriage with a Gorgio is a fundamental ideal. . . . Gypsies in England permit a small number of Gorgio-Gypsy marriages, provided the Gorgios repudiate their origins and adopt Gypsy values. Information on families in addition to those with whom I became closely acquainted also revealed a preponderance of marriages between two Gypsies rather than between a Gorgio and a Gypsy. Thus ethnic endogamy was both the ideal and the practice of the majority of traveling families who recognised themselves as Gypsies.

47. Thomas More, *A Dyalog of Syr Thomas More Knyghte* (1514), xci^r.

48. 22 Henry VIII, cap. 10, reprinted in Crofton, "Early Annals of the Gypsies in England," 9.

49. In "Early Annals of the Gypsies in England" Crofton cites two records indicating deportation of a number of gypsies (10–11).

50. Reprinted in Crofton, "Early Annals of the Gypsies in England," 10.

51. Salgado, *The Elizabethan Underworld,* 153.

52. Reprinted in Crofton, "Early Annals of the Gypsies in England," 12. Also reprinted in *Illustrations of British History, Biography, and Manners,* ed. Edmund Lodge (London: John Chidley, 1838), 165–66.

53. 1 and 2 Philip and Mary, cap. 4, cited in Crofton, "Early Annals of the Gypsies in England," 13; and 5 Elizabeth, cap. 20, in *Anno Quinto Reginae Elizabethe. At the Parliament Holden at Westmynster the.xii.of January . . . Were Enacted as Followeth* (1562).

54. Derbyshire order, cited in Beier, *Masterless Men,* 61.

55. *Anno Quinto Reginae Elizabethe. At the Parliament Holden at Westmynster the.xii.of January . . . Were Enacted as Followeth,* 55^r.

56. "Privy Council to London Aldermen" (20 June 1569) *Journal* 19, fol. 171 verso-172.

57. For Randall's view, see *Jonson's Gypsies Unmasked, 50–55.*

58. Salgado, *The Elizabethan Underworld,* 155.

59. 39 Elizabeth, cap. 4, in R. H. Tawney, *Tutor Economic Documents,* vol. 2 (London: Longmans, Green, 1924), 355. See also *Anno xxxix. Reginae Elizabethae. At the Parliament . . .* (1597), B6ᵛ.

60. Reprinted in Eric Otto Winstedt, "Early British Gypsies," *Journal of the Gypsy Lore Society,* n.s.,7, pt 1 (1913–14): 5–36, 8, 9, 11, 13, 15, 17.

61. Thompson, "Gleanings from Constables' Accounts and Other Sources," 37.

62. Salgado, *The Elizabethan Underworld,* 155.

63. Cited in Salgado, *The Elizabethan Underworld,* 155.

64. John Minsheu, *The Guide to Tongues* (1617), 16.

65. Beier, *Masterless Men,* 59.

66. Dekker, *Lanthorne and Candle-Light,* 236.

67. Aydelotte, *Elizabethan Rogues and Vagabonds,* 19; Salgado, *The Elizabethan Underworld,* 155.

68. Dekker, *Lanthorne and Candle-Light,* 236.

69. Jonson, *The Gypsies Metamorphos'd,* 155.

70. Pierre Bourdieu, *Language and Symbolic Power,* ed. John B. Thompson, trans.Gino Raymond and Matthew Adamson (Cambridge: Harvard University Press, 1991), 249.

71. Jonson, *The Gypsies Metamorphos'd,* 185.

72. *The Brave English Gypsy,* reprinted in *A Book of Roxburghe Ballads,* ed. John Payne Collier (London: Longman, Brown, Green, and Longmans, 1847), 184–85.

73. There has been much debate among Renaissance scholars over the authorship of the *The Spanish Gypsy.* Gary Taylor has decided not to include it in his *Collected Works of Thomas Middleton.* For my purposes it does not matter who wrote the play. What matters is that it was written in the 1620s and performed for Prince Charles. For citation purposes, I am using the following edition: Thomas Middleton, *The Spanish Gypsy,* in *The Works of Thomas Middleton,* ed. A. H. Bullen (Boston: Houghton, Mifflin, 1885).

74. For a detailed discussion of England's early modern racism and xenophobia, see Ian Archer's book *The Pursuit of Stability: Social Relations in Elizabethan London* (Cambridge: Cambridge University Press, 1991).

75. Jonson, *The Gypsies Metamorphos'd,* 203.

76. It is interesting that the aphetic "gypsy," with its absent letter *E,* which the *OED* maintains is a sixteenth-century English adaptation of the word "Egyptian," seems to indicate official culture's acknowledgment of the gypsy sign's uncertain and missing referent.

77. *The Spanish Gypsy,* 2.1.3.

78. Middleton, *More Dissemblers Besides Women,* 4.2.109–16.

79. In *A Caveat or Warening, For Commen Cursetors vulgarely called Vagabones,* Harman says about a wild rogue: "His grandfather was a beggar, his father was one, and he must be one by good reason" (79). In Ben Jonson's *Bartholomew Fair*

(1614), Humphrey Wasp declares: "How? I? I look like a cutpurse? Death! your sister's a cutpurse! and your mother and father and all your kin were cutpurses!" ((*Drama of the English Renaissance II: The Stuart Period*, ed. Russell A. Fraser and Norman Rabkin [New York: Macmillan, 1976]), II.6.152–54).

80. Anon., *The Brave English Gipsy*, 185.

81. Middleton, *More Dissemblers Besides Women*, 4.2.60–61, 77–81.

82. Reprinted in Thompson, "Gleanings from Constables' Accounts and Other Sources," 32–33.

83. *The Brave English Gipsy*, 185.

84. British Museum, MS. Lansdowne, 81, nos. 62 and 64.

85. In addition to the texts by Awdeley, Harman, Harrison, Rid, and Dekker already discussed, I am referring to Gilbert Walker, *A Manifest Detection of Diceplay* (1552), and William Fennor, *The Counter's Commonwealth* (1617) (both reprinted in Judges, ed., *The Elizabethan Underworld*) and Robert Greene, *A Notable Discovery of Coosnage* (1591), *The Black Book's Messenger* (1592), *The Second Part of Conny-Catching* (1592), *The Third Part of Conny-Catching* (1592), *A Disputation between a Hee-Conny-Catcher and a Shee-Conny-Catcher* (1592) (all reprinted in *Elizabethan and Jacobean Quartos,* ed. G. B. Harrison [Edinburgh: Edinburgh University Press, 1966]).

86. John Fletcher and Philip Massinger, *Beggars Bush,* ed. John H. Dorenkamp (The Hague: Mouton, 1967), 2.1.142–52.

87. To cite two examples, in *The Belman of London* Dekker writes about the community of rogues and vagabonds: "This is a *Ging* of good fellowes in whome there is more brotherhood: this is a *Crew* that is not the *Damned Crew,* (for they walke in Sattin) but this is the *Ragged Regiment: Villaines* they are by birth, *Varlets* by education, *Knaves* by profession, *Beggers* by the Statute, & *Rogues* by Act of Parliament. They are the idle *Drones* of a Countrie, the *Caterpillers* of a Common wealth, and the *ÆEgyptian* lice of a *Kingdome*" (81–82). In Brome's *A Jovial Crew* Sentwell declares, "But sir, we have taken with her such beggars, such rogues, / such vagabonds, and such hedge-birds (since you call 'em so) as you never knew, or heard of / though now the countries swarm with 'em under every hedge" (114).

88. John Taylor, *All The Workes Of John Taylor The Water Poet* (1630), ed. V. E. Neuberg (London: The Scholar Press, 1977), 96–98.

89. Richard Brome, *A Jovial Crew: or, The Merry Beggars,* ed. Ann Haaker (Lincoln: University of Nebraska Press, 1968), 35.

90. James Shirley, *The Sisters,* in *The Dramatic Works and Poems of James Shirley,* ed. William Gifford (London: John Murray, 1833), 361.

91. Awdeley, *The Fraternitye of Vacabondes,* 6.

92. Aydelotte, *Elizabethan Rogues and Vagabonds,* 20.

93. Harman, *A Caveat or Warening, For Commen Cursetors vulgarely called Vagabones* (1567), 94.

94. Beier, *Masterless Men*, 65. According to Beier, "When officials questioned couples closely they found about a third to be uncertainly wed: 11 of 35 in Wiltshire examinations, 1603–38; 18 of 56 in Leicester ones, 1584–1640" (65).

95. Dekker, *The Belman of London*, 101.

96. Middleton, *More Dissemblers Besides Women*, 4.2.167–70.

97. Dekker, *The Belman of London*, 107. The passage from which this quote ("without shame") is taken is quoted at length later in this chapter.

98. Head and Kirkman, *The English Rogue*, 27–28.

99. Fletcher and Massinger, *Beggars Bush*, 2.1.14–18.

100. Dekker, *O per se O*, 367.

101. Dekker, *The Belman of London*, 107.

102. Dekker, *Lanthorne and Candle-Light*, 239.

103. Dekker, *O per se O*, 378.

104. Jonson, *The Gypsies Metamorphos'd*, 123.

105. 2. Dekker, *O per se O*, 379.

106. For a discussion of the relationship between court masques, popular plays, and state power, see chapter 5.

107. Harman, *A Caveat or Warening, For Commen Cursetors vulgarely called Vagabones*, 64.

108. See Martin Ingram, *Church Courts, Sex and Marriage in England, 1570–1640* (Cambridge: Cambridge University Press, 1987).

109. Ian Archer, *The Pursuit of Stability: Social Relations in Elizabethan London* (Cambridge: Cambridge University Press, 1991), 204–5.

CHAPTER THREE

1. My comprehension of cant as what I call a "transversal language" is related to Gilles Deleuze and Félix Guattari's understanding of what they call "minor language." In *A Thousand Plateaus: Capitalism and Schizophrenia*, ed. and trans. Brian Massumi (Minneapolis: University of Minnesota Press, 1987), Deleuze and Guattari write:

Minor languages are characterized not by overload and poverty in relation to a standard or major language, but by a sobriety and variation that are like a minor treatment of the standard language, a becoming-minor of the major language. . . . Minor languages do not exist in themselves: they exist only in relation to a major language and are also investments of that language for the purpose of making it minor. . . . they are not simply sublanguages, idiolects or dialects, but potential agents of the major language's entering into a becoming-minoritarian of all of its dimensions and elements. We should distinguish between minor languages, the major language, and the becoming-minor of the major language. Minorities, of course, are objectively definable states, states of language, ethnicity, or sex with their own ghetto

territorialities, but they must also be thought of as seeds, crystals of becoming whose value is to trigger uncontrollable movements and deterrito-
rializations of the mean or majority. (104–6).

For Deleuze and Guattari a minor language depends on its power (*puissance*) to
variate the major language (what I call "official language"), and the major language
depends on its power (*pouvoir*) of constants. It is the job of the major language to
regulate and contain the productive mechanisms of variation of any minor language since they necessarily threaten the stability and territory of the major language. Deleuze and Guattari's idea of minor and major languages is based on their
view of the minor and the major as sociopolitical factors, such as identities, operations, and systems, which are always seen as of position and not essence, as com-
posites and not individual or total expressions, as fluid processes and not stagnant
or absolute states.

Accordingly, the terms "majority" and "minority" refer, respectively, to quali-
tative identifications of powerfulness and powerlessness rather than quantitative
identifications. Majority implies constancy of expression or content and sets the
standard measure for its own evaluation; when tested, the majority "appears twice,
once in the constant and again in the variable from which the constant is extracted"
(105). Specifically, Deleuze and Guattari write:

> When we say majority, we are referring not to a greater relative quantity but
> to the determination of a state or standard in relation to which larger quan-
> tities, as well as the smallest, can be said to be minoritarian: white-man,
> adult-male, etc. Majority implies a state of domination, not the reverse. It
> is not a question of knowing whether there are more mosquitoes or flies
> than men, but of knowing how "man" constituted a standard in the uni-
> verse in relation to which men necessarily (analytically) form a majority.
> (291)

Unlike the majority, with its system of constancy and homogeneity, minorities are
subsystems, with potential for heterogeneity, multiplicity, and becoming. As they
further explain:

> What defines a minority, then, is not the number but the relations internal
> to the number. A minority can be numerous, or even infinite; so can a ma-
> jority. What distinguishes them is that in the case of a majority the relation
> internal to the number constitutes a set that may be finite or infinite, but is
> always denumerable, whereas the minority is defined as a nondenumerable
> set, however many elements it may have. What characterizes the nondenu-
> merable is neither the set nor its elements; rather it is the *connection,* the
> "and" produced between elements, between sets, and which belongs to nei-
> ther, which eludes them and constitutes a line of flight. The axiomatic ma-
> nipulates only denumerable sets, even infinite ones, whereas the minorities
> constitute "fuzzy," nondenumerable, nonaxiomizable sets, in short,

"masses," multiplicities of escape and flux. . . . What is proper to the minority is to assert a power of the nondenumerable, even if that minority is composed of a single member. That is the formula for multiplicities. Minority as a universal figure, for becoming-everybody/everything (*devenir tout le monde*). Woman: we all have to become that, whether we are male or female. Nonwhite: we all have to become that, whether we are white, yellow, or black. (470)

As Deleuze and Guattari emphasize, "The problem is not the distinction between major and minor language, it is one of a becoming" (104). Thus, for the communicating subject undergoing becomings "it is a question not of reterritorializing oneself on a dialect or a patois but of deterritorializing the major language" (104). For instance, "Black Americans do not oppose Black to English, they transform the American English that is their own language into Black English" (104–5). In other words, black Americans, especially urban blacks, blend American English with and adapt it to their own vocabulary and grammar such that American English loses much of its power over and access into the community of black Americans that speaks a given form of black English. In effect, this community of black Americans is escaping the linguistic jurisdiction of the majority; they are deterritorializing the major language from their conceptual space and have begun their own minoritarian becoming of something other than what the state has prescribed. Their own language provides them with exclusivity, privacy, and protection against many of the state's mechanisms of subjugation and surveillance. It provides them with their own emotional, intellectual, and political territory, their own communicative domain. But black English also disempowers those who use it, especially in conventional circumstances, unless they can also speak standardized English. As I shall demonstrate, the situation for early modern England's criminal culture and cant was like that of black Americans and black English, with the important difference that cant was a more developed and standardized language that was deliberately invented by criminal culture for social *and* professional (criminal) purposes. Whereas black English is the language of some "criminals," it is used predominantly by a population that is discriminated against and criminalized because of its dark skin color.

For more on Deleuze and Guattari's theory of "minor literature," see their book *Kafka: Toward a Minor Literature,* trans. Dana Polan (Minneapolis: University of Minnesota Press, 1986).

2. Robert Hodge and Gunther Kress, *Social Semiotics* (Ithaca: Cornell University Press, 1988). See also Michael Halliday, *Language as Social Semiotic* (London: Edward Arnold, 1978), 164–82.

3. Hodge and Kress, *Social Semiotics,* 68.

4. I say "vernacular multilingualism" because the state did encourage multilingualism involving English and the classical languages taught in schools.

5. For a discussion of the rise of standard English, see Albert C. Baugh and Thomas Cable, *A History of the English Language* 3rd ed. (Englewood Cliffs, N.J.: Prentice-Hall, 1978), esp. 189–96.

6. 27 Henry 8, quoted in Bowen 75. *The Statutes of Wales,* ed. Ivor Bowen (London, 1908). For a thorough discussion of the early modern English debate over linguistic variety, see Richard F. Jones's groundbreaking study *The Triumph of the English Language* (Stanford, Calif.: Stanford University Press, 1966).

7. For accounts of England's immense growth, see Norman G. Brett-James, *The Growth of Stuart London* (London: George Allen & Unwin, 1935); Carl Bridenbaugh, *Vexed and Troubled Englishmen, 1590–1642* (New York: Oxford University Press, 1976); and A. L. Beier, *Masterless Men: The Vagrancy Problem in England, 1560–1640* (London: Methuen, 1985).

8. Steven Mullaney, *The Place of the Stage: License, Play, and Power in Renaissance England* (Chicago: University of Chicago Press, 1988), 78. See also Baugh and Cable, *A History of the English Language,* and Thomas Pyles and John Algeo, *The Origins and Development of the English Language,* 3rd ed. (New York: Harcourt Brace Jovanovich, 1982).

9. Among the participants were Richard Carew, Robert Cawdrey (author of *Table Alphabetical* [1604], the first English dictionary), Sir John Cheke, Samuel Daniel, Sir Thomas Elyot (author of *The Governor* [1531], the first book on English education), Thomas Nashe, Richard Mulcaster, George Pettie, George Puttenham, Sir Philip Sidney, and Thomas Wilson. Contributions to the debate by all of these writers are anthologized in *Education in Tudor and Stuart England,* ed. David Cressy (London: Edward Arnold, 1975).

10. For example, in *Vexed and Troubled Englishmen* Bridenbaugh documents that "something approaching a 'system' of education [for girls as well as boys] began during the reign of Edward VI" and continued to develop throughout the early modern period. He maintains that this happened not only because "strong support for better elementary schools came from the puritan clergy" as well as from the court but also because of the enforcement of laws regulating who had the authority to teach and what was taught (as in the Canons of 1604) (311, 339). Bridenbaugh found that "in hundreds of little rule parishes between 1590 and 1640, petty schools, or 'petties,' were established" and "in the towns and cities, greater endowments and benefactions enabled the civil authorities to make better provision for elementary education" (318–19). I am grateful to one of the anonymous readers of my manuscript for pointing out that a main reason for an increase in grammar schools was mercantile. The guilds established the schools, using dissolved monasteries and chantries for buildings, to teach people how to keep business records and conduct business correspondence. See also Sandra Clark, *The Elizabethan Pamphleteers: Popular Moralistic Pamphlets, 1580–1640* (London: Athlone Press, 1983), 19–21; David Cressy, *Literacy and the Social Order: Reading and Writ-*

ing in Tudor and Stuart England (Cambridge: Cambridge University Press, 1980), 25, and *Education in Tudor and Stuart England,* 9; and Joan Simon, *Education and Society in Tudor England* (Cambridge: Cambridge University Press, 1966), 291–97.

11. While my use of the term "recording" is inspired by Stephen Greenblatt's in his article "Invisible Bullets: Renaissance Authority and Its Subversion, *Henry IV* and *Henry V,*" in *Political Shakespeare: New Essays in Cultural Materialism,* ed. Jonathan Dollimore and Alan Sinfield (Ithaca: Cornell University Press, 1985), my understanding of the term is less one-sided and definite. For Greenblatt recording is a tactic employed only by mechanisms of hegemonic power for the purpose of consolidating that power: "I have called *recording,* a mode that culminates for Harriot in a glossary, the beginnings of an Algonkian-English dictionary, designed to facilitate further acts of recording and hence to consolidate English power in Virginia" (32). Greenblatt's understanding of recording does not take into consideration the impact that the process of recording might have on the recorder(s) and the recording culture. Through the intellectual and social engagement that the recording process necessitates, the ideology of the recorded culture is further disseminated. Recording thus requires, to some degree, the intervention of alternative ideas.

12. While all of the dictionaries include words cataloged by Thomas Harman in *A Caveat or Warening, For Commen Cursetors vulgarely called Vagabones* (1567), only Dekker's dictionary in *Lanthorne and Candle-Light* (1608) does not expand on it. However, throughout *The Belman of London* (1608), *Lanthorne and Candle-Light* (1608), and *O per se O* (1612), Dekker does discuss many cant words and phrases not included by Harman. Bibliographical information for the anonymously authored texts is as follows: *Street Robberies consider'd* (London: J. Roberts, n.d.) and *The Catterpillers of this Nation anatomized* (London: Printed for M. H. at the Princes Armes, in Chancery-lane, 1659).

13. For other accounts of the life of Mary Frith, see the anonymous pamphlet *The Life and Death of Mrs Mary Frith commonly called Moll Cutpurse* (1612), Nathan Field's play *Amends for Ladies, with the Merry Prankes of Moll Cutpurse* (1618), John Taylor's poem "The Water Comorant," and *The Consistory of London Correction Book* (1605). For criticism on *The Roaring Girl,* a good place to start is Marjorie Garber, "The Logic of the Transvestite," in *Staging the Renaissance: Reinterpretations of Elizabethan and Jacobean Drama,* ed. David Scott Kastan and Peter Stallybrass (New York: Routledge, 1991), 221–34; see also Coppélia Kahn's critical introduction to *The Roaring Girl* in *The Collected Works of Thomas Middleton,* ed. Gary Taylor (Oxford: Clarendon Press, 2002).

14. As noted by Dekker in *The Belman of London,* "An *Upright-man* is a sturdy *big bonde knave,* that never walkes but (like a *Commander*) with a short troncheon [a cudgel] in his hand, which hee cals his *Filchman*" (90).

15. Dekker and Middleton, *The Roaring Girl,* 5.1.220.

16. Bruce Smith, *The Acoustic World of Early Modern England* (Chicago: University of Chicago Press, 1999), 46.

17. While Halliday does not analyze cant, he does give it as an example of an antilanguage.

18. It is important to note that my account of cant is limited by the fact that it was secretive and coded, that it was primarily a spoken language, and that my access to it is only by way of literary texts written by people who were familiar with criminal culture to varying degrees.

19. See Pierre Bourdieu, *Language and Symbolic Power* (Cambridge, Mass.: Harvard University Press, 1991), esp. 229–51. Consider the following example given by Bourdieu: "The possession of a talent for being 'the life and soul of the party,' capable of incarnating, at the cost of a conscious and constant labor of research and accumulation, the ideal of the 'funny guy' which crowns an approved form of sociability, is a very precious form of capital" (99).

20. David Crystal, *An Encyclopedic Dictionary of Language and Languages* (London: Penguin Books, 1994), 28, 263. Examples of natural languages are English, French, Japanese, Russian—basically any language used socially, standardized, and passed down generationally. Examples provided by Crystal of recent artificial languages include Ido (1907), which is a modified version of Esperanto (its name means "derived from" in Esperanto), and Glosa (1981), which is a modified version of Interglossa (invented by Lancelot Hogben in 1943) containing a basic thousand-word vocabulary.

21. Dekker, *Lanthorne and Candle-Light,* 182–83. Also in Harman, *A Caveat or Warening, For Commen Cursetors vulgarely called Vagabones,* 117.

22. In *Pidgin & Creole Languages* (London: Longman, 1988), Suzanne Romaine differentiates between analytic and synthetic languages: "A language which is analytic in structure indicates syntactic relations by means of function words and word order as opposed to synthetic languages, where such formal relationships are expressed by the combination of elements (e.g. prefixes, suffixes and infixes) with the base or stem word. The structure of words in an analytical language is morphologically simple, but complex in a synthetic language" (28).

23. Despite the frequent, flippant, nominal attribution of cant to a language called "pedlars French" in early modern England's popular literature, such as Dekker's *Belman of London* (83) and *Lanthorne and Candle-Light* (179) and Harrison's *Description of England* (184), examples of cant recorded in this literature bear little resemblance to the French language, certainly less resemblance, generally speaking, to French than to early modern English. As I have noted, the fact that the word "French" was used generically and arbitrarily for purposes of derogation during the period may explain the coinage "pedlars French." In *Lanthorne and Candle-Light* Dekker lists some of the words that cant borrowed from Latin: "As for example, they call a cloake (in the *canting* tongue) a *Togeman,* and in Latin, *Toga*

signifies a gowne, or an upper. *Pannam* is bread: and *Panis* in Lattin is likewise read, *cassan* is cheese, and is a worde barbarously coyne out of the substantive *caseus* which also signifies cheese. And so of others" (180).

24. For instance, in *An Encyclopedic Dictionary of Language and Languages* Crystal defines "dialect" as "a language variety in which the use of grammar and vocabulary identifies the regional or social background of the user" (101).

25. *Oxford English Dictionary*, ed. H. W. Fowler (Oxford: Clarendon Press, 1949).

26. Head and Kirkman, *The English Rogue*, 29. Emphasis added.

27. Brome, *A Jovial Crew*, 61. Emphasis added.

28. *The Book of John Fisher, Town Clerk and Deputy Recorder of Warwick, 1580–1588* (Warwick: Henry T. Cooke, n.d.), 28.

29. Essex Record Office, Q/SR 113/40a, cited in Lee Beier, "Anti-language or Jargon? Canting in the English Underworld in the Sixteenth and Seventeenth Centuries," in *Languages and Jargons: Contributions to a Social History of Language*, ed. Peter Burke (Cambridge: Polity Press, 1995), 71.

30. Harman, *A Caveat or Warening, For Commen Cursetors vulgarely called Vagabones*, 65.

31. Ibid., 113–14.

32. Kent County Archives Office, QM/SB 643–44, cited in Lee Beier, "Anti-language or Jargon? Canting in the English Underworld in the Sixteenth and Seventeenth Centuries," 71.

33. Pyles and Algeo, *The Origins and Development of the English Language*, 235–36. In *An Encyclopedic Dictionary of Language and Languages* Crystal defines "slang" as "informal, nonstandard vocabulary, usually intelligible only to people from a particular region or social group; also, the jargon of a special group, such as doctors, cricketers, or sailors. Its chief function is to mark social identity—to show that one belongs—but it may also be used just to be different, to make an effect, or to be informal. Such 'in-group' language is subject to rapid change" (355–56).

34. Dekker and Middleton, *The Roaring Girl*, 5.1.195–96.

35. For instance, Shakespeare uses the word "filch" in the following plays: *The Merry Wives of Windsor* (1.3.28), *Henry V* (3.2.48), *A Midsummer Night's Dream* (1.1.36), and *Othello* (3.3.159, 3.3.315).

36. Suzanne Romaine, *Language in Society: An Introduction to Sociolinguistics* (New York: Oxford University Press, 1994), 169–70.

37. Crystal, *An Encyclopedic Dictionary of Language and Languages*, 200–201.

38. Dekker, *Lanthorne and Candle-Light*, 179.

39. William Fletewoode, Letter to Lord Burghley (7 July 1585) in *Tudor Economic Documents*, 3 vols., ed. R. H. Tawney and Eileen Power (London: Longman, 1924), 2:337–38.

40. Fletewoode, Letter to Lord Burghley, 339.

41. One might also consider whether cant is a pidgin or creole. To answer this question, we must turn to pidgin and creole studies. In this field, attempts to define the terms "pidgin" and "creole" are made cautiously. For my purposes, I am following Suzanne Romaine and Peter Mühlhäusler, who, in their respective studies on pidgin and creole languages, do not rely on a single or absolute definition of the terms "pidgin" and "creole" but instead consider the definitions most often maintained by sociolinguists. However, there is much more definitional debate over pidgins than creoles. As documented by Mühlhäusler in *Pidgin & Creole Linguistics* (Oxford: Blackwell, 1986), sociolinguists generally agree that "creoles are defined as pidgin languages (second languages) that have become the first language of a new generation of speakers" (6). For this reason I prefer to analyze cant primarily in light of the pervasive definitions of pidgins, and only in the process will I consider the possibility that cant was a creole language. I will briefly compare cant to two much-studied English-based pidgins. One, called Tok Pisin (Talk Pidgin), is spoken in Papua New Guinea. It is an expanded pidgin. "An expanded pidgin," as Romaine says, "has a complex grammar, a developing word formation, and an increase in speech tempo" (*Pidgin & Creole Languages,* 138). The other is not considered an expanded pidgin. It is spoken in Nigeria and is referred to as Nigerian Pidgin English. The following example of Tok Pisin is cited in Loreto Todd, *Pidgins and Creoles* (London: Routledge, 1990):

Na Jon i save putim klos ol i bin wokim long gras bilong kamel, na em i pasim let long namel bilong en; na em i save kaikai grasop wantaim hani bilong bus. (In English: "And Jon was clothed with camel's hair, and with a girdle of skin about his loins; and he did eat locusts and honey.") (12; Todd's translation)

The following example of Nigerian Pidgin English is cited in Romaine, *Language in Society*:

Dem come take night carry di wife, go give di man. (In English: "They came at night, got the wife and gave her to her husband.") (176; Romaine's translation)

These examples contain many of the crucial defining characteristics for pidgins upheld by most sociolinguists.

According to Peter Bakker, "Pidgins are always simplified compared to the lexifier language, as is apparent in their loss of morphology and their more analytic structure. . . . Also, there have to be two or more language groups who use the pidgin." "Pigeons," in *Pigeons and Creoles: An Introduction,* ed. Jacques Arends, Pieter Muysken, and Norval Smith (Amsterdam: John Benjamins, 1995), 26). Tok Pisin's simplification is evinced by its extreme loss of morphology, such as in the absence of inflectional morphology in the phrase "i save putim klos ol i bin" ("was clothed") and by its dependence on circumlocution, which, as Crystal puts it, occurs when "more words than necessary are used to express a meaning." (*An Ency-clopedic Dictionary of Language and Languages,* 64). For instance, the first clause uses fourteen words ("Na Jon i save putim klos ol i bin wokim long gras bilong kamel") to express what can be said with seven words in English ("And Jon was clothed with camel's hair"). English is Tok Pisin's superstrate, lexifier language, which means that it is the official language from which Tok Pisin draws most of its vocabulary and structure. Tok Pisin's almost total lack of inflectional morphology and subsequent enhanced syntactic, analytic structure contributes to its status as an expanded pidgin. The resultant developing word formation (derivational morphology) and complex grammar are exemplified by its use of combined words (such as "putim" for "put them") and word multifunctionality (as with its use of only two prepositional forms, "long" and "bilong," to indicate all grammatical relations). That Nigerian Pidgin English is not expanded can be seen in its greater dependence on English words, however adapted contextually, and its comparatively less complex grammatical structure. For instance, consider its substantially less elaborate use of circumlocution and obvious subject-verb-object construction in the clause "Dem come take night" ("They came at night"). Nevertheless, Nigerian Pidgin English's loss of inflectional morphology—as in "come take" for "came," "carry" for "got," and "go give" for "gave"—and subsequent enhanced analytic structure are very apparent.

Cant does not meet Bakker's criteria for a pidgin. It was neither morphologically simpler (consider "bing" for "goe" and "beng" for "come") nor more complexly analytically structured than English, its lexifier language. In fact, as in the example provided by Dekker, cant's overall grammatical structure was for the most part syntactically and morphologically identical to English. For instance, its word economy (as seen in its lack of circumlocution) and word order (its typical subject-verb-object sentence construction) were the same in English. Furthermore, there is no evidence that "two or more language groups" used cant, as there is with Tok Pisin and Nigerian Pidgin English. Thus, the only significant, immediate major-language influence on cant is that of English, which was early modern England's superstrate and official language.

Loreto Todd's and David DeCamp's definitions of pidgins are similar. According to Todd, "a *pidgin* is a marginal language which arises to fulfil certain restricted communication needs among people who have no common language. In the initial stages of contact the communication is often limited to transactions where a detailed exchange of ideas is not required and where a small vocabulary, drawn almost exclusively from one language, suffices" (*Pigeons and Creoles,* 1–2). According to DeCamp, a pidgin is a "contact vernacular, normally not the name language of any of its speakers . . . characterized by a limited vocabulary, an elimination of many grammatical devices such as number and gender, and a drastic reduction of redundant features ("The Study of Pidgin and Creole Languages," in *Pidginization and Creolization of Languages,* ed. Dell Hymes [Cambridge: Cambridge University Press, 1971], 15). Cant was not used, as Todd says of pidgins, for "restricted communication needs among people who have no common language." As was shown earlier, the range in which cant was used was not restricted and was typically used by people who also spoke English and needed to speak English for criminal purposes, especially when perpetrating cons. It may have been the case that some speakers of cant, such as those who were born into criminal culture (called "clapperdudgeons"), were more proficient in cant than in English. But, as was just mentioned, it is very unlikely that they only spoke cant since criminal culture existed and operated in, indeed, necessarily interacted with, a predominantly English-speaking society. The fact that there were first-language speakers of cant, combined with the fact that cant was a community language, might imply that cant was a creole. The following statement on the nature of creole languages by Charles-James Bailey and K. Maroldt is representative of pidgin and creole scholars: "A creole is the result of mixing ["of two or more languages"] which is substantial enough to result in a new system, a system that is separate from its antecedent parent system" ("The French Lineage of English," in *Pidgins—Creoles—Languages in Contact,* ed. Jürgen Meisel [Tübingen: Narr, 1977], 21). However, since cant's linguistic system (its grammatical structure) is consistent with that of English, "its antecedent parent system," it cannot be considered a creole.

If one considers only the neologistic canting vocabulary recorded by early modern writers, such as the two hundred and fifty words provided by Head and Kirkman (*The English Rogue,* 24–34), then it would be considered "small" or "limited" like the vocabulary of pidgins. But if the great degree to which cant used English words is also considered, than the canting vocabulary could not be considered small or limited. (Harman claims that the canting language is "half mingled with English when it is familiarly talked" [*A Caveat or Warening, For Commen Cursetors vulgarely called Vagabones,* 114]). Moreover, one must keep in mind that cant was a secret language; thus, it is unlikely, if not "impossible" (as Dekker admits in the introduction to his "Canters Dictionarie"), for the vocabulary recorded in the period's popular literature to be complete (*Lanthorne and Candle-Light,* 181, 183). We can speculate from the widespread, multifunctional use of cant that its vocabulary was large—certainly over nine hundred words, which is the average size of a pidgin (Romaine, *Language in Society,* 181). In fact, Beier's investigation revealed that 1,218 cant words were recorded during the sixteenth and seventeenth centuries, none of which were included by lexicographers in the first five English-language dictionaries published between 1604 and 1658 ("Anti-language or Jargon? Canting in the English Underworld in the Sixteenth and Seventeenth Centuries," 75).

DeCamp's stipulations about grammatical devices apply—albeit sketchily because the stipulations themselves are sketchy—to Tok Pisin and Nigeria Pidgin

English but certainly not to cant. For instance, Tok Pisin's lack or reduction of number, gender, and redundant features (this usually refers to syntactical features) can be seen, respectively, in the previousuly cited example's use of the noninflected phrase "kaikai grasop" for "locusts," the pronoun "em" for "he" (as Todd points out, "em" means "he," "she" or "it," depending on context [*Pidgins and Creoles,* 15]), and in the general absence of prefixes, suffixes, and infixes. Cant, on the other hand, regularly uses number, gender, and redundant features.

Unlike the definitions just considered, John Holm's definition directly addresses issues of social power:

> A *pidgin* is a reduced language that results from extended contact between groups of people with no language in common; it evolves when they need some means of verbal communication, perhaps for trade, but no group learns the native language of any other group for social reasons that may include lack of trust or of close contact. Usually those with less power (speakers of *substrate* languages) are more accommodating and use words from the language of those with more power (the *superstrate*), although the meaning, form, and use of these words may be influenced by the substrate languages" (*Pigeons and Creoles, vol. 1, Theory and Structure* [Cambridge: Cambridge University Press, 1988], 4–5).

English is the superstrate language for Tok Pisin and Nigerian Pidgin English because Papua New Guinea and Nigeria were colonized by the English. These languages did evolve to meet the "need [for] some means of communication . . . between groups of people with no language in common." As in Holm's definition, Tok Pisin and Nigerian Pidgin English did not arise for "social reasons." Whereas English was also the superstrate language for cant, cant was not derivative of English; it did not evolve to meet the need for a means of verbal communication between groups with no common language.

42. In "Anti-language or Jargon? Canting in the English Underworld in the Sixteenth and Seventeenth Centuries," Lee Beier argues that cant was not "an anti-language serving an anti-society" (92), but rather a jargon, "a learned vocabulary and a tool of the trades of thieving and begging" (73). But since Beier does not define the term "anti-language," it is difficult to comprehend the import of his conclusion.

43. Harman is undoubtedly one of Harrison's primary sources. In *A Caveat or Warening, For Commen Cursetors vulgarely called Vagabones* Harman notes that cant is a recently invented language: "As far as I can learn or understand by the examination of a number of them [the criminals], their language—which they term pedlars' French or canting—began but within these thirty years, little above; and that the first inventor thereof was hanged, all save the head; for that is the final end of them all, or else to die of some filthy and horrible diseases" (64).

44. Ibid., 114.

45. It is curious that Dekker links cant and criminal culture to "Civill Warre" thirty-four years before it happened.

46. For a discussion of the educational function of prisons, see E. D. Pendry, "The Idea of a Prison," *Elizabethan Prisons and Prison Scenes,* 2 vols. (Salzburg: Institut für Anglistik und Amerikanistik, 1974), 264–85.

47. Awdeley, *The Fraternitye of Vacabondes* (1561), 280.

48. Harrison argues that Cuthbert Cunny-catcher was not a pseudonym for Robert Greene but rather for one of his enemies.

49. In *Martin Markall, Beadle of Bridewell,* Rid provides a history of gypsy-rogue-vagabond culture in which he describes the merging of two criminal factions: the rogues "calling themselves by the name of Egyptians" and the "Catalogue of Vagabonds, or Quartern of Knaves, called the five-and-twenty orders of knaves" (420).

50. For instance, see Harman, *A Caveat or Warening, For Commen Cursetors vulgarely called Vagabones,* 64–65, 113–17.

51. To cite two examples, in the *The Belman of London* Dekker writes about the community of rogues and vagabonds: "This is a *Ging* of good fellowes in whome there is more brotherhood: this is a *Crew* that is not the *Damned Crew,* (for they walke in Sattin) but this is the *Ragged Regiment: Villaines* they are by birth, *Varlets* by education, *Knaves* by profession, *Beggers* by the Statute, & *Rogues* by Act of Parliament. They are the idle *Drones* of a Countrie, the *Caterpillers* of a Common wealth, and the *ÆEgyptian* lice of a *Kingdome*" (81–82). In Brome's *A Jovial Crew* Sentwell declares, "But sir, we have taken with her such beggars, such rogues, / such vagabonds, and such hedge-birds (since you call 'em so) as you never knew, or heard of, though now the countries swarm with 'em under every hedge" (114).

52. The translations are from Harman's *A Caveat or Warening, For Commen Cursetors vulgarely called Vagabones,* 114–15. Emphasis added.

CHAPTER FOUR

1. I have borrowed the following terms: "differential space" from Henri Lefebvre, *The Production of Space,* trans. Donald Nicholson-Smith (Oxford: Blackwell, 1993), esp. 50–60, 352–400; "discursive ruptures" from Michel Foucault, *The Archeology of Knowledge,* trans. A. M. Sheridan Smith (New York: Pantheon Books, 1972); "out-of-field" from Gilles Deleuze, *Cinema 1: The Movement-Image,* trans. Hugh Tomlinson and Barbara Habberjam (Minneapolis: University of Minnesota Press, 1996), esp. 15–19; and "place-image" from Rob Shields, *Places on the Margin: Alternative Geographies of Modernity* (London: Routledge, 1991), esp. 60–61. My term " wilderness effects" is derived from the term "frontier effects" in Michael Keith and Steve Pile's essay "The Place of Politics," in *Place in the Politics of Identity,* ed. Michael Keith and Steve Pile (London: Routledge, 1993), 22–41. To vary-

ing degrees, I have adapted the meanings and functions of these terms to suit my purposes and assume full responsibility for any pitfalls.

2. See the chapter entitled "Laws Against Vagabonds" in Aydelotte, *Elizabethan Rogues and Vagabonds,* 56–75; Sharpe, *Crime in Early Modern England 1550–1750,* 99–111; and the chapter entitled "State Policy: From *Utopia* to the Penal Colony" in Beier, *Masterless Men,* 146–69.

3. Beier, *Masterless Men,* 149.

4. 22 Henry VIII, c. 12; reprinted in Aydelotte, *Elizabethan Rogues and Vagabonds,* 142–45.

5. 20 June 1569. *Journal* 19, fol. 171 verso-172; reprinted in Aydelotte, *Elizabethan Rogues and Vagabonds,* 153.

6. As was documented in the section of chapter 3 entitled "Dissent Cultural Functionality," this phrase refers to a ceremony in which a person was anointed with liquor or ale and made an authentic member of a specific criminal cultural group, as well as criminal culture in general.

7. 20 June 1569. *Journal* 19, fol. 171 verso-172; reprinted in Aydelotte, *Elizabethan Rogues and Vagabonds,* 153.

8. Beier, *Masterless Men,* 143.

9. Awdeley, *The Fraternitye of Vacabondes,* 5. In MS. Lansdowne 81, No. 64 in the British Museum there is a forged passport that was used by a vagabond to travel from Cumberland to Somerset, where he was apprehended; it is reproduced in Aydelotte, *Elizabethan Rogues and Vagabonds,* between pages 40 and 41.

10. Essex Record Office (Q/SR 79/92); cited in Beier, 143–144.

11. Dekker, *O per se O,* 374.

12. Beier, *Masterless Men,* 142.

13. Robert Copland, *The Highway to the Spital-House,* in *The Elizabethan Underworld: A Collection of Tudor and Early Stuart Tracts and Ballads,* ed. A. V. Judges (London: E. P. Dutton, 1930), 1–26, 4, 13, 9.

14. 22 Henry VIII, c. 12; reprinted in Aydelotte, *Elizabethan Rogues and Vagabonds,* 142–45.

15. 22 Henry VIII, cap. 10; rpt. in Crofton, "Early Annals of the Gypsies in England," 9.

16. Rid, *Martin Markall, Beadle of Bridewell,* 420–21.

17. *27 Henry 8 in The Statutes of Wales,* ed. Ivor Bowen (London, 1908), 75.

18. Awdeley, *The Fraternitye of Vacabondes,* 9–10.

19. Harman, *A Caveat or Warening, For Commen Cursetors vulgarely called Vagabones,* 66–67.

20. Greene, *A Notable Discovery Coosnage,* 30–31.

21. Dekker, *The Belman of London,* 89.

22. Samuel Rid, *The Art of Juggling,* in *Rogues, Vagabonds, and Sturdy Beggars,* ed. Arthur F. Kinney (Amherst: University of Massachusetts Press, 1990): 261–93,

275. This assertion is copied almost verbatim from Gilbert Walker's *A Manifest Detection of Dice-play* (1552), 44. Apparently Rid thought the information on conycatching supplied by Walker still topical and worth repeating.

23. John Taylor, "The Beggar," in *All The Workes Of John Taylor The Water Poet* (1630; rpt. London: The Scholar Press, 1977), 99.

24. Dekker, *Lanthorne and Candle-Light*, 165.

25. Deleuze, *Cinema 1: The Movement-Image*, 8.

26. Middleton, *The Black Book* (Epistle), ll. 27–28.

27. Dekker, *Lanthorne and Candle-Light*, 164.

28. Among the texts about or that refer to criminals in rural regions are the following: *The Life and Death of Gamaliel Ratsey a famous thief, of England, Executed at Bedford the 26 of March last past* (1605) and *Ratseis Ghost. Or the Second Part of his madde Prankes and Robberies* (1605) ed. S. H. Atkins, Shakespeare Association Facsimiles, no. 10 (London, 1935).

29. 8 Elizabeth, c. 4 (1566); reprinted in Aydelotte, *Elizabethan Rogues and Vagabonds*, 110.

30. For documentation of the criminality that occurred in these areas, see John McMullan, "Criminal Areas," *The Canting Crew*, 52–77.

31. Greene, *The Second Part of Conny-Catching*, 30.

32. Greene, *The Third Part of Conny-Catching*, 42.

33. Greene, *A Notable Discovery of Coosnage*, 18.

34. Hutton, *The Black Dog of Newgate*, 279.

35. Dekker, *The Belman of London*, 48. Dekker elaborates on cutpurses and pickpockets:

> You must understand likewise, that both of *Nips* and *Foists* there are two sortes, for there be City *Nips* and country *Nips,* whose office is to haunt nothing but *Faires:* these country *Nips* never come into London to doe any peece of service, but at *Bartholmewtide* onely. . . . There are also women *Foists* and *Nips* as well as men, but farre more dangerous then the men: All the troopes of both *sexes* beeing subject to the discipline of the *Grand Nips* and *Foists,* and from whom, the better to receive directions both what to doe, and what quarters to keepe (for they shift their walkes according to the pleasure of the cheefe *Rangers*) they have a certaine house, sometimes at one end of the towne sometimes at another, which is their hall; at this Hall the whole company do meete very orderly. (149–50)

36. Barry, *Ram-Alley,* I3, E2.

37. Middleton and Dekker, *The Roaring Girl,* 3.3.33–35.

38. Rid, *The Art of Juggling,* 280. This is presumably a reference to the same Cuthbert Cony-catcher who authored *The Defense of Cony-Catching* (1592). In a textual note Arthur Kinney suggests that Rid uses Cuthbert as a generic term for conycatcher (311).

39. For more on Paul's, see William Simpson, *Gleanings from old St. Paul's* (London: E. Stock, 1889), and Maria Hackett, *A Popular Description of St. Paul's Cathedral* (London: J. B. Nichols and Son, 1828).

40. Walker, *A Manifest Detection of Dice-play,* 28.

41. Greene, *The Second Part of Cony-Catching,* 31.

42. Middleton, *The Black Book,* ll. 551–58.

43. Westminster Abbey is similarly represented. For example, in *The Second Part of Cony-Catching,* Greene writes: "But againe, to the places of resort, westminster, I marry, that is their chiefest place that brings in their profite, the tearm-time is their haruest" (32).

44. Greene, *The Third Part of Cony-Catching,* 21.

45. John Earle, *Micro-cosmography,* quoted in Judges, *The Elizabethan Underworld,* 495.

46. Among the more prominent antitheatricalist tracts are Stephan Gosson, *The Schoole of Abuse* (1579; rpt. London: Shakespeare Society, 1853); William Rankins, *A Mirrour of Monsters* (London, 1588); John Rainoldes, *Th' Overthrow of Stage-Playes* (London, 1600); John Greene, *A Refutation of the Apology for Actors* (London, 1615); William Prynne, *Histrio-mastix: The Player's Scourge or Actor's Tragedy* (1633; rpt. New York: Garland, 1974).

47. Greene, *The Second Part of Cony-Catching,* 30.

48. Dekker, *The Belman of London,* 148.

49. Wheatley and Cunningham, *London Past and Present,* i, 112

50. See the section entitled "The Disguise Factor."

51. Copland, *The Highway to the Spital-House,* 7.

52. For an official reference, see the 1567 ordinance quoted at the beginning of this chapter.

53. Harman, *A Caveat or Warening, For Commen Cursetors vulgarely called Vagabones,* 83.

54. In *A Caveat or Warening, For Commen Cursetors vulgarely called Vagabones* Harman gives a fascinating account of a notorious counterfeit crank named Nicholas Jennings who pretended to be an epileptic beggar in one town while he lived comfortably in another (86–90).

55. Dekker, *Lanthorne and Candle-Light,* 238.

56. John Taylor, "A Whore," in *All The Workes Of John Taylor The Water Poet,* 106.

57. Stephan Gosson, *Playes Confuted in Fiue Actions* (London, 1582), D5^v; E5.

58. [G. Ratsey], *The Life and Death of Gamaliel Ratsey a famous thief, of England, Executed at Bedford the 26 of March last past* (1605) and *Ratseis Ghost. Or the Second Part of his madde Prankes and Robberies* (1605), A4.

59. Dekker, *The Belman of London,* 80.

60. The popularity of *The Belman of London* is supported by a sentence in

William Fennor's *Compters Common-wealth* (1617). In response to an ex-con who offers to expose some of his criminal tactics, Fennor replies: "Why sir, there is a booke called *Greenes Ghost Haunts Cony-catchers,* another called *Legerdemaine,* and *The Blacke Dog of Newgate,* but the most wittiest, elegantest and eloquentest *Peece* (Master *Dekkers,* the true heire of *Apollo* composed) called *The Belman of London,* haue already set foorth the vices of the time so viuely, that it is vnpossible the *Anchor* of any mans braine can sound the sea of a more deepe and dreadful mischeefe." Cited in Aydelotte, *Elizabethan Rogues and Vagabonds,* 129–30.

61. John Taylor, "A Thiefe," in *All The Workes Of John Taylor The Water Poet,* 115.

62. Richard Brome, *A Jovial Crew: or, The Merry Beggars* (1641), 121.

63. Robert Greene, "The art of Cros-biting," *A Notable Discovery of Coosnage* (1591), 40–51.

64. See Aydelotte, *Elizabethan Rogues and Vagabonds,* esp. the chapter entitled "The Art of Conny-Catching," 26–55.

65. Walker, *A Manifest Detection of Dice-play,* 35.

66. Dekker, *The Belman of London,* 118.

67. Awdeley, *The Fraternitye of Vacabondes,* 268.

68. Ibid.

69. Greene, *A Notable Discovery of Coosnage,* 22; 36.

70. Greene, *The Third Part of Cony-Catching,* 26.

71. Greene, *A Disputation between a Hee-Conny-Catcher and a Shee-Conny-Catcher* (1592), 18.

72. Cuthbert Cony-Catcher, *The Defense of Conny-Catching* (1592) in *Elizabethan and Jacobean Quartos,* ed. G. B. Harrison (New York: Barnes & Noble, 1966), 13; see note 36.

73. John Taylor, "A Bawd," in *All The Workes Of John Taylor The Water Poet,* 95.

74. Middleton, *The Black Book,* ll. 526–29.

75. William Shakespeare, *The Winter's Tale,* ed. J. H. P. Pafford (London: Methuen, 1963), 4.4.670–74.

76. Shirley, *The Sisters,* 383.

CHAPTER FIVE

1. By "public theater" I mean all commercial theaters that were open to public patronage; these included The Red Lion, The Theater, The Curtain, The Rose, The Swan, The Globe, The Fortune, The Red Bull, and The Hope.

2. The following is a selective list of significant work concerned with censorship and the politics of the drama: Martin Butler, *Theatre and Crisis, 1632–1642* (Cambridge: Cambridge University Press, 1984); Janet Clare, "'Greater Themes for Insurrection's Arguing': Political Censorship of the Elizabethan and Jacobean Stage," *Renaissance English Society* 38 (1987), 169–83; Jonathan Dollimore, *Radical Tragedy: Religion, Ideology and Power in the Drama of Shakespeare and His Contem-*

poraries (Chicago: University of Chicago Press, 1984); John Drakakis, ed., *Alternative Shakespeares* (London: Methuen, 1985); Philip J. Finkelpearl, "'The Comedians Liberty': Censorship of the Jacobean Stage Reconsidered," *English Literary Renaissance* 16 (1986), 123–38, and "The Role of the Court in the Development of Jacobean Drama," *Criticism* 24 (1982), 138–58; Jean E. Howard and Marion F. O'Connor, eds., *Shakespeare Reproduced: The Text in History and Ideology* (New York: Methuen, 1987); Alvin Kernan, *Shakespeare, the King's Playwright: Theater in the Stuart Court, 1603–1613* (New Haven: Yale University Press, 1995); Margot Heinemann, *Puritanism and Theatre: Thomas Middleton and Opposition Drama under the Early Stuarts* (Cambridge: Cambridge University Press, 1980); Annabel Patterson, *Censorship and Interpretation: The Conditions of Reading and Writing in Early Modern England* (Madison: University of Wisconsin Press, 1984); Alan Sinfield, *Faultlines: Cultural Materialist and the Politics of Dissident Reading* (Berkeley: University of California Press, 1992). For a complete list of related work written before 1980, see Jonathan Goldberg, "The Politics of Renaissance Literature: A Review Essay", *English Literary History* 49 (1982), 514–42.

3. Phillip Stubbes, *The Anatomie of Abuses* (1583; rpt. London: The New Shakespeare Society, 1877), 144–45.

4. John Rainoldes, *Th' Overthrow of Stage-Playes* (London, 1600), 11.

5. John Greene, *A Refutation of the Apology for Actors* (London, 1615), 61.

6. In this study the term "antitransvestismist" refers only to those who attack the practice of transvestism (which requires not only cross-dressing but also adopting mannerisms usually attributed to the impersonated gender). Since all of the discourses against the theater discussed here include an attack on the theatrical practice of transvestism, it is a given that an antitheatricalist is also an antitransvestismist, but not vice versa.

7. The following represents a summary of their respective arguments. In his essay "Fiction and Friction," *Shakespearean Negotiations* (Berkeley: University of California Press), 66–93, Stephen Greenblatt focuses on *Twelfth Night, As You Like It,* and a case study by the sixteenth-century French doctor Jacques Duval. He argues that the English Renaissance commonly held a conception of sexual identity as essentially male, and that women were seen as incomplete or "inverted mirror images of men" (92). He also asserts that this "conception of gender that is teleologically male and insists upon a verifiable sign that confirms nature's final cause finds its supreme literary expression in a transvestite theater" (88). This is so, says Greenblatt, because "the open secret of identity—that within differentiated individuals is a single structure, identifiably male—is presented literally in the all-male cast" (93). He discovers that the Elizabethan theater reflects an axiom central to state thought: the identifiably male origins of woman (as in Gen. 2:22).

In her book *The Stage and Social Struggle in Early Modern England* (London: Routledge, 1994), Jean E. Howard maintains that "Stubbes," the representative antitheatricalist cited by Greenblatt, "and the other antitheatrical writers suggest that a transvestite theater could also be read, in the Renaissance, as *un*natural, as a transgression of a divinely sanctioned social order" (98). This sanctioned order also comes from the Bible, which states that there are two sexes (Gen. 1:27), and that "woman shall not wear that which pertaineth unto a man, neither shall a man put on a woman's garment" (Deut. 22:5). Howard observes that although "in some discourses, masculine and feminine identity *were* seen as points on a continuum, not separate essences" (as Greenblatt sees it), the frequent quoting of the Deuteronomic dress code shows that in "the antitheatrical tracts the language of two kinds predominates" (98). This is due to the prevalent sex-gender system: "To transgress the codes governing dress disrupted an official view of the social order in which one's identity was largely determined by one's station or degree—and where that station was, in theory, providentially determined and immutable" (97). "The real point," asserts Howard, "is that the Renaissance needed the idea of two genders, one subordinate to the other, as a key part of its hierarchical view of the social order and to buttress its gendered division of labor"; moreover, the antitheatricalists, as fully subjectified state thinkers, supported this need (98).

In her book *Men in Women's Clothing: Anti-theatricality and Effeminization, 1579–1642* (Cambridge: Cambridge University Press, 1994), Laura Levine's analysis of the antitheatrical tracts reveals a radically different idea of identity difference. She concludes that the tracts (and perhaps the greater English populace) hold two views of the self: "They subscribe simultaneously to a view of the self as pliable, manipulable, easily unshaped, and at the same time to a view of the self as monstrous" (16). According to these "contradictory" views, Levine says, "the self can easily be made into anything because it has no inherent nature, and at the same time can be made into anything monstrous because it has an inherently monstrous nature" (17). Basically, Levine contends that for the antitheatricalists essential metamorphosis was not possible because for them the self is similar to a body of water: its form is fixed in that it is always malleable and thus ostensibly "shapeless," but its essence (like the chemical composition of water) is also fixed, for it remains constantly "monstrous."

Greenblatt, Howard, and Levine all keenly demonstrate that the antitheatrical tracts' conceptual interiorities are informed by and linked to state thought and official culture. For them a primary connection is that the tracts assert their belief in absolute dispositions: male (Greenblatt), male or female (Howard), and nothing or monstrous (Levine). To differing degrees and in a somewhat contradictory way, Greenblatt, Howard, and Levine also imply that the tracts suggest that although God determines sexual difference anatomically and designates the corresponding gender-specific demeanor and sexual orientation in Scripture, sexuality, gender, and social status are not fixed but rather are sensitive, flexible, and forever subject to one's ability to adequately *construct* or *maintain* one's prescribed identity. This implication, however underdeveloped by Greenblatt, Howard, and Levine, intimates a dormant discourse of social mobility among the antitheatricalists. Other critics who argue that the antitheatricalists were motivated by the conception of an absolute or fixed identity include Jonas Barish, *The Anti- theatrical Prejudice* (Berkeley: University of California Press, 1981), and Katherine Eisaman Maus, "Playhouse Flesh and Blood: Sexual Ideology and the Restoration Actress," *English Literary History* 46 (1979), 604–17.

8. Jean-Jacques Rousseau, *The Social Contract,* trans. Maurice Cranston (London: Penguin, 1968), 153.

9. Greene, *A Refutation,* 44.

10. Ibid., 43. In *The Anatomie of Abuses* Phillip Stubbes also refers to the theater as "Sathan's Synagogue" (143), and in *A Second and Third Blast of Retrait from Plaies and Theatres* (London: 1580) Anthony Munday calls "the Theater" "the chappel of Satan" (quoted in Stubbes, *The Anatomie of Abuses,* 302).

11. See Marshall McLuhan and Quentin Fiore, *The Medium Is the Massage* (New York: Bantam Books, 1967).

12. Stephen Orgel, *The Illusion of Power: Political Theater in the English Renaissance* (Berkeley: University of California Press, 1975), 2.

13. For substantiation of The Red Lion's precedence, antedating The Theater by a decade, see John Orrell, *The Human Stage: English Theater Design, 1567–1640* (Cambridge: Cambridge University Press, 1988), 20–28; see also Herbert Berry, "The First Public Playhouses, Especially The Red Lion," *Shakespeare Quarterly* 40 (1989), 133–40.

14. See Richard Dutton, *Mastering the Revels: The Regulation and Censorship of English Renaissance Drama* (London: Macmillan, 1991), esp. 17–41, 97–117; see also Janet Clare, *'Art made tongue-tied by authority': Elizabethan and Jacobean Dramatic Censorship* (Manchester: Manchester University Press, 1990), 8–11.

15. Steven Mullaney, *The Place of the Stage: License, Play, and Power in Renaissance England* (Chicago: University of Chicago Press, 1988), 23.

16. Martin Butler, *Theatre and Crisis, 1632–1642,* 306.

17. In *Princes to Act: Royal Audience and Royal Performance, 1578–1792* (Baltimore: Johns Hopkins University Press, 1993), which he calls a "conjectural" study of the relationship between King James I and the public theater (19), Matthew Wikander asserts as his main premise that "any play written for performance," for instance, "by Shakespeare's company, the King's Men, could be requested for performance at court; no play could justify its existence, however, as a purely occasional piece. Nor could any play, as far as we can discern, be guaranteed performance before the king" (49). Wikander maintains that every acting company, indeed, every play to some extent, was institutionalized by the state since at some unexpected moment a performance at court could be ordered, however unlikely (performances at court were rare, even by James's own professional acting companies). Nevertheless, as

Wikander admits, "It is not surprising that censorship was inefficient, where the institution to be controlled was so diverse" (63). This is illustrated, notes Wikander, even by James's own professional acting companies: *"Measure for Measure* evokes the tensions between public playhouse and court theater, and the Beaumont and Fletcher plays allude satirically to the language of the court masque: the metatheatrical dimension of these entertainments points directly to failures of royal control" (89).

18. Jean-Christophe Agnew, *Worlds Apart: The Market and the Theater in Anglo-American Thought, 1550–1750* (Cambridge: Cambridge University Press, 1986), 147.

19. Smith, *The Acoustic World of Early Modern England,* 208.

20. The distinct and enhanced acoustic environments of the purpose-built theaters may have contributed to the popularization of verse in plays. For instance, euphonious rhyme schemes may have generated delightful bodily sensations.

21. Mullaney, *The Place of the Stage,* 55.

22. Agnew, *Worlds Apart,* 11.

23. In *Puritanism and Theatre* Heinemann explains Gosson's relationship with the London authorities. See also Agnew, *Worlds Apart,* 125.

24. Stephan Gosson, *The Schoole of Abuse* (1579; rpt. London: Shakespeare Society, 1853), 10.

25. Rainoldes, *Th'Overthrow of Stage-Plays,* 18.

26. Stephan Gosson, *Playes Confuted in Five Actions* (London, 1582), B3.

27. Greene, *A Refutation,* 56.

28. Thomas Heywood, *An Apology for Actors* (1612; rpt. London: Shakespeare Society, 1853), 44.

29. Greene, *A Refutation,* 28.

30. Stephen Greenblatt, *Renaissance Self-Fashioning: From More to Shakespeare* (Chicago: University of Chicago Press, 1980), 8–9.

31. In *Men in Women's Clothing* Levine makes a similar observation: "But the problem with the attempt to argue 'no inherent self' is that Greenblatt often replicates the very notion he himself considers a fallacy. At regular junctures in *Renaissance Self-Fashioning,* the notion of the self as a manipulable construct seems underwritten by an older sense of the self as a 'deep psychic structure'" (11).

32. Gosson, *Playes Confuted,* G4.

33. Ibid., G7v.

34. John L. McMullan, *The Canting Crew: London's Criminal Underworld, 1550–1700* (New Brunswick, N.J.: Rutgers University Press, 1984), 56. See Beier, *Masterless Men: The Vagrancy Problem in England* (London: Methuen, 1985); see also Mullaney, *The Place of the Stage.*

35. See, for instance, "An Act for the punishment of Rogues, Vagabonds, and Sturdy Beggars" (1597), which called for the punishment of players, tricksters, jugglers, minstrels, bearwards, and many other wayfarers.

36. Thomas Dekker, *The Belman of London* (1608) and *The Gull's Horn-Book* (1609) (London: J. M. Dent, 1904), 144, 148.

37. See Agnew, *Worlds Apart*, 145. In *Village Revolts: Social Protest and Popular Disturbances in England, 1509–1640* (Oxford: Clarendon Press, 1988), Roger Manning notes: "Between 1581 and 1602, the city was disturbed by no fewer than 35 outbreaks of disorder. Since there were at least 96 insurrections, riots, and unlawful assemblies in London between 1517 and 1640, this means that more than one third of the instances of popular disorder during the century-and-a-quarter were concentrated within a 20-year period" (187).

38. Recall the notorious female-to-male transvestite Mary Frith, who was known as a rogue, a prostitute, the ringleader of a gang of thieves, and a stage player. Her representation in such popular texts as the anonymous pamphlet *The Life and Death of Mrs Mary Frith commonly called Moll Cutpurse* (1612), Nathan Field's play *Amends for Ladies* (1612), Dekker and Middleton's play *The Roaring Girl* (1611), along with the many legal documents related or devoted to her (such as *The Consistory of London Correction Book* [1605]), make the discourse of Frith particularly engaging for an analysis of the intersections between the state machinery, popular culture, female-to-male transvestitism, and criminality.

39. Thomas Adams, *Mystical Bedlam; or, The world of mad-men* (London, 1615), 50.

40. N. E. McClure, *The Letters of John Chamberlain* (Philadelphia: Lancashire Press, 1939), 2:289, 286. For an intriguing overview of sumptuary legislation in Renaissance England, see Marjorie Garber, "Dress Codes, or the Theatricality of Difference," *Vested Interests: Cross-Dressing and Cultural Anxiety* (New York: Routledge, 1992), 21–41.

41. John Williams, *A Sermon of Apparell* (London, 1619), 7, 22.

42. *Hic Mulier: or, the Man-Woman* (London, 1620), A3.

43. William Harrison, *The Description of England*, ed. Georges Edelen (1587; rpt. Ithaca: Cornell University Press, 1986), 170–71.

44. Stubbes, *The Anatomie of Abuses,* 34, 73.

45. Jean E. Howard, "Renaissance Antitheatricality and the Politics of Gender and Rank in *Much Ado About Nothing*," in *Shakespeare Reproduced: The Text in History and Ideology*, ed. Jean E. Howard and Marion F. O'Connor (New York: Methuen, 1987), 166.

46. Stubbes, *The Anatomie of Abuses,* 73.

47. *Hic Mulier,* A3.

48. Linda Woodbridge, *Women and the English Renaissance: Literature and the Nature of Womankind* (Chicago: University of Illinois Press, 1986), 144.

49. *Hic Mulier,* A3, C2.

50. *Hic Mulier,* B1.

51. William Rankins, *A Mirrour of Monsters* (London, 1588), B2.

52. *Haec-Vir: or the Womanish-Man* (London, 1620), A4. The words "de-forme[d]" and "deformitie[s]" signify mutation; as noted by Woodbridge, they are used to describe transvestite women twenty-one times in eighteen pages of *Hic Mulier.* However pejorative, these words still indicate that transvestite women were thought to be transformed women.

53. Judith Butler, *Gender Trouble: Feminism and the Subversion of Identity* (New York: Routledge, 1990), 137.

54. Woodbridge, *Women and the English Renaissance,* 147.

55. Howard, *The Stage and Social Struggle,* 105. In *Sexual Dissidence: Augustine to Wilde, Freud to Foucault* (Oxford: Clarendon Press, 1991). Jonathan Dollimore perceptively notes that there is no reason to assume that the pamphlet's ending debunks any of the points previously argued: what is said at the end is not necessarily more sincere than what went before; after all, to privilege the pamphlet's conclusion "is probably to interpret the pamphlet according to modern and anachronistic notions of authorial intention, character utterance, and textual unity" (298). Regardless of the relationship between the pamphlet's ending and its entirety, what is most important, says Dollimore, is that for Hic Mulier to state that "gender difference *can be and is being* maintained through cross-dressing and inversion is to maintain or imply the crucial claim even while apparently surrendering it: the difference in question is capable of working in terms of custom and culture (and is thereby contestable) rather than nature and divine law (which are immutable)" (298). Nevertheless, Dollimore seems to have overlooked the fact that for Hic Mulier "the difference in question" is indeed "nature and divine law" ("Nature to euery thing she hath created, hath giuen a singular delight in change") and a nature and divine law that are neither immutable, nor tyrannical.

56. Valerie Traub, *Desire and Anxiety: Circulations of Sexuality in Shakespearean Drama* (London: Routledge, 1992), 106.

57. Alan Bray, *Homosexuality in Renaissance England* (London: Gay Men's Press, 1982), 54. See Bruce Smith, *Homosexual Desire in Shakespeare's England: A Cultural Poetics* (Chicago: University of Chicago Press, 1991), 146–57.

58. Alan Bray, "Homosexuality and the Signs of Male Friendship in Elizabethan England," in *Queering the Renaissance,* ed. Jonathan Goldberg (Durham: Duke University Press, 1994), 41.

59. Donald Mager, "John Bale and Early Tudor Sodomy Discourse," in *Queering the Renaissance,* 141.

60. Bray, "Homosexuality and the Signs of Male friendship in Elizabethan England," 41.

61. For a concise explanation of becomings-woman, see the chapter "Becoming a Woman" in Félix Guattari's *Molecular Revolution: Psychiatry and Politics* (New York: Penguin, 1984). For a more complex explanation of all becomings, see Gilles

Deleuze and Félix Guattari, *A Thousand Plateaus: Capitalism and Schizophrenia* (Minneapolis: University of Minnesota Press, 1987), 232–309.

62. Harrison, The *Description of England*, 171.

63. Gosson, *The Schoole of Abuse*, 19, 22.

64. Rainoldes, *Th' Overthrow of Stage-Playes*, 21 (cf. also 37 and 38), 34.

65. Ibid., 44. The fact that Rainoldes makes this argument even though, while a seventeen year-old student at Oxford, he played the part of a woman in a play composed for Queen Elizabeth testifies to the complexity of the sexual-gender issues at hand. For more on this, see Peter Stallybrass, "Transvestism and the 'body beneath': Speculating on the Boy Actor," in *Erotic Politics: Desire on the Renaissance Stage, ed.* Susan Zimmerman (New York: Routledge, 1992).

66. Jonathan Goldberg, *Sodometries: Renaissance Texts, Modern Sexualities* (Stanford, Calif.: Stanford University Press, 1992), 111.

67. Levine, *Men in Women's Clothing*, 22.

68. William Prynne, *Histrio-mastix: The Player's Scourge or Actor's Tragedy* (1633; rpt. New York: Garland, 1974), 209.

69. [Ratsey], *The Life and Death of Gamaliel Ratsey a famous thief, of England, Executed at Bedford the 26 of March last past* (1605), ed. Atkins, A4.

70. Jacques Derrida, *Writing and Difference,* trans. Alan Bass (Chicago: University of Chicago Press, 1978), 289. For a detailed explanation of Derrida's theory of "supplementarity," see the chapter entitled "Structure, Sign, and Play in the Discourse of the Human Sciences," 278–93.

71. For a discussion on English sodomy law, see Goldberg, *Sodometries,* 120.

72. Friedrich Nietzsche, *Ecco Homo,* ed. and trans. Walter Kaufman (New York: Vintage Books, 1967), 328.

73. For more on statutory poor relief, see Beier, *Masterless Men,* esp. 173–74. For many accounts of people feigning need, see Harman, *A Caveat or Warening, For Commen Cursetors vulgarely called Vagabones,* and Dekker, *The Belman of London.*

74. Salgado, *The Elizabethan Underworld,* 157–58.

75. For information about the witch craze in early modern England, see Sidney Anglo, ed., *The Damned Art* (London: Routledge and Kegan Paul, 1977); see also Alan Macfarlane, *Witchcraft in Tudor and Stuart England: A Regional and Comparative Study* (New York: Harper & Row, 1970).

76. Unlike Derrida, who sweepingly claims that "différance" describes or occurs in the process of interpreting every text, and thereby weakens the purport of this very useful concept (albeit to some extent it must hold true in every context), I prefer to apply the term only when its suitability is obvious. See Derrida's *Writing and Difference.*

77. Brome, *A Jovial Crew,* 44.

78. Shirley, *The Sisters,* 361.

Adams, Thomas. *Mystical Bedlam: or, The world of mad-men*. London, 1615.

Agnew, Jean-Christophe. *Worlds Apart: The Market and the Theater in Anglo-American Thought, 1550–1750*. Cambridge: Cambridge University Press, 1986.

Althusser, Louis. "Ideology and Ideological State Apparatuses (Notes Towards an Investigation)." In *Lenin and Philosophy and Other Essays*. New York: Monthly Review Press, 1971.

Anderson, Benedict. *Imagined Communities: Reflections on the Origin and Spread of Nationalism*. London: Verso, 1983.

Anglo, Sydney. *The Damned Art*. Boston: Routledge, 1977.

Archer, Ian. *The Pursuit of Stability: Social Relations in Elizabethan London*. Cambridge: Cambridge University Press, 1991.

Awdeley, John. *The Fraternitye of Vacabondes* (1561), ed. Edward Viles and F. J. Furnivall. Early English Text Society, extra series, 9 (1869). Millwood, N. Y.: Kraus Reprint, 1988.

Aydelotte, Frank. *Elizabethan Rogues and Vagabonds*. Oxford Historical and Literary Studies, 1. Oxford: Oxford University Press, 1913.

Bailey, Charles-James, and K. Maroldt. "The French Lineage of English." In *Pidgins—Creoles—Languages in Contact*, ed. Jürgen Meisel. Tübingen: Narr, 1977.

Bakker, Peter. "Pigeons." In *Pigeons and Creoles: An Introduction*, ed. Jacques Arends, Pieter Muysken, and Norval Smith. Amsterdam: John Benjamins, 1995.

Barish, Jonas. *The Antitheatrical Prejudice*. Berkeley: University of California Press, 1981.

Barry, Lo. *Ram-Alley, or Merry Tricks*. London, 1608.

Baudrillard, Jean. *For a Critique of the Political Economy of the Sign*. Trans. Charles Levin. St. Louis, Mo.: Telos Press, 1981.

Baugh, Albert C., and Thomas Cable. *A History of the English Language*. 3rd ed. Englewood Cliffs, N. J.: Prentice-Hall, 1978.

Beier, A. L. "Anti-language or Jargon? Canting in the English Underworld in the Sixteenth and Seventeenth Centuries." In *Languages and Jargons: Contributions to a Social History of Language*, ed. Peter Burke. Cambridge: Polity Press, 1995.

———. *Masterless Men: The Vagrancy Problem in England, 1560–1640*. London: Methuen, 1985.

Berry, Herbert. "The First Public Playhouses, Especially The Red Lion." *Shakespeare Quarterly* 40 (1989), 133–40.

Bond, Ronald B., ed. Certain Sermons or Homilies (1547) *and* A Homily against Disobedience and Wilful Rebellion (1570): *A Critical Edition*. Toronto: University of Toronto Press, 1987.

Borrow, George. *The Romany Rye*. 1837. Reprint, London: Dent, 1969.

Bourdieu, Pierre. *The Field of Cultural Production*, ed. Randal Johnson. New York: Columbia University Press, 1993.

———. *Language and Symbolic Power*, ed. John B. Thompson. Cambridge: Harvard University Press, 1991.

Bowen, Ivor, ed. *The Statutes of Wales*. London, 1908.

The Brave English Gypsy. In *A Book of Roxburghe Ballads*, ed. John Payne Collier. London: Longman, Brown, Green, and Longmans, 1847.

Bray, Alan. *Homosexuality in Renaissance England*. London: Gay Men's Press, 1982.

———. "Homosexuality and the Signs of Male Friendship in Elizabethan England." In *Queering the Renaissance*, ed. Jonathan Goldberg. Durham: Duke University Press, 1994.

Brett-James, Norman G. *The Growth of Stuart London*. London: George Allen & Unwin, 1935.

Bridenbaugh, Carl. *Vexed and Troubled Englishmen, 1590–1642*. Oxford: Oxford University Press, 1976.

Bristol, Michael D. *Carnival and Theater: Plebeian Culture and the Structure of Authority in Renaissance England*. New York: Routledge, Chapman and Hall, 1989.

———. "Shakespeare: The Myth." In *A Companion to Shakespeare*, ed. David Scott Kasten. Oxford: Blackwell, 1999.

———. *Shakespeare's America, America's Shakespeare*. London: Routledge, 1990.

Brome, Richard. *A Jovial Crew: or, The Merry Beggars*. Ed. Ann Haaker. Lincoln: University of Nebraska Press, 1968.

Bushnell, Rebecca C. *Tragedies of Tyrants: Political Thought and Theater in the English Renaissance*. Ithaca: Cornell University Press, 1990.

Butler, Judith. *Bodies That Matter*. New York: Routledge, 1993.

———. *Gender Trouble: Feminism and the Subversion of Identity*. New York: Routledge, 1990.

Butler, Martin. *Theatre and Crisis, 1632–1642*. Cambridge: Cambridge University Press, 1984.

The Catterpillers of this Nation Anatomized. London: Printed for M. H. at the Princes Armes, in Chancery-lane, 1569.

Chamberlain, John. *The Letters of John Chamberlain*. Ed. N. E. McClure. Philadelphia: Lancashire Press, 1939.

Clare, Janet. *'Art made tongue-tied by authority': Elizabethan and Jacobean Dramatic Censorship*. Manchester: Manchester University Press, 1990.

——. "'Greater Themes for Insurrection's Arguing': Political Censorship of the Elizabethan and Jacobean Stage." *Renaissance English Society* 38 (1987), 169–83.

Clark, Sandra. *The Elizabethan Pamphleteers: Popular Moralistic Pamphlets, 1580–1640*. London: Athlone Press, 1983.

Cohen, Walter. "Political Criticism of Shakespeare." In *Shakespeare Reproduced: The Text in History and Ideology*, ed. Jean E. Howard and Marion F. O'Connor. New York: Methuen, 1987.

Collinson, Patrick. *The Elizabethan Puritan Movement*. Oxford: Clarendon Press, 1990.

Cony-Catcher, Cuthbert [pseud.?]. *The Defense of Conny-Catching*. In *Elizabethan and Jacobean Quartos*, ed. G. B. Harrison. New York: Barnes & Noble, 1966.

Copland, Robert. *The Highway to the Spital-House*. In *The Elizabethan Underworld: A Collection of Tudor and Early Stuart Tracts and Ballads*, ed. A. V. Judges. London: E. P. Dutton, 1930.

Crabb, James. *The Gipsies' Advocate: or Observations on the Origin, Character, Manners, and Habits, of the English Gipsies*. London: Mills, Jowett, and Mills, 1832.

Cressy, David. *Literacy and the Social Order: Reading and Writing in Tudor and Stuart England*. Cambridge: Cambridge University Press, 1980.

——, ed. *Education in Tudor and Stuart England*. London: Edward Arnold, 1975.

Crofton, Henry T. "Early Annals of the Gypsies in England." *Journal of the Gypsy Lore Society* 1, no. 1 (1888), 5–24.

Crystal, David. *An Encyclopedic Dictionary of Language and Languages*. London: Penguin Books, 1994.

Cummings, John, and Ernest Volkman. *Goombata: The Improbable Rise and Fall of John Gotti and His Gang*. Boston: Little, Brown, 1990.

DeCamp, David. "The Study of Pidgin and Creole Languages." In *Pidginization and Creolization of Languages*, ed. Dell Hymes. Cambridge: Cambridge University Press, 1971.

Dekker, Thomas. The Belman of London *and* Lanthorne and Candle-Light. 1608. Reprint, London: J. M. Dent, 1904.

——. *The Gull's Horn-Book*. 1609. Reprint, London: J. M. Dent, 1904.

——. *O per se O*. In *The Elizabethan Underworld: A Collection of Tudor and Early Stuart Tracts and Ballads*, ed. A. V. Judges. New York: E. P. Dutton, 1930.

Deleuze, Gilles. *Cinema 1: The Movement-Image*. Trans. Hugh Tomlinson and Barbara Habberjam. Minneapolis: University of Minnesota Press, 1996.

——. *Negotiations, 1972–1990*. Trans. Martin Joughin. New York: Columbia University Press, 1995.

Deleuze, Gilles, and Félix Guattari. *Kafka: Toward a Minor Literature*. Trans. Dana Polan. Minneapolis: University of Minnesota Press, 1986.

——. *A Thousand Plateaus: Capitalism and Schizophrenia*. Trans. Brian Massumi. Minneapolis: University of Minnesota Press, 1987.

Derrida, Jacques. "Signature, Event, Context." In *Limited, Inc.*, ed. Gerald Graff and trans. Samuel Weber and Jeffrey Mehlman. Evanston, Ill.: Northwestern University Press, 1988.

——. *Writing and Difference*. Trans. Alan Bass. Chicago: University of Chicago Press, 1978.

Dollimore, Jonathan. *Radical Tragedy: Religion, Ideology and Power in the Drama of Shakespeare and His Contemporaries*. Chicago: University of Chicago Press, 1984.

——. *Sexual Dissidence: Augustine to Wilde, Freud to Foucault*. Oxford: Clarendon Press, 1991.

Drakakis, John, ed. *Alternative Shakespeares*. London: Methuen, 1985.

Dutton, Richard. *Ben Jonson*. Cambridge: Cambridge University Press, 1983.

——. *Mastering the Revels: The Regulation and Censorship of English Renaissance Drama*. London: Macmillan, 1991.

Eagleton, Terry. *William Shakespeare*. New York: Blackwell, 1986.

Earle, John. *Micro-cosmographie, or, A Peece of the World Discovered in Essayes and Characters* (1628). In *The Elizabethan Underworld: A Collection of Tudor and Early Stuart Tracts and Ballads*, ed. A. V. Judges. New York: E. P. Dutton, 1930.

Fennor, William. *The Counter's Commonwealth*. In *The Elizabethan Underworld: A Collection of Tudor and Early Stuart Tracts and Ballads*, ed. A. V. Judges. New York: E. P. Dutton, 1930.

Field, Nathan. *Amends for Ladies, with the Merry Prankes of Moll Cutpurse*. 1618.

Finkelpearl, Philip J. "'The Comedians Liberty': Censorship of the Jacobean Stage Reconsidered." *English Literary Renaissance* 16 (1986), 123–38.

——. "The Role of the Court in the Development of Jacobean Drama." *Criticism* 24 (1982), 138–58.

Fisher, John. *The Book of John Fisher, Town Clerk and Deputy Recorder of Warwick, 1580–1588*. Warwick: Henry T. Cook, n.d.

Fletcher, John, and Philip Massinger. *Beggars Bush*. Ed. John H. Dorenkamp. The Hague: Mouton, 1967.

Foucault, Michel. *The Archeology of Knowledge*. Trans. A. M. Sheridan Smith. New York: Pantheon Books, 1972.

Garber, Marjorie. "Dress Codes, or the Theatricality of Difference." In *Vested Interests: Cross-Dressing and Cultural Anxiety*. New York: Routledge, 1992.

——. "The Logic of the Transvestite." In *Staging the Renaissance: Reinterpretations of Elizabethan and Jacobean Drama*, ed. David Scott Kastan and Peter Stallybrass. New York: Routledge, 1991.

Glucksmann, André. *Master Thinkers*. Trans. Brian Pearce. New York: Harper & Row, 1980.

Goldberg, Jonathan. "The Politics of Renaissance Literature: A Review Essay." *English Literary History* 49 (1982), 514–42.

——. *Sodometries: Renaissance Texts, Modern Sexualities*. Stanford, Calif.: Stanford University Press, 1992.

Gosson, Stephan. *Playes Confuted in Fiue Actions*. London, 1582.

——. *The Schoole of Abuse*. 1579. Reprint, London: Shakespeare Society, 1853.

Greenblatt, Stephen. "Fiction and Friction." In *Shakespearean Negotiations: The Circulation of Social Energy in Renaissance England*. Berkeley: University of California Press, 1988.

——. "Invisible Bullets: Renaissance Authority and Its Subversion, *Henry IV* and *Henry V*." In *Political Shakespeare: New Essays in Cultural Materialism*, ed. Jonathan Dollimore and Alan Sinfield. Ithaca: Cornell University Press, 1985.

——. *Renaissance Self-Fashioning: From More to Shakespeare*. Chicago: University of Chicago Press, 1980.

——. "Shakespeare Bewitched." In *New Historical Literary Study: Essays on Reproducing Texts, Representing History*, ed. Jeffrey N. Cox and Larry J. Reynolds. Princeton: Princeton University Press, 1993.

Greene, John. *A Refutation of the Apology for Actors*. London, 1615.

Greene, Robert. *The Black Book's Messenger*. In *Elizabethan and Jacobean Quartos*, ed. G. B. Harrison. Edinburgh: Edinburgh University Press, 1966.

——. *A Disputation between a Hee-Conny-Catcher and a Shee-Conny-Catcher*. In *Elizabethan and Jacobean Quartos*, ed. G. B. Harrison. Edinburgh: Edinburgh University Press, 1966.

——. *A Notable Discovery of Coosnage*. In *Elizabethan and Jacobean Quartos*, ed. G. B. Harrison. Edinburgh: Edinburgh University Press, 1966.

——. *The Second Part of Conny-Catching*. In *Elizabethan and Jacobean Quartos*, ed. G. B. Harrison. Edinburgh: Edinburgh University Press, 1966.

——. *The Third Part of Conny-Catching*. In *Elizabethan and Jacobean Quartos*, ed. G. B. Harrison. Edinburgh: Edinburgh University Press, 1966.

Guattari, Félix. *Molecular Revolution: Psychiatry and Politics*. Trans. Rosemary Sheed. New York: Penguin Books, 1984.

——. *Psychanalyse transversalité*. Paris: Maspero, 1972.

Hackett, Maria. *A Popular Description of St. Paul's Cathedral*. London: J. B. Nichols and Son, 1828.

Haec-Vir: or the Womanish-Man. London, 1620.

Halliday, Michael. *Language as Social Semiotic*. London: Edward Arnold, 1978.

Harman, Thomas. *A Caveat or Warening, For Commen Cursetors vulgarely called Vagabones*. In *The Elizabethan Underworld: A Collection of Tudor and Early Stuart Tracts and Ballads*, ed. A. V. Judges. London: E. P. Dutton, 1930.

Harrison, William. *The Description of England*. 1587. Ed. Georges Edelen. Reprint, Ithaca: Cornell University Press, 1968.

Head, Richard, and Francis Kirkman. *The English Rogue*. 1665. Reprint, London: George Routledge & Sons, 1928.

Heinemann, Margot. *Puritanism and Theatre: Thomas Middleton and Opposition Drama under the Early Stuarts*. Cambridge: Cambridge University Press, 1980.

Heywood, Thomas. *An Apology for Actors*. 1612. Reprint, London: Shakespeare Society, 1853.

Hic Mulier: or, the Man-Woman. London, 1620.

Hill, Christopher. *Intellectual Origins of the English Revolution*. Oxford: Clarendon Press, 1980.

——. *The World Turned Upside Down: Radical Ideas During the English Revolution*. London: Penguin Books, 1975.

Hodge, Robert, and Gunther Kress. *Social Semiotics*. Ithaca : Cornell University Press, 1988.

Holm, John. *Pigeons and Creoles. Vol. 1, Theory and Structure*. Cambridge: Cambridge University Press, 1988.

Howard, Jean E. "Renaissance Antitheatricality and the Politics of Gender and Rank in *Much Ado About Nothing*." In *Shakespeare Reproduced: The Text in History and Ideology*, ed. Jean E. Howard and Marion F. O'Connor. New York: Methuen, 1987.

——. *The Stage and Social Struggle in Early Modern England*. London: Routledge, 1994.

Howard, Jean E., and Marion F. O'Connor. Introduction to *Shakespeare Reproduced: The Text in History and Ideology*, ed. Jean E. Howard and Marion F. O'Connor. New York: Methuen, 1987.

——, eds. *Shakespeare Reproduced: The Text in History and Ideology*. New York: Methuen, 1987.

Hutton, Luke. *The Black Dog of Newgate*. In *The Elizabethan Underworld: A Collection of Tudor and Early Stuart Tracts and Ballads*, ed. A. V. Judges. London: E. P. Dutton, 1930.

Ingram, Martin. *Church Courts, Sex amd Marriage in England, 1570–1640*. Cambridge: Cambridge University Press, 1987.

Intriligator, James, and Bryan Reynolds. "Transversal Power: Molecules, Jesus Christ, The Greatful Dead, and Beyond." Paper presented at the Manifesto Conference at Harvard University, May 9, 1998.

Jameson, Frederic. *The Political Unconscious: Narrative as a Socially Symbolic Act*. Ithaca: Cornell University Press, 1981.

Jones, Richard F. *The Triumph of the English Language*. Stanford, Calif.: Stanford University Press, 1966.

Jonson, Ben. *Bartholomew Fair*. In *Drama of the English Renaissance II: The Stuart Period*, ed. Russell A. Fraser and Norman Rabkin. New York: Macmillan, 1976.

——. *Masque of Gipsies, In the Burley, Belvoir, and Windsor Versions. An Attempt at Reconstruction*. Ed. W. W. Greg. London: Oxford University Press, 1952.

Kahn, Coppélia. Introduction to *The Roaring Girl*. In *The Collected Works of Thomas Middleton*, ed. Gary Taylor. Oxford: Clarendon Press, 2002.

Kant, Immanuel. *Critique of Pure Reason*. Trans. J. M. D. Meiklejohn. Buffalo, N. Y.: Prometheus Books, 1990.

Kastan, David Scott, and Peter Stallybrass. "Introduction: Staging the Renaissance." In *Staging the Renaissance: Reinterpretations of Elizabethan and Jacobean Drama*, ed. David Scott Kastan and Peter Stallybrass. New York: Routledge, 1991.

Keith, Michael, and Steve Pile. "The Place of Politics." In *Place in the Politics of Identity*, ed. Michael Keith and Steve Pile. London: Routledge, 1993.

Kernan, Alvin. *Shakespeare, the King's Playwright: Theater in the Stuart Court, 1603–1613*. New Haven: Yale University Press, 1995.

Laclau, Ernesto. *New Reflections on the Revolution of Our Time*. London: Verso, 1990.

Larner, Christina. *Witchcraft and Religion: The Politics of Popular Belief*. Oxford: Blackwell, 1984.

Lefebvre, Henri. *The Production of Space*. Trans. Donald Nicholson-Smith. Oxford: Blackwell, 1993.

Leland, Charles G. *The English Gipsies and Their Language*. New York: Hurd and Houghton, 1873.

Levine, Laura. *Men in Women's Clothing: Anti-theatricality and Effeminization, 1579–1642*. Cambridge: Cambridge University Press, 1994.

The Life and Death of Mrs. Mary Frith Commonly Called Moll Cutpurse. 1612.

Lodge, Edmund, ed. *Illustrations of British History, Biography, and Manners*. London: John Chidley, 1838.

Lott, Eric. *Love and Theft: Blackface Minstrelsy and the American Working Class*. New York: Oxford University Press, 1993.

Maas, Peter. *The Valachi Papers*. New York: Putnam, 1968.

Macfarlane, Alan. *Witchcraft in Tudor and Stuart England: A Regional and Comparative Study*. London: Routledge, 1970.

Mager, Donald. "John Bale and Early Tudor Sodomy Discourse." In *Queering the Renaissance*, ed. Jonathan Goldberg. Durham: Duke University Press, 1994.

Manning, Roger. *Village Revolts: Social Protest and Popular Disturbances in England, 1509–1640*. Oxford: Clarendon Press, 1988.

Maus, Katherine Eisaman. "Playhouse Flesh and Blood: Sexual Ideology and the Restoration Actress." *English Literary History* 46 (1979), 604–17.

McLuhan, Marshall, and Quentin Fiore. *The Medium Is the Massage*. New York: Bantam Books, 1967.

McMullan, John L. *The Canting Crew: London's Criminal Underworld, 1550–1700*. New Brunswick, N.J.: Rutgers University Press, 1984.

Middleton, Thomas. *The Black Book*. In *The Collected Works of Thomas Middleton*, ed. G. B. Shand. Oxford: Clarendon Press, 2002.

———. *More Dissemblers Besides Women*. Ed. John Jowett. In *The Collected Works of Thomas Middleton*, ed. Gary Taylor. Oxford: Clarendon Press, 2002.

———. *The Spanish Gypsy*. In *The Works of Thomas Middleton*, ed. A. H. Bullen. Boston: Houghton, Mifflin, 1885.

Middleton, Thomas, and Thomas Dekker. *The Roaring Girl*. In *Drama of the English Renaissance II: The Stuart Period*, ed. Russell A. Fraser and Norman Rabkin. New York: Macmillan, 1976.

Minsheu, John. *The Guide to Tongues*. 1617.

Montrose, Louis. "Professing the Renaissance: The Poetics and Politics of Culture." In *The New Historicism*, ed. Aram H. Veeser. New York: Routledge, 1989.

More, Thomas. *A Dyalog of Syr Thomas More Knyghte*. 1514.

Mühlhäusler, Peter. *Pidgin & Creole Linguistics*. Oxford: Blackwell, 1986.

Mullaney, Steven. *The Place of the Stage: License, Play, and Power in Renaissance England*. Chicago: University of Chicago Press, 1988.

Munday, Anthony. *A Second and Third Blast of Retrait from Plaies and Theatres* (1580). In Phillip Stubbes, *The Anatomie of Abuses* (1583). Reprint, London: New Shakespeare Society, 1877).

Munday, Anthony [and Henry Chettle?]. *The Death of Robert, Earl of Huntington*. 1595.

———. *The Downfall of Robert, Earl of Huntington*. 1598.

Nietzsche, Friedrich. *Ecce Homo*. Ed. and trans. Walter Kaufman. New York: Vintage Books, 1967.

———. *On the Genealogy of Morals*. Trans. Walter Kaufman. New York: Vintage Books, 1989.

Okely, Judith. *The Traveller-Gypsies*. Cambridge: Cambridge University Press, 1983.

Orgel, Stephen. *Ben Jonson: The Complete Masques*. New Haven: Yale University Press, 1969.

———. *The Illusion of Power: Political Theater in the English Renaissance*. Berkeley: University of California Press, 1975.

———. *The Jonsonian Masque*. Cambridge: Harvard University Press, 1965.

Orrell, John. *The Human Stage: English Theater Design, 1567–1640*. Cambridge: Cambridge University Press, 1988.

Patterson, Annabel. *Censorship and Interpretation: The Conditions of Reading and Writing in Early Modern England*. Madison: University of Wisconsin Press, 1984.

Pendry, E. D. "The Idea of a Prison." In *Elizabethan Prisons and Prison Scenes*. 2 vols. Salzburg: Institut für Anglistik und Amerikanistik, 1974.

Pileggi, Nicolas. *Wiseguy: Life in a Mafia Family*. New York: Simon & Schuster, 1985.

Prynne, William. *Histrio-mastix: The Player's Scourge or Actor's Tragedy*. 1633. Reprint, New York: Garland, 1974.

Puzo, Mario. *The Last Don*. New York: Random House, 1996.

Pyles, Thomas, and John Algeo. *The Origins and Development of the English Language*. 3rd ed. New York: Harcourt Brace Jovanovich, 1982.

Rainoldes, John. *Th'Overthrow of Stage-Playes*. London, 1600.

Randall, Dale B. J. *Jonson's Gypsies Unmasked: Background and Theme of* The Gypsies Metamorphos'd. Durham: Duke University Press, 1975.

Rankins, William. *A Mirrour of Monsters*. London, 1588.

Ratseis Ghost. Or the Second Part of His Madde Prankes and Robberies. Ed. S. H. Atkins. Shakespeare Asoociation Facsimiles, no. 10. London, 1935.

[Ratsey, G.] *The Life and Death of Gamaliel ratsey a famous thief, of England, Executed at Bedford the 26 of March last past*. 1605. Ed. S. H. Atkins.

Reynolds, Bryan. "The Devil's House, 'or worse': Transversal Power and Antitheatrical Discourse in Early Modern England." *Theatre Journal* 49, no. 2 (1997), 143–67.

———. "The Terrorism of Macbeth and Charles Manson: Reading Cultural Construction in Polanski and Shakespeare." *Upstart Crow* 13 (1993), 109–27.

———. "'What is the city but the people?': Transversal Performance and Radical Politics in Shakespeare's *Coriolanus* and Brecht's *Coriolan*." In *Shakespeare Without Class: Misappropriations of Cultural Capital*, ed. Bryan Reynolds and Donald Hedrick. New York: St. Martin's Press, 2000.

Reynolds, Bryan, and Joseph Fitzpatrick. "The Transversality of Michel de Certeau: Foucault's Panoptic Discourse and the Cartographic Impulse." *Diacritics* 29, no. 3 (Fall 1999), 63–80.

———. "Venetian Ideology or Transversal Power?: Iago's Motives and the Means by Which Othello Falls." In *Critical Essays on* Othello, ed. Philip Kolin. New York: Garland, 2001.

Reynolds, Bryan, and D. J. Hopkins. "The Making of Authorships: Transversal Navigation in the Wake of *Hamlet*, Robert Wilson, Wolfgang Wiens, and Shakespace." In *Shakespeare After Mass Media*, ed. Richard Burt. New York: Palgrave/St. Martin's Press, 2001.

Rid, Samuel. *Martin Markall, Beadle of Bridewell: His Defense and Answers to the Bellman of London*. In *The Elizabethan Underworld: A Collection of Tudor and Early Stuart Tracts and Ballads*, ed. A. V. Judges. London: E. P. Dutton, 1930.

Romaine, Suzanne. *Language in Society: An Introduction to Sociolinguistics*. New York: Oxford University Press, 1994.

——. *Pidgin and Creole Languages*. London: Longman, 1988.

Rousseau, Jean-Jacques. *The Social Contract*. Trans. Maurice Cranston. London: Penguin Books, 1968.

Salgado, Gamini. *The Elizabethan Underworld*. London: J. M. Dent, 1977.

Sampson, John. *The Wind on the Heath*. London: Chatto & Windus, 1930.

Shakespeare, William. *Henry V*. Ed. J. H. Walter. London: Methuen, 1954.

——. *The Merry Wives of Windsor*. Ed. H. J. Oliver. London: Methuen, 1971.

——. *A Midsummer Night's Dream*. Ed. Harold F. Brooks. London: Methuen, 1979.

——. *Othello*. Ed. M. R. Ridley. London: Methuen, 1958.

——. *The Two Gentlemen of Verona*. Ed. Clifford Leech. London: Methuen, 1986.

——. *The Winter's Tale*. Ed. J. H. P. Pafford. London: Methuen, 1963.

Sharpe, J. A. *Crime in Early Modern England, 1550–1750*. London: Longman, 1984.

Shields, Rob. *Places on the Margin: Alternative Geographies of Modernity*. London: Routledge, 1991.

Shirley, James. *The Sisters*. In *The Dramatic Works and Poems of James Shirley*, ed. William Gifford. London: John Murray, 1833.

Simon, Joan. *Education and Society in Tudor England*. Cambridge: Cambridge University Press, 1966.

Simpson, William. *Gleanings from Old St. Paul's*. London: E. Stock, 1889.

Sinfield, Alan. *Cultural Politics–Queer Reading*. London: Routledge, 1994.

——. "*Macbeth*: History, Ideology, and Intellectuals." In *Faultlines: Cultural Materialism and the Politics of Dissident Reading*. Berkeley: University of California Press, 1992.

Smith, Alan G. R. *The Emergence of a Nation State: The Commonwealth of England, 1529–1660*. London: Longman, 1984.

Smith, Bruce. *The Acoustic World of Early Modern England*. Chicago: University of Chicago Press, 1999.

——. *Homosexual Desire in Shakespeare's England: A Cultural Poetics*. Chicago: University of Chicago Press, 1991.

Stallybrass, Peter. "Transvestism and the 'body beneath': Speculating on the Boy Actor." In *Erotic Politics: Desire on the Renaissance Stage*, ed. Susan Zimmerman. New York: Routledge, 1992.

Street Robberies Consider'd. London: J. Roberts, n.d.

Stubbes, Phillip. *The Anatomie of Abuses*. 1583. Reprint, London: New Shakespeare Society, 1877.

Tawney, R. H., and Eileen Power, eds. *Tudor Economic Documents*. 3 vols. London: Longmans, Green, 1924.

Taylor, John. *All The Workes Of John Taylor The Water Poet*. Ed. V. E. Neuberg. London: The Scholar Press, 1977.

Thompson, T. W. "Gleanings from Constables' Accounts and Other Sources." *Journal of the Gypsy Lore Society*, 3rd ser., 7, no. 1 (1928), 30–47.

——. "Gypsy Marriage in England." Parts 1–3. *Journal of the Gypsy Lore Society*. 3rd ser., 5, no. 1 (1927), 9–37; 6, no. 4 (1927), 101–29, 151–82.

Tillyard, E. M. W. *The Elizabethan World Picture*. New York: Random House, 1945.

Todd, Loreto. *Pidgins and Creoles*. London: Routledge, 1990.

Traub, Valerie. *Desire and Anxiety: Circulations of Sexuality in Shakespearean Drama*. London: Routledge, 1992.

U. K. *Anno Quinto Reginae Elizabethe. At the Parliament Holden at Westmynster the.xii.of January . . . Were Enacted as Followeth*. 1562.

——. *Anno xxxix. Reginae Elizabethe. At the Parliament. . . .* 1597.

——. *The Consistory of London Correction Book*. 1605.

——. *State Papers—Domestic—Elizabeth*, vol. 7. n.d.

——. "27 Henry 8." In *The Statutes of Wales*, ed. Ivor Bowen. London, 1908.

Vesey-Fitzgerald, Brian. *Gypsies of Britain: An Introduction to Their History*. Newton Abbott, England: David and Charles, 1973.

Walker, Gilbert. *A Manifest Detection of Dice-Play*. In *The Elizabethan Underworld: A Collection of Tudor and Early Stuart Tracts and Ballads*, ed. A. V. Judges. London: E. P. Dutton, 1930.

Wayne, Don E. "Power, Politics, and the Shakespearean Text: Recent Criticism in England and the United States." In *Shakespeare Reproduced: The Text in History and Ideology*, ed. by Jean E. Howard and Marion F. O'Connor. New York: Methuen, 1987.

Wheatley, Henry Benjamin. *London, Past and Present: Its History, Associations, and Traditions*. New York: Scribner and Welford, 1891; London: J. Murray, 1891.

White, Hayden. *Tropics of Discourse: Essays in Cultural Criticism*. Baltimore: Johns Hopkins University Press, 1978.

Wikander, Matthew. *Princes to Act: Royal Audience and Royal Performance, 1578–1792*. Baltimore: Johns Hopkins University Press, 1993.

Williams, John. *A Sermon of Apparell*. London, 1619.

Williams, Raymond. *Keywords: A Vocabulary of Culture and Society*. New York: Oxford University Press, 1983.

——. *Marxism and Literature*. New York: Oxford University Press, 1977.

Winstedt, Eric Otto. "Early British Gypsies." *Journal of the Gypsy Lore Society*, n.s., 7, no. 1 (1913–14), 5–36.

Woodbridge, Linda. *Women and the English Renaissance: Literature and the Nature of Womankind*. Chicago: University of Illinois Press, 1986.

Žižek, Slavoj. "Beyond Discourse-Analysis." In Ernesto Laclau, *New Reflections on the Revolution of Our Time*. London: Verso, 1990.

——. *The Sublime Object of Ideology*. London: Verso, 1989.